D1564283

CONTAINMENT AND CONDEMNATION

CONTAINMENT AND CONDEMNATION

LAW AND THE OPPRESSION OF THE URBAN POOR

David Ray Papke

Michigan State University Press ✒ *East Lansing*

⊛ The paper used in this publication meets the minimum requirements of
ANSI/NISO Z39.48-1992 (R 1997) (Permanence of Paper).

Michigan State University Press
East Lansing, Michigan 48823-5245

Printed and bound in the United States of America.

28 27 26 25 24 23 22 21 20 19   1 2 3 4 5 6 7 8 9 10

LIBRARY OF CONGRESS CATALOGING-IN-PUBLICATION DATA
Names: Papke, David Ray, 1947– author.
Title: Containment and condemnation : law and the oppression of the urban poor / David Ray Papke.
Description: East Lansing : Michigan State University Press, [2019] | Includes bibliographical references and index.
Identifiers: LCCN 2018011225 | ISBN 9781611863093 (cloth : alk. paper) | ISBN 9781609175887 (pdf)
| ISBN 9781628953527 (epub) | ISBN 9781628963526 (kindle)
Subjects: LCSH: Public welfare—Law and legislation—United States.
| Legal assistance to the poor—United States. | Urban poor—Civil rights—United States.
| Urban poor—United States. | Social legislation—United States. | Poverty—Social aspects—United States.
Classification: LCC KF390.5.P6 P36 2018 | DDC 344.7303/25—dc23
LC record available at https://lccn.loc.gov/2018011225

Book design by Charlie Sharp, Sharp Des!gns, East Lansing, MI
Cover design by Shaun Allshouse, www.shaunallshouse.com
Cover image is "Alleys of Baltimore," by Peeter Viisimaa, and is used
under a licensing agreement via iStock by Getty Images.

Michigan State University Press is a member of the Green Press Initiative and is committed to developing
and encouraging ecologically responsible publishing practices. For more information about the Green
Press Initiative and the use of recycled paper in book publishing, please visit www.greenpressinitiative.org.

Visit Michigan State University Press at www.msupress.org

Contents

Acknowledgments

A s many before me have observed, nobody publishes a book alone, and that is certainly true with regard to *Containment and Condemnation: Law and the Oppression of the Urban Poor*.

The administration, faculty, and students at the Marquette University Law School supported my work on this book, work that was atypical for a professor in mainstream legal education. Dean Joseph Kearney generously provided summer grants that helped me complete research for the book. Faculty colleagues critiqued early drafts of individual chapters in formal faculty workshops and in informal conversation. Attorneys Marlo Buser, Sibyl McCarley, Casey Shorts, and Kate Thometz provided excellent research assistance while they were still students at Marquette.

Early treatments of selected topics in the book appeared in articles in the *Fordham Urban Law Journal*, the *Indiana Law Review*, *The Scholar: St. Mary's Law Review on Race and Social Justice*, and *The Urban Lawyer*. Editors at all of these journals not only granted permission to revisit those topics in my book but also expressed delight that my earlier efforts in their journals had developed into a book publication.

At the Michigan State University Press, Gabriel Dotto courteously moved my manuscript through the selection and revision processes, always encouraging me to continue on. Editors Anastasia Wraight and Bonnie Cobb reined in my tendency to hyphenate words, insisted on precise accuracy in my citations, and worked diligently to improve my prose. I have been fortunate in my career to publish a half dozen books, but the anonymous outside readers and members of the editorial board of the Michigan State University Press easily surpassed readers and board members at other presses in providing pointed critiques and thoughtful suggestions for my book.

And last but certainly not least, my wife Elise Papke engaged with and contributed to my book, even as she completed professional tasks and duties more demanding and time-consuming than my own. Elise's love, support, and insistence that I be as good as possible in my academic endeavors have been sustaining forces at every turn in my career.

Introduction

The population of American cities has always included poor people, but the perceptions, conditions, and attitudes of the urban poor have worsened over time. Considered lazy, annoying paupers in the early nineteenth century, the urban poor came to be seen as a violent, criminal "underclass" by the end of the twentieth. In the present, comfortable and prosperous Americans care less and less about the urban poor's plight and increasingly think of the urban poor in "us and them" terms. Comprising over 40 percent of the nation's inner-city population and an estimated 14–15 percent of the total population, the urban poor themselves are weathering declining economic equality and also watching as their social capital—that is, the connections and organizations that facilitate community—falls apart right before their eyes. With good reason, many of the urban poor have abandoned hope and begun to accept their predicament as permanent.

In this book I explore the relationship of law to the contemporary urban poor. Americans customarily respect both law itself and the "rule of law" and think of them as positive aspects of American life. While that sentiment might be appropriate in some settings, it is not necessarily the case for the urban poor. I contend that law, broadly understood, creates and contributes to urban poverty more frequently than it ends or reduces that poverty.

I discuss the general features of American urban poverty in the nineteenth and twentieth centuries, emphasizing the ways elites, religious figures, and political leaders tried to address the problems associated with urban poverty. Throughout these initial discussions, I presume that history is the engine of the present. History is perhaps best perceived not as something that is over and done with but rather as the ongoing process that delivers the sad situation involving the urban poor to our present-day doorstep.

I then attempt to capture in a general sense how laws, legal proceedings, and legal institutions function in society before exploring how they work for, against, and with regard to the urban poor. Law is a formidable and troubling factor in the most fundamental parts of their daily life. Law is problematic in criminal justice for the urban poor, in the maintenance and location of the places they call home, in the operation of their families, in their options in the marketplace, and in their attempts to lead healthy lives. In all of these fundamental areas, patterns of legalistic containment and condemnation appear, and the containment and condemnation is so forceful as to be literally oppressive. In my opinion, law, legal proceedings, and legal institutions play major roles in the oppression of the urban poor.

Nineteenth-Century Antecedents

Prior to the nineteenth century, American society was more compact and tightly wound than it would later come to be, and colonial leaders were most certainly aware of the poor men and women in their towns and villages. However, members of the colonial elite did not perceive the poor as a problem but rather as an embodiment of God's will. Professedly secure in their Christian faith and publicly optimistic about their prospects, the more prosperous and established members of colonial society showed no overarching tendency to isolate or punish the poor. In the opinion of David and Sheila Rothman, a twentieth-century historian and social worker, respectively, the poor were taken to be "pawns in a divine game."[1] Yes, in the happiest of all worlds their lives could be more comfortable and rewarding, but their condition was simply their divine fate.

An attitude of this sort was of course easier to maintain since colonial clergy and civic leaders were for the most part able to rein in the poor. Elite control of humbler compatriots was evident, to cite one significant example, when it came to the drinking of alcoholic beverages. While in later periods drunkenness would become a type of conduct often associated with the urban poor, members of the colonial elite were able to restrict drinking among the poor by limiting their access to taverns and public houses, where colonial drinking usually took place. Leadership cadres recognized that taverns and public houses were often centers of community life, but they granted licenses to operate taverns and public houses only to eligible voters or to those who belonged to the approved Protestant church. These responsible and moral citizens, the thinking went, would know that order and decorum required excluding the poor.[2]

But then, in the decades immediately following the founding of the Republic, norms and perceptions began changing. Rum, the preferred alcoholic drink of the era and a strong one at that, became cheaper, and rising levels of alcohol consumption led some to call the American Early Republic a "nation of drunkards." Employers typically summoned workers twice a day, once in the morning and then again in late afternoon, for alcoholic beverages, and in 1820 Americans spent $12 million on liquor, more than the total expenditures of the federal government.[3] In this sodden environment, elites lost control of the taverns and public houses. Public drinking—right on the streets of town—became common and was frequently tinged with not just joy and frivolity but also anguish and hostility. The drunken poor, it seemed to some, were likely to be thieves and lechers. "To those who presumed that they had the right to mold society's institutions, the unregulated tavern's independence, like the growing independence of the lower classes, was a sign of chaos and disorder."[4]

The largest factor in these changing perceptions was accelerating urbanization. While at the time of the Republic's founding approximately 90 percent of Americans still lived on farms or in country towns, the nation was on the cusp of urbanization. From 1790 to 1840, every decade but one witnessed a rate of urban population growth nearly double the rate of population growth as a whole.[5] Some of the urban growth involved immigration from abroad, but even more involved Americans moving from their farms and small towns to the east-coast cities. Boston, New York, Philadelphia, and Baltimore grew rapidly, and smaller cities such as Portland, Salem, Providence, New Haven, and Charleston burst at their seams.[6]

Increasingly fluid and complex, city life undermined the older notion that the needy were a normal and natural part of the population. Elites had less control than in more rural settings, and city fathers found it difficult to maintain order and tolerable living conditions. People were less known to one another and unlikely to remain in particular places and neighborhoods. In the new context, the poor seemed in the minds of many to be especially prone to inappropriate, disrespectful conduct. My goodness, their fondness for rum was bad enough, but now the poor wandered all about the city, begging for handouts.

What could be done about the people taken to constitute a social problem? City fathers turned to the so-called poorhouse to bring the urban poor back into the fold. While smaller, charitable "almshouses" dated back to the Middle Ages, poorhouses began in the 1820s to grow much larger than those from earlier eras and to be administered by local governments instead of private charities. The poorhouses were customarily hulking yet unadorned structures built on the grounds of a poor farm near the city limits or, just as frequently, adjacent to the city jail or prison near the heart of town. Poorhouses housed the orphaned, disabled, epileptic, feeble-minded, alcoholic, and unemployed. Their true foundation was not so much the ground on which they were built but rather the relatively new assumption that poverty was immoral, licentious, and even depraved.

The workings of the poorhouse were an effort to do something about the poor's degeneracy. Residents of the poorhouse were not expected simply to eat their gruel and live out their impoverished lives behind thick walls, but rather to suffer and, in the process, acquire proper values and good habits. The poorhouses in this sense resembled the era's growing number of penitentiaries, which incarcerated convicted criminals for long periods of time in hopes of reforming them. Just as a penitentiary would reform convicts and turn them into law-abiding citizens, the poorhouse would rehabilitate the poor and make them self-sufficient.[7] The more prosperous and righteous saw the poorhouses as not just shelters but also instructional facilities.

Overseers and superintendents required the residents of the poorhouses to work—and to work hard. Some of the residents chopped wood, washed laundry, or tilled vegetable gardens, but other residents had to endure make-work projects such as moving rocks from one side of the yard to the other, or carrying heavy bundles while walking on a treadmill. As unbelievably harsh as poorhouse rules and procedures might seem today, they were in fact designed to reintegrate the poor into their communities. Presumably, all the disciplined labor would equip the poor to avoid vice and eventually lead conventional lives. The fortunate ones, at least, might even find jobs as servants for the very people who put them in the poorhouses in the first place.[8]

The era's surging evangelical Protestantism endorsed and buoyed the moral retooling being attempted by the poorhouse managers. Although evangelical Protestantism was a more powerful force in rural America, it did bring its weight to bear in the urban setting as well. The urban poor were the evangelicals' chief targets, and evangelical Protestantism sought "to revive the power of shame through organized social disapproval."[9] In the 1820s and 1830s, voluntary associations in virtually every city attempted to address the urban poor's perceived laziness and moral decay. The associations focused on gambling, profanity, disrespect of the Sabbath, and what the evangelicals took to be illicit sex.

Prostitution was an especially pronounced concern among the reformers, and, not surprisingly given the limited employment opportunities for women in the emerging market economy, almost all of the prostitutes had poor and humble backgrounds. A woman might earn $2 for a week of twelve-hour days as a seamstress, but she might make $10 for one session as a prostitute. "By conservative estimate, in the 1840s between 5 percent and 10 percent of all New York women between fifteen and thirty worked for a time as prostitutes, and in hard times the percentage was higher. By the 1850s, prostitution was New York City's second largest cash-value business."[10]

Moral reformers opened shelters for penitent prostitutes, distributed an extraordinary number of tracts and leaflets, and even directly confronted the poor women plying sexual services. Ward Stafford, a self-styled missionary who preached on the streets of New York City, urged "the moral and pious" to walk through the areas in which prostitutes solicited customers. "Should respectable persons simply pass through particular streets every day and look at those who now exhibit in these streets all the degradation of their character," Stafford said, "it would soon cause them to hide their heads."[11]

The evangelical reformers also took the poor to be particularly prone to masturbation and, indeed, considered the "solitary vice" to be in itself a variety of illicit sex. The Presbyterian minister Sylvester Graham, whose most enduring contribution to the American diet was what came to be known as the "Graham cracker," lectured widely on the dangers of masturbation. He thought it caused mental derangement and led many to the poorhouses and asylums. Graham was concerned chiefly with masturbation among men, but others insisted women as well were going crazy and even dying from masturbation. Also shocking was the idea that masturbation was supposedly taking place in groups of individuals. Selected boys and girls were thought to teach and participate in group masturbation sessions and find special satisfaction in manipulating one another. And where might this be happening? The poorhouses, no doubt, were the most likely locales.[12]

In the decades prior to the Civil War, and to an even greater extent during the last third of the nineteenth century, poorhouse managers and evangelical reformers noted changes among the poorhouses' residents and shameless streetwalkers. A larger and larger percentage of the poor were immigrants from Europe. Furthermore, while earlier immigrants had tended to come from northern and western Europe, the new immigrants were more likely to hail from eastern and southern Europe. They were Czechs and Poles, Serbs and Russians, Italians and Greeks. Most did not speak English as a first language, and many appeared to have little interest in learning English as their proverbial second language. Unlike the largely Protestant native population, many of the new immigrants were Catholics and Jews.

As if the arrival of large numbers of these decidedly "foreign" outsiders was not troubling enough for the powers that be, the immigrant poor tended to live near one another in ethnic slums. In the larger cities, poorly constructed, low-rent tenements clustered tightly together on block after block. Extended ethnic families and the "roomers" who lived with these families jammed into tenement buildings, often sleeping two or three to the bed or even occupying and vacating the beds in "shifts." The tenements were noisy and congested, and the outhouses and outdoor latrines were often disturbingly unsanitary.

Concern about the tenements and the way in which the immigrant poor lived in them even led to a revealing change in the labels for rental housing. Prior to the Civil War, journalists, city officials, and Americans in general used the term "tenement" to refer to any building that housed three or more family groups. However, those developing multifamily rental housing for the middle and upper classes grew concerned that the allure of these new buildings would be diminished by any linkage, linguistic or otherwise, to the tenements in which the poor immigrants lived. As buildings with rental housing sprung up in Baltimore, Boston, Chicago, Philadelphia, and New York City in the final decades of the nineteenth century, the owners of the buildings searched for language that would distinguish them from tenements. Gradually, they settled on the phrase "apartment building" as an alternative. The hope was that no one would mistake "apartment buildings" and the financially secure people who lived in them for "tenements" and the presumably loud, degraded, and unhygienic urban poor who called them home.[13]

The great majority of middle- and upper-class Victorians did not attempt to improve conditions in the slums or to help the urban poor, but a small number of the economically successful and socially secure suggested small steps that could be taken to those ends. The proposals were more secular than those from earlier in the century and involved better construction methods for housing, more conscious planning for city growth, and publicly financed expansion of urban parks. Some do-gooders also attempted to rusticate the urban poor by developing farm schools and garden training institutes, promoting agricultural work as a desirable profession, and urging the development of rapid transit systems that would facilitate suburban migration.[14]

Reformers also suggested the enactment of housing codes for the tenement districts. New York City, for example, enacted the Tenement Housing Act, the nation's first housing code, in 1867. It pertained to the hygiene, safety, and general housing conditions in the tenements. The Tenement Housing Act also addressed the height, lot coverage, and spacing of the tenements. According to Roy Lubove, a social historian who wrote in the mid-twentieth century,

"American municipal reformers commonly assumed that if we imposed zoning regulations to prevent overcrowding, we would plug the fountain from which many of the physical and social evils of urban life flowed."[15]

The thinking was naive, well-intentioned, and hard to kill off. When the respected reformer Lawrence Veiller pointed out how poorly the Tenement Housing Act was working, people suggested improving rather than jettisoning it. In 1901, New York City enacted the Tenement House Law, a new and presumably better housing code. These reformist efforts also led to the drafting of a model housing code, which cities all around the country might consider enacting.[16]

Other reformers had approaches that resembled those of the early nineteenth century in that they addressed conduct and behavior rather than the physical environment. In particular, a well-intentioned group of reformers opened "settlement houses" in poor neighborhoods. While in 1891 there were only six settlement houses in the United States, by the turn of the twentieth century there were over one hundred.[17] The settlement house movement rejected the idea that urban poverty was inevitable and attempted instead to provide the poor with the skills and education necessary to lift themselves out of their condition. The best-known settlement house figure was Jane Addams. She founded Hull House in Chicago and became both the settlement movement's most articulate leader and a remarkably astute commentator on her own life and times.[18]

Like their reformist predecessors in the first half of the nineteenth century, the reformers from the end of the century hoped the urban poor could find a place in the mainstream, and some of the poor immigrants undoubtedly benefited from the new parks, tenement codes, and settlement-house programs. But unfortunately, end-of-the-century reformers could not lift many of the poor immigrants out of their slums or relieve their collective plight. To the extent the urban poor were able to build better lives, they did so through dogged, almost desperate hard work and with support from their families and ethnic communities. The United States was industrializing rapidly, but even though employers exploited workers and subjected them to uncertainty in the workplace, a significant number of workers rode jobs as laborers and factory hands from poverty to the blue-collar working class.

While clear evidence of hard work and success among the immigrants existed, most mainstream Americans remained leery of the urban poor and especially of the ethnic slums. Writing at the turn of the twentieth century in a book titled *Poverty*, even the well-intentioned socialist and international commentator Robert Hunter betrayed his doubts. While Hunter realized the urban poor were not the "paupers" of the early nineteenth century, he still thought they were unable or unwilling to take advantage of the opportunities available to them: "There are in all large cities . . . streets and courts and alleys where a class of people live who have lost all self-respect and ambition, who rarely, if ever, work, who are aimless and drifting, who like to drink, who have no thought for their children, and who live more or less contently on rubbish and alms."[19]

Urban Poverty in the Twentieth Century

In the early decades of the twentieth century, urban poverty became increasingly intertwined with issues of race, as large numbers of African Americans settled in American cities and became impoverished. During the so-called Great Migration between 1915 and 1960, five to six million African Americans migrated from the predominantly rural South to northern and western cities, with particularly large numbers settling in Chicago, Detroit, Los Angeles, New York City, and Pittsburgh.[20] In sheer numbers, the migration was larger than the migration of any single turn-of-the-century European ethnic group, and by 1970 more than 80 percent of African Americans lived in cities.[21]

The initial lure for the migration was employment in urban factories, but employment opportunities declined when white workers returned from World War I, and especially as a result of the economic collapse of the 1930s. More generally, the white working class felt threatened by the influx of new labor competition, and white business interests used mortgage discrimination and redlining to impede African Americans' efforts to find fairly priced housing. Then, too, as African American urban populations grew, middle- and upper-class whites moved to other neighborhoods and eventually to the suburbs, increasingly attributing crime, violence, and the use of drugs to African American populations. Often unemployed or struggling to find minimum-wage jobs, poor African Americans were semipermanently stuck in the inner cities.

As was the case in the nineteenth century, the majority of Americans considered the urban poor to be lazy and duplicitous, and this bias against the poor increased because of the nation's deeply entrenched racism.[22] However, a small number of Americans were genuinely sympathetic and supportive, and their thoughts surely merit mention.

Michael Harrington, for example, was one of the first prominent Americans to be sympathetic to the urban poor in the second half of the twentieth century. His *The Other America: Poverty in the United States*, published in 1962, rejected the idea that African Americans and the urban poor were indolent connivers and insisted instead that they were people denied the material support and social security the nation provided to most others. Widely read, *The Other America* demanded conscious, sustained social justice for the poor.[23]

According to an often-heard tale, one that subtly incorporates the hope among intellectuals that they might influence political leaders, President John F. Kennedy read Harrington's book and started to imagine federal anti-poverty measures.[24] After Kennedy's assassination, President Lyndon Johnson took up the cause and called, in his 1964 State of the Union Address, for "an unconditional war on poverty."[25] Congress then passed the Economic Opportunity Act, which set up the Office of Economic Opportunity to award federal funds to fight poverty. Some wondered even at the time if war-making metaphors were quite right for the anti-poverty program,[26] but would-be war makers did in fact express new policy commitments, launch federal programs, and form hundreds of local anti-poverty organizations.[27]

As for the policy commitments, the Congress was especially concerned with the dilapidated housing and neighborhoods in which the urban poor lived. Like the local reformers concerned with tenements and slums in another era, federal policymakers promoted programs addressing the urban poor's physical environment. Congress required that communities have "workable programs" for tending to their housing and neighborhood woes in order to be eligible for federal aid, which could then in turn be used for slum clearance, urban renewal, and public housing. Local programs, according to federal funding guidelines, had to include not only a housing code but also a mechanism for code enforcement.[28]

The War on Poverty's neighborhood and community organizations, meanwhile, sometimes took on a mildly subversive character. The organizations engaged in so-called community organizing and assorted efforts to enhance the social capital of the urban poor. Frequently thorns in the sides of local government leaders, the community organizations pointed out how the urban poor were overlooked and sometimes exploited. Public arguments and even physical skirmishes sometimes followed in housing projects, school boards, and city councils as the poor and their representatives tried to wrest control from elites.

It is an open question how much housing code enforcement took place and how enduring the community organizing proved to be. What's more, support for the War on Poverty declined and then disappeared during the 1970s. While some continue to credit the War on Poverty with reducing infant mortality, improving high-school graduation rates, and enabling single mothers to return to school or join the workforce,[29] the more general consensus is that the War on Poverty failed.[30]

During the waning days of the War on Poverty, observers and commentators began referring to the urban poor as the "underclass." The term itself is intriguing. While the dominant American belief system emphasizes the individual and dwells incessantly on individual struggles for success and advancement, the term "underclass" suggests something less individualized and more collective. While users of the term "underclass" were not for the most part attempting to add to the immense social-science literature on socioeconomic class, the very notion of a "class"—underclass or otherwise—connotes some degree of social rigidity and permanence. In addition, to speak of a class "under" the others implied a hierarchy of social groups.

As may already be obvious, the "underclass" is not the same as the "proletariat," to invoke a central and much favored notion from Marxian theory. Marx not only condemned the exploitation of industrial workers but also thought the "proletariat" would seize control from the wealthy "bourgeoisie" and then lead the way to socialism and eventually to communism. If there is a group in Marxian theory that resembles the "underclass," it might be what Marx called the "lumpenproletariat." He took this group to consist primarily of vagabonds, beggars, and petty criminals, and he hardly anticipated that they would lead the struggle for liberation.[31] For Marx, the members of the "lumpenproletariat" were "social scum, that passively rotting mass thrown off by the lowest layers of old society."[32]

The American "underclass" was not scummy, at least as originally conceived. Consisting of the unemployed and barely employed and their children, the "underclass" caught the eye of American journalists in the late 1970s.[33] A lengthy journalistic treatment of the underclass titled "The American Underclass: Destitute and Desperate in the Land of Plenty" appeared in the August 29, 1977, issue of *Time*, middle-class America's favorite newsweekly. Presumably group-written, the article had no byline, but it did have a large number of striking photographs of littered streets, decaying tenements, and African Americans and Latinos decidedly down on their luck. The article was sympathetic to the underclass, bemoaning the unemployment, alienation, violence, and drug addiction in the daily lives of the era's urban poor.[34]

The scholar Herbert Gans collected data showing what was already obvious to the naked eye—journalists liked the term "underclass." And indeed, according to his study of three newsmagazines (*Newsweek*, *Time*, and *U.S. News and World Report*) and three of the nation's most respected daily newspapers (*Chicago Tribune*, *Los Angeles Times*, and *New York Times*), references to and commentaries on the "underclass" were skyrocketing. There was a substantial increase during the early 1980s compared to the late 1970s and another big jump in the late 1980s compared to the early 1980s.[35]

Sociologists also took to the term and predictably attempted to quantify underclass life. The most distinguished of these sociologists was Harvard University's William Julius Wilson, whose studies of poor African Americans in Chicago are among the most distinguished sociological works of the final decades of the twentieth century.[36] Wilson acknowledged that a disproportionately large percentage of the urban poor were African American, but he also argued that the growth of a large urban underclass did not come about simply due to racism. A large, predominantly African American underclass had emerged, Wilson maintained, in good part because of post–World War II deindustrialization. The urban poor's access to traditional blue-collar jobs that they could ride out of poverty declined precipitously, and the urban poor also lacked the skills, degrees, and education necessary for the jobs becoming newly available in the postindustrial economy. The "underclass," according to Wilson, was "the very bottom of the economic hierarchy and not only includes those lower-class workers whose income falls below the poverty level but also the more or less permanent welfare recipients, the long-term unemployed, and those who have officially dropped out of the labor market."[37]

To make matters worse, Wilson thought, the urban poor became concentrated and isolated. Starting in the 1960s and continuing in subsequent years, the middle- and upper-class residents of inner-city neighborhoods, as small in number as they might have been, moved away. The poor people who were left behind lived mostly with other poor people. Packed together and often profoundly alienated, the urban poor were less successful in building relationships and networks with one another. Their limited social capital resulted in less social cohesion in general, and the unfortunate situation continued to build on itself. Stated bluntly, the urban poor were becoming increasingly unable to build and maintain their communities.

Then, as if the situation were not bad enough, in the late 1980s conservative journalists and sociologists turned on the underclass. Against the backdrop of a general downturn in the economy, conservatives started to blame the underclass for sapping resources, and for refusing to work their way up the rickety ladder to success. According to one liberal commentator, conservatives increasingly took the urban poor to be "shiftless, irresponsible, and prone to addiction. . . . So, if they suffer from grievous material deprivation, if they run out of money between paychecks, if they do not always have food on their tables—they have no one to blame but themselves."[38]

One widely read conservative sniper was Myron Magnet, who published, among other pieces, a lengthy feature article in *Fortune*. He did not think of the underclass as a needy, sympathetic sector of the population, but rather cast underclass neighborhoods as "urban knots that threaten to become enclaves of permanent poverty and vice." What primarily distinguished members of the underclass, Magnet wrote, "is not so much their poverty or race as their behavior—their chronic lawlessness, drug use, out-of-wedlock births, non-work, welfare dependency, and school failure. 'Underclass' describes a state of mind and a way of life. It is at least as much a cultural as an economic condition."[39]

Among sociologists, William Julius Wilson's scholarly work was so accomplished that many sociologists continued to praise and extend it, but another group of sociologists who did not share Wilson's politics and perceptions scurried to their keyboards to take Wilson to task. Like the conservative journalists, these sociologists questioned the very notion of a deprived underclass. Christopher Jencks, for example, argued that talk of an "underclass" did not truly help the society to understand urban poverty:

> Everyone who stops to think recognizes that the world is untidy in this sense. We use class labels precisely because we want to make the world seem tidier than it is. The purpose of labels is to draw attention to the differences between classes. But by emphasizing differences between classes, such labels inevitably encourage us to forget about the much larger differences that exist *within* classes.[40]

With Jencks and other academics grousing and complaining, even Wilson grew tired of the notion of an "underclass." In one of those episodes that qualify as high drama among academics, Wilson delivered a presidential address at the annual meeting of the American Sociological Association in 1990 that surprised the assembled. Fearing that the term "underclass" had been co-opted by conservatives and was being used to denigrate inner-city African Americans, Wilson said he would relinquish the term and begin using the phrase "ghetto poor" as a substitute.[41] At the same time, of course, Wilson remained committed to addressing the plight of the urban poor in his scholarly work.[42]

In more recent years, the term "underclass" has virtually disappeared from journalism, sociology, and political debate, but the social group designated by the term has not become less numerous or blended into American life. African Americans continue to make up a disproportionately large percentage of the urban poor. A full 22 percent of African Americans live in poverty, a percentage significantly higher than that for Latinos, Asians, and—of course—whites.[43] African Americans are also more than two times as likely as whites to be either unemployed or underemployed.[44]

Beyond African Americans, others constitute important parts of the ranks of the urban poor. Many Latinos, especially Mexicans, continue to find employment as farm laborers, but even larger numbers of Latinos live in American cities, often in abject poverty. In addition, many recent immigrants and refugees from Africa, the Middle East, and southeastern Asia belong to the urban poor. The general public routinely conceives of the immigrants and refugees with reference to their ethnicity and religion, but the public tends to overlook the poor housing, unemployment, and poverty that await many of the immigrants and refugees. Since late 2016, to cite just one example, a large number of Syrian refugees have settled in Fresno, the largest city in California's agricultural interior. Fresno apparently has abundant inexpensive rental housing, but the city's lack of employment opportunities and suffocating poverty make it virtually certain that the Syrian refugees will find their place among Fresno's poor.[45]

Even whites, somewhat surprisingly, have a small place among the urban poor. In cities such as Indianapolis, Jacksonville, Memphis, and Nashville, whites actually have higher rates of unemployment and are more impoverished than Latinos.[46] We perhaps overlook white poverty in our cities because it is less concentrated in particular neighborhoods than is African American or Latino poverty. Poor rural whites cluster in particular towns and counties, but poor urban whites reside in and about working- and middle-class white neighborhoods.

In essence, today's urban poor consist of unemployed or marginally employed African Americans, Latinos, recent immigrants and refugees, and even some whites. Most continue to live in the slums, ghettos, and decaying neighborhoods of America's postindustrial cities. In addition, a smaller number have taken up residence in areas outside the center cities of metropolitan areas.

Some commentators have in fact coupled the presence of the poor in the suburbs with the movement of the middle and upper classes into downtown neighborhoods and cast the two phenomena as a "demographic inversion."[47] The idea is that the poor are moving up and out while members of the middle and upper classes are "gentrifying" urban areas. This supposed socioeconomic reshaping of American metropolitan areas is for some a reassuring, albeit curious, confirmation of social mobility and equality in American life.

But wishing for "demographic inversion" does not make it a reality. For starters, the traditional urban poor, the group Wilson called the "underclass," have not been able to move into newer and more affluent suburbs. To the extent the urban poor have moved to the suburbs, they have moved to poor or working-class suburbs immediately adjacent to their former neighborhoods in the center city. In metropolitan Milwaukee, for example, substantial numbers of poor people have made the formerly blue-collar suburbs of West Milwaukee and West Allis home, but almost none have found their way to the second and third suburban rings to the west and north of Milwaukee. In metropolitan Chicago, the older working-class suburb of Harvey was perhaps the first suburb to accommodate the urban poor,[48] and in more recent years other suburbs immediately to the south and southwest of the city such as Lansing, Matteson, Park Forest, Richton Park, and South Holland have become home for significant populations of poor people. However, few poor people have taken up residence in the prestigious North Shore suburbs.[49]

Basically, the great majority of the urban poor have stayed put and watched as conditions worsened all around them. A 2011 report titled "The Re-Emergence of Concentrated Poverty" documented the growth in number and size of both "high-poverty neighborhoods," in which at least 20 percent of the residents live in poverty, and "distressed neighborhoods," in which at least 40 percent of the residents live in poverty. The obstacles to getting by, much less to finding success, are much greater in these neighborhoods than in middle- and upper-class neighborhoods, or even in neighborhoods that are simply less poor. Concentrated poverty is largely an urban as opposed to a suburban phenomenon. One in four poor urban neighborhoods has concentrated poverty, while only 6.3 percent of poor suburban neighborhoods face a comparable problem.[50]

The effects of living in concentrated poverty are particularly consequential for children. Children are especially vulnerable to the stress that comes along with concentrated poverty, and long-term emotional and behavioral problems can result. A study by the Annie E. Casey Foundation documented this and found that fully two-thirds of children living in concentrated poverty do in fact live within center cities.[51]

As for "gentrification"—the other half of the purported "demographic inversion"—it, too, is a more complicated phenomenon than what at first meets the eye. The sociologist Ruth Glass first used the term "gentrification" during the 1960s to describe the movement of middle- and upper-class English families to what had been predominately working-class coastal villages.[52] Americans then applied the term to the process through which developers convert older parts of the center city into condominiums, restaurants, and stores appealing to the middle and upper classes. Most commonly, the impoverished and working poor who had lived in the gentrifying area vacate it, and in many cases the new arrivals are mostly white, while those departing are usually African American.[53]

Yet the ability of gentrification to turn the fundamental demographics of metropolitan areas upside down is questionable. While the suburbs harbor plenty of would-be gentrifiers, the substantial increase in housing values that could be seen as evidencing gentrification has only occurred in a small group of prosperous cities: Boston, New York, San Francisco, Seattle, and Washington, DC. One study looked at 1,119 impoverished census tracts in fifty-one metropolitan areas and found that from 1970 to 2010, only 105 of those tracts have experienced a significant degree of gentrification.[54]

If anything is particularly noteworthy in the early twenty-first century, it is not the abandonment of the term "underclass" or the movement of some of the urban poor into the suburbs. The critical observer of urban life might note instead the sobering absence of large-scale, systematic, and genuine efforts to free the urban poor from their alienating, dead-end lives. Nineteenth-century Americans thought immoral paupers could be brought back into the social fold. At the turn of the twentieth century, some Americans believed schools, parks, and settlement-house instruction on how to cook healthier meals would help. Today, most middle- and upper-class Americans write off urban poverty as a thorny and intractable reality, and one common twenty-first-century hope is that the urban poor will somehow disappear.

The Functioning of Law in American Life

Law is extraordinarily important in the lives of the urban poor and in American society in general. There seems to be little disagreement that Americans not only use law to articulate their policy choices but also rely on law for an understanding of their fundamental rights and responsibilities. According to the Danish scholar Helle Porsdam, "What in other countries may be seen as merely legal or political-legal analyses in the United States become the articulation of the ideas and aspirations that define the national identity."[55] Furthermore, socio-legal scholars have insisted that law is ubiquitous in everyday life, often in ways that go unrecognized. Law, they maintain, is less removed from social life than it is "fused with and inseparable from the activities of living and knowing."[56]

But how does law, broadly understood, function? How do the laws, legal proceedings, and legal institutions actually work in American life? Those questions are daunting. However, an attempt to abstractly capture how the law functions might be worth the effort. If nothing else, this attempt could beneficially set the stage for this book's overarching pursuit, namely, a consideration and appraisal of how law works for, against, and with regard to the urban poor.

In general, law *does* things, and it *says* things. On the first score, law causes things to happen. It directs and manages what we should do, where we should live, and how we might earn, save, and spend our money. Traditional sociologists, without intending to be pejorative, characterize this as a matter of "social control." They also emphasize that social control through law and legal institutions is likely to be more evident in a modern society such as the United States.[57] And indeed, the ability of law and legal institutions to bring about social compliance and social order should not be underestimated.

An observer could collapse with mental exhaustion if he or she tried to list all of the more specialized things that fit or could fit under the rubric "social control." Law, legal proceedings, and legal institutions permit and oblige, reform and redirect; they also channel, constrain, forbid, incarcerate, penalize, isolate, relocate, and even unify. Law and legal institutions often achieve some of their goals by making certain choices more undesirable than others by increasing their social and financial cost. Basically, law and legal institutions prompt and require people to behave and conduct themselves in particular ways.

Law also says things—that is, it functions "expressively." While it is difficult to draw a bright line between social control through law and expression via the law, the latter is more a matter of what the words of the law suggest than what the law actually allows or requires. Traditional law professors spend a great deal of time underscoring and dissecting just what the law says, but one can find a greater appreciation of how and why the law is expressive in the works of an interdisciplinary humanist such as James Boyd White. Writing in the late 1980s, White described law as a kind of "constitutive rhetoric," and he insisted that law as rhetoric is crucial in how "culture and community are established."[58] More recent scholars have continued to insist that law is engaged in "making statements," be they direct or indirect, denotative or connotative.[59]

As is true with the social control function, law's expressive function includes a huge range of possibilities. Laws, legal proceedings, and legal institutions communicate positions, send messages, and convey images. Law articulates values and preferences, and it says what is right and what is wrong. In this book, I am especially interested in the way certain groups in society use law to say how other groups are supposed to behave. In some cases this type of expression is straightforward and explicit, while in other cases it is subtle and symbolic.

Identifying the exact meaning of legal expression is never easy. It is not as if a statute or an administrative regulation unambiguously sets out what it means. The meaning of a law or set of laws is socially constructed. That is, meaning results from the reigning attitudes, norms, and practices of a given community or of the dominant groups within a community. The community need not consciously and collectively share what it takes a law to mean, but, at minimum, the meaning has to be something the community can grasp and recognize.[60] Lawrence Lessig, a particularly influential commentator on the expressive function of the law, once said, "One cannot use meaning talk to speak in ways that purport to be general laws of humanity. Meanings, prescriptions, and descriptions are more local, more contingent. Meanings are often highly contestable and sometimes hard to know."[61]

Then, too, it is not only the actual enacted and printed laws that convey meanings that can conjure up plausible interpretations in the community. We must also consider the ways these rules are presented, debated, and justified by legislators. Furthermore, deliberations in legislatures, as revealing as they might be, are not necessarily the most important sources regarding what laws mean to the public. Other important sources of information might be publicity about forthcoming laws, news reports regarding them, or even pop-cultural representations of the laws. Law *says* things, but various sources and media convey the legal message.[62]

The social control and expressive functions are abstractions, and sprawling ones at that, but law can in fact provide social control, express thoughts, or do both at once. The key point is that law works in myriad, important ways. Law, broadly understood, shapes both individual lives and the collective lives of social groups, and law conveys things about people and how they should conduct themselves. A diverse, complex society such as that of the United States would be unstable and perhaps impossible without its law and legal institutions.

Containment, Condemnation, and Oppression

Providing social control and expressing values and judgments, law is tremendously important in the lives of the urban poor, and in the chapters that follow I will try to demonstrate this by exploring law's relationship to five crucial concerns of the urban poor. These five concerns are not so much subject areas in a law school curriculum but rather fundamental concerns for the urban poor. Many poor people begin and then work through their days wondering about the possibility of criminal justice, the homes in which they live, the state of their families, their ability to buy what they want, and their health and well-being. Accordingly, chapters 1 through 5 of this book are titled, respectively, "Labeling the Urban Poor as Criminals," "No Place to Call Home," "Channeling Family Life," "Marketplace Exploitation," and "Health Inequity."

Law, legal proceedings, and legal institutions are not mere gadgets but rather main cogs in these five areas. Variations and exceptions of course exist in all of the areas, and law, legal proceedings, and legal institutions are not simply instruments uniformly and unremittingly used to hold down the urban poor. But, at the same time, a pattern of containment and condemnation is evident. The law, broadly understood, requires that the urban poor remain in their neighborhoods and in their socioeconomic class. Basically, the urban poor are supposed to stay put. In many instances, the law also expresses disapproval of the urban poor. It implicitly and sometimes explicitly criticizes, rebukes, and deplores the urban poor for the impractical and unhealthy ways they lead their lives.

This containment and condemnation is more harmful and hostile than one realizes at first. By containing and condemning the urban poor, the law to some extent institutes, establishes, and enacts urban poverty. The containing and condemning contribute mightily to making the urban poor who they are and who they are perceived to be. If it were not for law, the urban poor might not even exist as a recognizable sector of the population.

What, overall, should we make of the apparent pattern of containment and condemnation? How might we characterize the relationship of law to the urban poor? The notion seems harsh, but oppression might be afoot. We normally associate "oppression" with tyrants and despots, and in this traditional variety of oppression, an ethnic group, race, class, or even an entire population is under the thumb of a central armed or authoritarian force. However, oppression of a more subtle sort is also possible in a democratic society. When oppression exists in a society such as that of the United States, it derives from a combination of factors and phenomena working together to constrain and devalue a given social group. Since the oppressive forces are varied and numerous, oppression is less evident and perhaps not even noticed.

Law, it seems to me, is a major oppressive force in the lives of the contemporary urban poor. Containment and condemnation through law take place in each of the five areas discussed in subsequent chapters of this book. When it comes to the urban poor, law, broadly understood, might be best construed as an extremely important, multifaceted agent of oppression.

CHAPTER ONE

Labeling the Urban Poor as Criminals

very morning on my drive to work, I confront a towering, illuminated billboard with large, rotating photos of criminals. Mostly men wanted for murder, attempted murder, and armed robbery, the individuals in the photos look angry. No well-groomed bankers or professionals among them, they project an ominous roughness. A line of print stretching across the bottom of the billboard provides the authorities' telephone number and asks motorists to call if they know where the criminals are hiding.

Like everyone else in my comfortable middle-class part of town, I have absolutely no idea where the pictured men are, and it is not even clear if the men have perpetrated their heinous acts locally. Nevertheless, the billboard effectively labels these men as criminals. Popular with scholars in the 1960s and 1970s, "criminal labeling theory" insists that there be a "process of social definition" before a person can be deemed a criminal.[1] The identification of criminals, in other words, requires some sort of gesture or statement from certain people or institutions and a reaction to the gesture or statement.[2] The giant billboard labels supposed perpetrators, and, along with others passing through the intersection, I notice the billboard and am chilled by a sense that criminals are among us.

Being labeled a criminal is highly consequential because it both denigrates and restricts, and police departments, district attorneys' offices, criminal courts, and prisons are more important in criminal labeling than the largest of billboards. These legal institutions continually and sometimes eagerly characterize and identify criminals. The institutions' labeling can come in many ways, ranging from something as simple as pushing down an arrested person's head as he or she enters the back seat of a squad car all the way to a formal conviction and sentencing in a court of law. The legal institutions often act in combination and in sequence, and as criminals pass through the system, their criminal labels grow larger, darker, and more indelible.

Men and women who are unemployed or marginally employed are more likely to be labeled as criminals than are other members of society. The process is not a tightly coordinated conspiracy, but police officers, prosecutors, and jailers repeatedly apply rules of one sort or another and in the process deem individual impoverished city dwellers to be criminals. While in many cases those labeled have committed the criminal acts that are alleged, the criminal justice system too unthinkingly and too hastily attaches criminal labels to the urban poor.

In the end, this labeling during arrests, in the courthouses, and through imprisonment affects more than individual suspects, defendants, and inmates. Criminal labeling by the law and legal institutions contributes mightily to a broader sociocultural process of criminalization, one that sometimes implies all of the urban poor are criminal. Those angry and menacing young men who stare down at me from the giant illuminated billboard do so not only as individuals but also as representatives of a whole sector of the American population. The criminalization of the urban poor is a forceful first step in their oppression.

Arrest

The labeling of the urban poor as criminals does not begin with formal convictions in a court of law but rather with arrests on the streets of town. When the police arrest a poor person—usually a youth or young adult—consequences abound. The arrested person loses touch with school or work, assuming either has a place in his or her life. Many friends, neighbors, and relatives conclude the arrested person had "gone bad" or turned toward crime, and complete restoration of lost trust and respect is almost impossible. While in custody, the arrested person interacts with others who may have more fully accepted identities as criminals and are prepared to influence arrested neophytes. One arrest sets the stage for subsequent arrests, and it is not an exaggeration to say that being arrested can change the tenor and direction of one's life.

Where are the arrests most likely to occur? The answer is hardly surprising: Arrests are most likely where crime and criminal victimization are the most common. Study after study shows this locale to be the poor neighborhoods of our inner cities. The indefatigable William Julius Wilson, whose characterization of the urban poor as an "underclass" was mentioned in the introduction, has attempted to explain this phenomenon. In an article written with fellow sociologist Robert J. Sampson, Wilson observed that "macrosocial patterns of residential inequality give rise to social isolation and the ecological concentration of the truly disadvantaged, which in turn leads to structural barriers and cultural adaptation that undermine social organization and hence control of crime."[3] Wilson and Sampson remind us, to put it more directly, to bear in mind the concentrated poverty and lack of social coherence in the communities in which crime and criminal victimization are most prevalent. We should not be surprised, Wilson and Sampson tell us, that a great deal of criminal conduct occurs in poor urban neighborhoods. As these neighborhoods took on their modern form in the 1970s and 1980s, they experienced dramatic increases in arrests per capita. The arrest rates then remained at high levels through the remainder of the twentieth century and into the twenty-first century.[4]

But concentrated poverty and deteriorating social capital do not fully explain the high arrest rates in poor inner-city neighborhoods. The controversial mindsets, expectations, and tactics of the police are also important factors. These features of policing push what are already high arrest rates even higher.

Facing criticism for their attitudes and actions, police departments have in fact greatly increased public-relations appearances and also the production of pamphlets and videos about their role as friendly helpers of the public. Then, too, so-called community policing has become all the rage. In community policing, police cordially patrol on foot, decentralize their departments, and most generally attempt to coordinate police work with the preferences of neighborhood residents and community organizations. Community policing stresses cooperation and partnership, and who, after all, wants to oppose anything with the word "community" in its name?

In reality, though, many police are not truly prepared to relinquish the power to community leaders or even to pay attention to what the leaders have to say.[5] Stated simply, police prefer to root out crime and apprehend lawbreakers on their own. Individual police might have a passion for stamping out specific varieties of wrongdoing as indicated by the law, but more commonly police are enamored with enforceable laws whatever they might be. They think laws are to be followed, and they want to enforce them and crack down on those who break them. In their private heart-of-hearts, most police take their role to literally be "law enforcement."

The police are likely to be especially sanguine about law enforcement in poor urban communities. In particular, police are prone to perceiving poor urban neighborhoods as "offensible space."[6] When a policeman observes the boarded-up storefronts and broken windows, he or she is likely to think of crime and violence. When a policeman contemplates the bulletproof shields in front of cash registers in corner stores, or the curving, metallic graffiti on the buses and trains, he or she might assume that criminals lurk and abound. Police come to the inner city thinking it is crime-laden, see visual cues, and take their expectations to be confirmed.[7]

Beyond their general expectations and the visual cues, many police react to the behavior and characteristics of actual people they encounter in the inner city. Some police might see men wearing low-slung pants or sporting neck tattoos as likely to have criminal tendencies and inclinations. More crudely, some policemen might consider African Americans and Latinos as especially strong candidates for arrest. Certain people might strike police as a "good collar"—that is, an arrest that can stick and lead ultimately to a conviction.[8]

In 2013, this type of thinking struck Judge Shira A. Scheindlin as an unconstitutional variety of racial profiling. Her 140-page opinion for the United States District Court for the Southern District of New York reviewed data for four million police stops and the purported efforts of New York City police to stop and frisk the right people at the right times in the right locations. In Scheindlin's mind, the notion of "the right people" was especially disconcerting in that it targeted members of groups heavily represented in the New York Police Department's crime-suspect data and thereby resulted in the disproportionate stopping and frisking of African Americans and Latinos. A person's race, like a person's height and weight, could be a permissible consideration in the descriptions of a specific suspect. But the practices of New York City's police did not relate to specific suspects and had to cease because it was impermissible to subject members of a racially defined group to heightened law enforcement simply because of their group affiliation.[9] As Scheindlin put it, "The Equal Protection Clause does not permit race-based suspicion."[10]

Scheindlin's 2013 decision outraged Michael Bloomberg and Raymond Kelly, the mayor and police commissioner respectively, and New York City legal officials successfully petitioned for a stay of Scheindlin's order.[11] "Stop-and-frisk" policies then became one of the most pointed issues in the immediately subsequent mayoral election. After Bill de Blasio was victorious in that election, he settled the case by agreeing to the reforms Judge Scheindlin had ordered in the first place. In the present, the police department is ambitiously revising its policies, training, supervision, and discipline regarding "stop-and-frisk." In addition, an appointed official now monitors police practices, and in one pilot program, officers have to wear tiny video cameras that record what is said and done while officers are on patrol.[12] The video camera idea has caught the eye of other communities and police departments and may eventually take hold in many cities. Overall, Judge Scheindlin estimated when she retired in 2016 that her orders had led street stops in New York City to drop from 685,000 in 2011 to only 24,000 in 2015.[13]

One reason New York City police officials and unions were so upset with Judge Scheindlin's ruling is that a reliance on the notion of "offensible space" and a sense of who might be a "good collar" were truly central in police department operations. Police departments in New York City and elsewhere want to convince the public they are doing their job and doing it well. This may or may not involve meetings behind closed doors to discuss how to pump up arrest figures, but police departments serve their own interests by arresting frequently and efficiently. Hence, in the words of one prominent criminologist, "The large population of poor black males is the perfect bureaucratic solution. . . . In a class society, the powerless, the poor, and those who fit the public stereotype of 'the criminal' are the human resources needed by law enforcement agencies to maximize rewards and minimize strains."[14]

Contributing even further to the problem is what criminologists call the "asymmetrical status norm" in police work.[15] As middle- and upper-class drivers stopped for a traffic offense know or quickly come to know, many police expect to receive more respect and deference than they are prepared to give. They expect to be addressed formally and approached politely. This is not the time for banter or, Heaven forbid, wisecracks. "A good deal of law enforcement is devoted not to the actual enforcement of rules, but to coercing respect from the people with whom the enforcer deals. This means that one may be labeled a criminal not because he has actually broken a rule, but because he has shown disrespect to the enforcer of the rule."[16] According to one older study, failure to show respect for a policeman is the most certain way to get arrested by that policeman.[17] Furthermore, police are often older than the people they have stopped or are questioning, and police are more likely to be white than are the people they encounter. Age and a sense of racial superiority can add to the asymmetrical expectations.

Within the "offensible space" of a center city populated by the urban poor, the asymmetrical expectations of the police are frequently unmet in encounters with poor people, especially teenagers and young adults. The police perceive young people wearing the badges of poverty to be rude and disrespectful. Police are unwilling to "take any shit" from these "wise-ass punks." Police almost instinctively feel the need to take firm control when dealing with the urban poor, and the resulting encounters are more fractious and menacing than one might expect. Given the tension, arrests become even more likely.

What's more, the law related to how and why police might arrest has evolved in ways that allow and almost invite the police to arrest. In his prize-winning book *No Equal Justice*, Georgetown University law professor David Cole has systematically set out an argument for how arrest law supports the police's proclivity for arresting the urban poor.[18] While the police cannot simply search a person because they want to, the Supreme Court of the United States has ruled that suspects can "voluntarily" consent to searches. Police can and do exploit the consent-search rules for intimidated and poorly educated suspects, and when searches yield guns, illegal drugs, or stolen property, the police arrest.[19]

Stop-and-frisk rules also allow a policeman who wants to arrest an inner-city resident to do so. Theoretically, the police cannot stop and frisk a suspect unless they have "reasonable suspicion" of wrongdoing, but a substantial body of laws and court rulings allows policemen to stop a person if they observe a suspect in a high-crime area or if the suspect is engaging in suspicious, evasive behavior.[20] This standard creates a special vulnerability for the urban poor. For starters, and recalling where most crime is perpetrated, the urban poor for the most part live in what would classify as a "high-crime area." Then, too, the urban poor frequently have reason to avoid the police even if they have done nothing criminal. The urban poor, after all, are aware of patterns of harassment, tasing, rough treatment, and even shooting by police, and often head the other way whenever the police appear on their personal radar screens. This avoidance, though, might register as evasive and suspicious and thereby provide a legally justified opportunity to stop and frisk. To make a potentially longer story short, stop-and-frisks "are applied disproportionately to the poor, to African Americans and to Hispanic Americans."[21] If frisking turns up a weapon, contraband, or both, the police can arrest, and no legal issues present themselves.

Police can also arrest individuals in motor vehicles using what are sometimes called "pretext stops." Police can almost always follow a car long enough to observe a rolling stop or failure to change a lane properly. Equipment problems also provide a pretext to stop a motor vehicle, and some police admit off the record that if all of a car's equipment is working, it is still easy to stop a car and break out the left rear taillight on the slow, ominous stroll to the driver's window.[22] Then, too, the possibility always exists that fuzzy dice, medallions, or even pacifiers will be hanging from the rearview mirror—a virtual requirement on older cars driven by younger men of modest means, and technically an equipment violation in most jurisdictions.[23] Given a purported traffic or equipment violation, a policeman can look inside the vehicle. If he or she spots weapons, drugs, open liquor bottles, or stolen property, he or she can arrest.

The media have reported frequently on the "driving while black" problem. As noted, African Americans are suspicious in some law-enforcement eyes simply because of their race. Sometimes police stop African American drivers not because of motor vehicle violations but rather because they are African Americans. Heated arguments might ensue, as might arrests, for what is really a matter of belonging to a subordinate race. In fairness to the media, the news stories have for the most part been critical of this phenomenon. However, the media have not satisfactorily noted that when a traffic stop occurs because somebody is African American, the traffic stop may be a pretext for looking for something else in order to make an arrest. The traffic stop, in other words, is often a means to a more consequential end.

Police attitudes, practices, and the legal standards that facilitate arrest are especially important to the urban poor. While middle- and upper-class Americans have the luxury of taking city councils and mayors to be the embodiment of their local government, the urban poor often take the police to be the government in their lives. And indeed, law enforcement and perhaps the welfare system in a very real sense constitute the predominant government of the poor.[24] When that "government" is not only eager to arrest but also, as is increasingly the case, willing to assert its power through such measures as street roll calls and saturation patrols, members of poor urban communities might understandably take the police to be an oppressive force.

Hostility to the police is common in poor communities. It manifests, for example, in Latino folktales called "corridos," in which crafty criminals outwit the cops, and in rap songs with anti-police lyrics.[25] "Fuck the Police" and "Cop Killer" are pointed examples of the latter and are often considered rap "classics." In "Fuck the Police," Dr. Dre presides at the trial of several policemen, and assorted rappers testify regarding police misconduct. One of the rappers fantasizes about putting a clip in his gun and shooting a policeman. "Taking out police will make my day."[26] In "Cop Killer," Ice-T similarly fantasizes about killing a policeman who had harassed him: "I'm about to kill somethin'. A pig stopped me for nuthin'."[27] Hostility toward the police is also evident in anti-snitching campaigns or networks of safe houses for illegal immigrants hiding from the authorities.[28]

Indeed, there is something of a tradition of anti-police resistance movements, especially among African Americans. In these movements, complaints about the police sometimes spawn multipurpose sociopolitical organizations and protests. A good example is the Black Panther Party, for example, which originated in the slums of Oakland, California, in the late 1960s. The Panthers offered free breakfasts, preschool programs, and basic health care, but their legendary slogan "Off the Pigs" sounded in middle-class America like a threat to kill policemen. In reality, the slogan referred more generally to the large and heavy presence and menacing hostile attitudes of the police in the Panthers' home communities. When it became clear that the Black Panther Party was at its core an anti-police organization, the police set out to eliminate the organization, and for the most part succeeded.[29]

More recently, the Black Lives Matter movement started with complaints about police misconduct. The movement originated in 2013 after the self-styled community watchman George Zimmerman was acquitted for shooting Florida teenager Trayvon Martin. The movement grew in 2014 after police shootings of Michael Brown in Ferguson, Missouri, and Eric Garner in New York City. Protests and unrest followed, as they did after still more deaths of African Americans from police gunfire or while in police custody. The initial focus of the movement was racial profiling and police brutality in the criminal justice system, but the movement also began to deplore the general inequality of African Americans in contemporary society. The movement found traction as a broader civil rights movement.

Particularly interesting with regard to Black Lives Matter's larger goals is the economic policy statement Black Lives Matter issued in 2016. The statement deplored the high levels of unemployment in African American urban communities, called for full employment, and demanded a "universal basic income." The statement also noted the decades of disinvestment and deterioration. Large-scale economic revitalization, the statement said, was desperately needed. Racial justice, the statement maintained, could only be possible in conjunction with economic justice.[30]

No doubt aware of the movement's appeal and growth, the United States Justice Department's Community Oriented Policing Services Office in September 2015 issued a lengthy report on police errors and mistakes in Ferguson, Missouri, and elsewhere. Many of the report's 113 "lessons" concern the police's handling of demonstrations following racially charged arrests. The report urges police, for example, to be cautious in the use of dogs and tear gas, and

to avoid militarizing crowd control. One especially intriguing and also disconcerting suggestion is that police departments disingenuously seize control of
the narrative concerning police conduct, lest sectors of the population using
social media successfully develop and disseminate their own anti-police
narratives.[31]

The typical person arrested in the inner city is less endowed with narrative
skills and less equipped with social-media technology than are the anti-police
protestors who so worried police and government officials. However, everyday
arrests are nevertheless important initial ways one legal institution—the
police—disproportionately labels the urban poor as criminals. Later in time,
charges might be pursued or dropped; an arrested man or woman might be
convicted or set free. But as early as his or her first arrest, a poor person acquires
the markings of a misfit, an outlier, a person not willing to play the game. Surely
he or she is not the type of person members of the middle and upper classes
take themselves to be.

Jail and Prosecution

After being arrested, the arrested person enters the sealed back seat of a police
squad car or takes a bench seat in the windowless compartment of a police
van. The subsequent ride to the police station or county lockup is only the first
part of a tortuous bureaucratic and legal journey, in which agents of the state
decide whether the arrested person will be charged, prosecuted, or, in many
cases, simply released. The arrested person watches and waits as the system
decides whether the criminal label acquired via arrest should be made bigger
and more permanent.

Scholars who have considered the period in the criminal justice process between arrest and trial have bemoaned this period's murkiness and arbitrariness.
The courts have, over the years, articulated fairly comprehensible rules about
how arrests might be made, and while those rules do the urban poor no favors,
at least arresting officers and arrestees have some guidelines to keep in mind.
In the period between arrest and trial, by contrast, much of what happens is
unofficial and provisional, open to negotiation and bargaining. Searching for

terms to describe this period, some scholars have called it "purgatory," referring, one assumes, to the condition or place in which, according to traditional Roman Catholic doctrine, penitent souls might temporarily suffer for their sinfulness before, at last, moving on to something more pleasant.[32] An even larger number of scholars have chosen to cast the period between arrest and trial as a "Twilight Zone," presumably referencing the television anthology series named *The Twilight Zone*, which found great success on American prime-time television in the late 1950s and early 1960s. The creation of Rod Serling, the series featured tales of suspense, horror, fantasy, and science fiction, and in many episodes, the tale ended with an unexpected or truly macabre twist. For some commentators, developments and final determinations in the period between arrest and trial are comparably weird.[33]

"Purgatory" or the "Twilight Zone" in the criminal justice system includes booking, presentment, arraignment, and perhaps a trial. The exact features of each stage vary somewhat from one jurisdiction to another, but in general, the process begins with the arrested person in a group holding cell with benches and a toilet. The cell can be dangerous, populated as it sometimes is with ill, enraged, and violent individuals. New arrivals are customarily called "fish," suggestive perhaps of how they might be hooked, speared, or eaten.[34] Periodically, a guard will take individual arrested people from the holding cell to a processing station. The guards confiscate wallets, cell phones, belts, and sometimes shoes, as much to prevent their theft as for any other reason. A guard or, more likely, a supervising police officer also "books" the arrested person by recording identifying information, obtaining fingerprints, and taking "mug shots," the latter being an especially effective and widely recognizable variety of criminal labeling. The practice itself dates back to the decades following the Civil War, when urban police departments began photographing criminals for their developing and often quite extensive "rogues' galleries."[35] The guards and supervising officers in the modern setting tend not to like either their jobs or the arrested men and women. In fact, the guards and supervising officers, to quote an older book-length study of jails, "often develop a distaste for incoming prisoners, and sometimes express hostility."[36]

Eventually, somewhere between a few hours and a full day after arriving at the lockup, the arrested person moves into another, smaller, more permanent group cell, usually in the local jail. According to a 2015 report from the Vera Institute, the number of people in jail on any given day increased from 224,000 in 1983 to 731,000 in 2013, the latter total being nearly equal to the population of Charlotte, North Carolina. Violent crime fell nationally by almost 50 percent during the same years, and property crime fell by 40 percent. But arrests for drug-related offenses skyrocketed and more than made up for the declines in other areas. What's more, many of the arrested individuals being sent to local jails have been there before. In Chicago, for example, 21 percent of the people sent to jail accounted for 50 percent of Windy City jail admissions. In New York City, law enforcement officials jailed four hundred people at least eighteen times each between 2009 and 2013.[37]

While roughly two-thirds of the men and women in urban jails are awaiting further proceedings, the other third consists of convicted criminals serving time. The latter sector of the jail population seems likely to grow in the future because various states are in the process of relocating convicted prisoners from state prisons to county jails, largely for financial reasons.[38]

More so than the general public seems to realize, urban jails are quite perilous, and in addition to the frequent fights and beatings among those who are jailed, the suicide rate is troubling. It is not surprising that men and women in jail commit suicide at a higher rate than the general population. Hopeless predicaments and general woes weigh heavy. It *is* surprising, meanwhile, that the suicide rate among those in local jails is higher than it is for those in state and federal prisons. Also, jailed people who have only been booked are more likely to commit suicide than are those who have been convicted and are serving time.[39]

The disabling effect of being booked and jailed should not be underestimated. Depending on local rules, the arrested person may have made one or more telephone calls to inform friends and family members of his or her whereabouts, but, unlike the occasional middle- or upper-class person who is arrested, arrested members of the urban poor tend not to have visitors or meetings with lawyers during this early stage of the process. The arrested person understandably feels vulnerable and powerless. One public defender turned law professor remembers his clients' mental state as one of "learned helplessness."[40] To be sure, some of the urban poor who find themselves in jail maintain their swagger, but a larger number manifest passivity and even fatalism. A leery, anxious resignation is perhaps the dominant mood.

The next formal stop for the man or woman who has entered the "Twilight Zone" is usually a pretrial release hearing, known in some jurisdictions as a presentment. In the typical case involving a poor person, no lawyer is present to represent that person. Only eight states and the District of Columbia systematically provide the arrested person with a lawyer for this hearing.[41] In fact, even the arrested person may not be present for the hearing, at least in a physical sense. In some urban areas, judges use a video feed from the jail in order to avoid transporting the jailed person to a courtroom. His or her image is a sort of video mug shot and another instance in which the system labels a person as a criminal.

At the hearing or presentment, the judge looks to the assistant district attorney for guidance and insight and decides whether to order release and whether bail is appropriate. In determining whether to release a person and on what terms, the judge typically considers whether the arrested and booked individual is a so-called flight risk, and also whether he or she is dangerous to family members, compatriots, witnesses, and others. The amount of money and the assets in the person's possession may also play a role in determining whether he or she will be released.[42] In general, the urban poor are unable to post bail, and therefore they stay in jail. Among arrestees in New York City with bail set at $1,000 or less, only 13 percent were able to post it.[43] Money issues, of course, make it harder for the individual to find and meet with an attorney, to contact people involved in the alleged criminal incident, to gather information about the case, and so on. For the urban poor much more so than for others, "pretrial detention sets the status quo at imprisonment."[44]

Another month can pass before the jailed person appears again in court for, in order, an initial appearance, preliminary hearing, and then an arraignment. During these proceedings, the detained individual will have a lawyer, most likely a public defender, and the lawyer will presumably explain to the defendant what the significance of each type of proceeding is. Is the person sent over from the jail for these proceedings able to grasp the distinctions? Perhaps those who have passed through the system before are the most likely to understand what is going on.

Among these different proceedings, the arraignment is not surprisingly the one with the greatest pointedness. At the arraignment the assistant district attorney will read an official charge. The detained person—now labeled a "defendant"—must establish his or her position vis-à-vis the charge by entering a formal plea of guilty, not guilty, or, where permitted, "nolo contendere." The latter plea indicates that the defendant does not admit to the charges but also will not contest them.

From the time of the arrest through the booking, presentment, arraignment, and early stages of an actual trial, negotiating and dealing that has acquired the moniker "plea bargaining" takes place, and many consider it to be the most important feature of the entire criminal justice process.[45] In a 2012 decision regarding the adequacy of a criminal defense attorney's work, Justice Kennedy of the Supreme Court of the United States quoted approvingly the work of scholars who had concluded that plea bargaining "is not some adjunct to the criminal justice system, it *is* the criminal justice system."[46] Then, speaking in his own words, Kennedy added: "In today's criminal justice system, therefore, the negotiation of a plea bargain, rather than the unfolding of a trial, is almost always the critical point for a defendant."[47]

So, yes, plea bargaining is extremely important, but it would be mistaken to picture plea bargaining as some type of full and thoughtful exchange of positions and requests. For the most part, defendants do not sit properly on one side of a conference room table with their lawyers while assistant district attorneys sit across from them representing the public. Instead, there are bits and pieces of conversations taking place here, there, and everywhere. Sometimes the defendant is present, but more frequently he or she is not. Furthermore, "plea bargaining" can involve many possibilities other than the trading of guilty pleas for reduced sentences. The possibilities include the facts of the case; charges; possible apologies, restitution, and promises to reform; conditions for probation and supervised release; fines; lengths of sentences; location and nature of a facility at which a sentence might be served; openings in rehabilitation facilities; required sex-offender registration; release of civil claims, etc. Frequently, more than one of those matters is metaphorically "on the table." Bargaining might also simultaneously address multiple cases involving the arrested person or the arrested person's willingness to play a role in the prosecution of another person in still another case. Malcolm M. Feeley, one of the first to systematically study plea bargaining, lamented the staggering array of possibilities. "To lump them all under the blanket phrase plea bargaining," Feeley said, "may conceal more than it reveals."[48]

The multitude of patterns and options contributes to the arrested person's confusion and sense of vulnerability, but one aspect of the varied bargaining and negotiating is consistent: the state occupies the superior position. Various agents speak for the state during the process—police officers, jailers, probation officers, rehabilitation counselors, child support collectors, and prosecutors— but all have some degree of leverage over the arrested party. Conversely, the defendant has few strings to pull or buttons to push. "Typically, defendants have little leverage to negotiate meaningful concessions from the government, which, more often than not, has significant trial and resource advantages."[49]

Class difference and socioeconomic status reinforce this leverage. All of the functionaries who process the poor are at minimum members of the middle class. Their differences from those whose fate is being bargained is evident in their language, attitudes, and conduct, and when "the state" interacts with poor men and women charged with a crime, it inevitably holds the upper hand. Writing of another era and its criminal justice system, the quirky but insightful postmodernist Michel Foucault made a point that still rings true: "So that the language of the law, which is supposed to be universal, is, in this respect, inadequate; it must, if it is to be effective, be the discourse of one class to another, which has neither the same ideas as it nor the same words."[50]

One might in fact argue that the defining feature of all the bargaining and negotiating is the state's coercive power to seek whatever it is that it might ultimately want.[51] The impoverished defendant, whose sense of life acting *on* him or her was perhaps present even before being arrested and booked, senses this dunning coercive power more so than others. White-collar criminals and, more generally, criminals with assets would on average feel more able to counter the state's coercive power.

The single most powerful participant in the bargaining is the assistant district attorney. In some district attorneys' offices, "a tradition of machismo" reigns, and assistant district attorneys frequently "succumb to the warrior mindset."[52] Chests can be so puffed with crime-stopping righteousness that dozens of buttons might burst. This does not mean, however, that an assistant district attorney will necessarily "throw the book" at the arrested person. In a large percentage of cases, assistant district attorneys dismiss the charges with just an unofficial reprimand and a stern warning. On one level, these dismissals are simply a way to eliminate the weakest cases and concomitantly reduce the workload. On a deeper level, the high release rates may reflect some courthouse disapproval of the police's rambunctious inclination to arrest. As previously noted, police aggressiveness may not always sit well in poor urban neighborhoods. Nobody wants to be plagued by criminal conduct, but "too much" law enforcement leads to "too many" children, spouses, and neighbors heading to jail. Frequent and routine dismissals might help placate inner-city communities. Overall, the system may be hesitant to clamp down on police misconduct, but at the same time the system sometimes has no inclination to go any further. "By the time the case reaches the prosecutor, no one in the criminal justice system may want to devote further time or resources to pursuing it."[53]

If the assistant district attorney does decide to prosecute, meanwhile, the attitudes and perspectives of an adversarial lawyer become evident. Although assistant district attorneys have theoretical obligations to take a balanced view rather than to win all cases, "they are still working within an adversarial paradigm."[54] This means that the assistant district attorney will see himself or herself opposing the defendant and the defendant's counsel. The assistant district attorney will want to "win" on one level or another, and this goal can promote some degree of caginess, manipulation, and—especially—guarding and withholding information. "The major weapon of combat is information control."[55] This approach can have dire consequences. "Victory" for the assistant district attorney can lead ultimately to more time for the defendant in a more dangerous incarceration facility.

Indigent defendants are usually represented by public defenders. When scholars first turned their attention to these overworked and underpaid attorneys, they expressed grave reservations about the quality of legal representation for the urban poor. Critics cited public defenders' limited resources and large caseloads as reasons for what they took to be unsatisfactory work.[56] Most troubling for purposes at hand were the allegations that public defenders did not maintain a strong adversarial stance.[57] In some jurisdictions, public defenders were eligible for and sought "promotions" to the ranks of prosecutors, and it is not difficult to imagine what professional aspirations of this sort did to public defenders' adversarial inclinations. Most public defenders did not seek to become prosecutors, but many were nevertheless familiar and friendly with prosecutors. This led, according to early critics, to unduly cooperative plea bargaining that may not have served the defendants' best interests. Public defenders and prosecutors, for example, often began their negotiations with the shared assumption that a defendant was guilty of something. Furthermore, the subsequent discussion was likely to concern who a defendant was and how that defendant had led his or her life. The "facts" of the case could receive surprisingly little attention.[58]

In more recent years, the situation has improved. The lousy compensation defense lawyers receive for representing indigent defendants still reduces the zeal some of them bring to their work, but defense lawyers for the poor seem to have developed better and more ethical relations with their clients and a more adversarial stance toward their prosecutorial colleagues. Indeed, some have argued that in the present, public defenders routinely obtain better results for their clients than do private attorneys.[59]

Professor Debra S. Emmelman of Southern Connecticut State University conducted an admirably nuanced study of defense work for the urban poor in an unidentified city. She concluded that the defense lawyers for the urban poor whom she studied maintained an adversarial stance toward the prosecutor and attempted to serve their clients' interests. However, she also found that the low socioeconomic standing of the clients influenced the manner in which lawyers represented them. According to Emmelman, lawyers for the urban poor anticipate how a judge or jury might react to their clients' cases and defenses, and public defenders' expectations become more important in shaping a defense strategy than do guilt or innocence. Furthermore, the anticipated reactions are decidedly bourgeois and can be biased against poor defendants:

> In particular, while judges and jurors are expected to uphold a traditional, commonsense value and belief system (or the values, beliefs and norms of the status quo), lower-class defendants and their personal allies tend to employ

a culturally disparate system. Thus, poor criminal suspects typically lack the cultural resources (or compelling language) with which to present themselves and be presented as socially acceptable and "upstanding" members of our society to judging authorities.[60]

Emmelman's study captures the interrelationship of urban poverty with legal representation. The criminal justice system does not convict defendants and send them away simply because they are poor, but biases subtly and indirectly come into play because of the milieu in which defense lawyers work for the poor. These biases are especially important in the range of informal, sometimes unofficial negotiations. Defense lawyers might be more inclined to plea-bargain in the first place, thinking that that their clients' language, demeanor, and narratives would not play well at trial. In actual bargaining sessions, defense lawyers might be less likely to present mitigating information involving their clients' lifestyles or lack of conventional values. In plea bargaining and in general, Emmelman concludes, "indigent defendants can be characterized as the victims of substantive injustice."[61]

Actual trials involving the urban poor (or any kind of defendants for that matter) are much less common than members of the lay public think. Dramatic and stirring trials are staples of contemporary popular culture, and while the average person has never witnessed an actual trial, he or she has watched or read about hundreds of them in Hollywood films, television series, and inexpensive fiction. These pop-cultural trials coalesce into a series of conventions, which consumers of popular culture take for granted.[62] Viewers and readers are quite familiar, for example, with heroic prosecutors and defense lawyers, revealing cross-examinations, and nail-biting jury verdicts. These pop-cultural mainstays are hard to find in actual courthouses, and an abundance of data shows a pronounced decline in actual trials.[63] As unbelievable as it might be, 94 percent of state convictions and an even higher 97 percent of federal convictions are the result of guilty pleas."[64]

A higher percentage of the urban poor might actually go to trial than do middle- and upper-class defendants, but this might not be a desirable turn of events for them.[65] The overwhelming majority of people who go to trial are found guilty, and defendants from humble backgrounds in particular have significant disadvantages at trial. As was the case with plea bargaining, defense lawyers often do not develop defense stories or themes for poor clients that comport with the expectations of the decision-makers. The defendants themselves may be less able or willing to work with their lawyers to develop their defenses and even to approach the trial as a whole with a winning degree of respect and attentiveness. Some public defenders complain that they have to wake up their clients—at trial. Then, too, poor defendants tend not to create particularly positive impressions in the courtroom. Defense lawyers routinely coach their clients on proper, middle-class dress, grooming, and even posture, but often judges and juries see through this and presume poor defendants are disdainful of social order and mainstream values. Lack of a job, drug use, prior rehabilitative stints, and earlier convictions are especially likely to convince decision-makers that a "bad apple" is seated next to his or her lawyer at the defense table. All of these characteristics are especially common among members of the urban poor.

Determinations of guilt and innocence in our criminal justice system, and particularly in criminal trials, are not supposed to be affected by the poverty of defendants. Everyone is supposedly entitled to his or her individual day in court. Defendants are presumed innocent until proven guilty beyond a reasonable doubt. But the realities of what transpires in American urban courtrooms are sometimes less winning than our law-related aspirations and fantasies. We have in mind the way a criminal trial should be conducted, but what happens in American courtrooms can be a lot tawdrier.

Overall, an arrest launches the poor man or woman's journey through the jail and local criminal court. Guards and jailers and others might process the arrested thoughtfully, or they might let the arrested sit for long periods of time or even forget about them. Prosecutors might decide to bring or not bring charges; later, they might decide to drop them. Deals might be struck leading only to fines or parole or rehabilitative placements. Once in a great while, a jury might find a poor defendant innocent. Through it all, the labeling process grinds out its designations and determinations, and the urban poor are especially likely to acquire criminal labels. Whatever labels the system settles upon, they seem attached with a powerful cement, with a cultural superglue. The labels stick for a long time, maybe forever.

Imprisonment

In the opinion of several historians referenced in the *New York Times*, contemporary American mass incarceration is a "new and historically distinct phenomenon."[66] Starting in the mid-1970s, the incarceration rate accelerated madly, "reaching the unprecedented rate of 197 inmates per one hundred thousand persons in 1990 and the previously unimaginable rate of 504 inmates per one hundred thousand persons in 2008."[67] At present, an extraordinary number of men and women, mostly with impoverished backgrounds, are behind bars. Approximately 1.6 million adults are now locked up.[68] The share of the population in prison is larger than in any other country and about five times the average for other industrialized nations. The per capita imprisonment rate in the United States is seven times greater than France's, fourteen times greater than Japan's, and twenty-five times greater than India's.[69]

Furthermore, the United States has abandoned any commitment to rehabilitate inmates while they are behind bars. The older variety of imprisonment geared to rehabilitation has virtually disappeared. Even though roughly three-quarters of those imprisoned have been sentenced for nonviolent offenses, the federal and state governments and the private prison companies with whom they sometimes contract treat the inmates as a violent and dangerous group that needs to be kept out of circulation. Prisons do not undertake the positive mission of retraining and redeveloping potential members of the workforce; they instead warehouse the nation's convicted and rejected. Berkeley criminologist Jonathan Simon has observed that between 1970 and the end of the twentieth century "the collapse of the power of the working class to demand improvement in their income and security, combined with the growing economic irrelevance of the urban poor, has driven a return to a more exclusionary role for punishment." In Simon's opinion, the nation perceives inmates as a type of "toxic waste" and thinks the men and women who tend to our prisons have the nasty job of "waste management."[70]

Those who reflect on the growing reliance on prisons and the changing style of imprisonment often assume that both trends are prompted by increases in crime or the commission of more and more serious crime. Statistical evidence supports neither assumption. The stark expansion of warehouse-style imprisonment is attributable instead to an increase in the likelihood of arrest and criminal processing that will result in imprisonment.[71] That is, we have large numbers of people in warehouse-style prisons basically because the system concludes through its various processes and determinations that such punishment is what we want.

What explains the turn to mass incarceration? The most general cause is a widespread "get-tough" attitude toward crime, which appears to have originated as much with ambitious politicians seeking to curry the favor of the electorate as with the general public itself. There is a cause-and-effect connection between political statements regarding crime and the public's subsequent attitudes about how to handle the "crime problem."[72] Politicians have for decades been able to garner favor with the voters by deploring one criminal menace or another, but starting in the 1970s and continuing through the 1980s and 1990s, the notion of "getting tough on crime" became an increasingly pronounced variety of political rhetoric. To appear "soft on crime" was to court disaster on election day. "Other than the promise to reduce taxes, few positions are easier for an American politician to espouse today than being tough on crime."[73]

With politicians promising to "get tough on crime" and presumably garnering votes in the process, the media, judicial figures, and religious leaders also got on board. Even the culture industry joined in, producing dozens of police and detective dramas in which retribution and punishment were the goals, and also a spate of movies in which self-righteous vigilantes take crime control into their own hands.[74] It is hardly surprising that public attitudes about crime grew more punitive, and tossing lawbreakers into prison and "throwing away the key" seemed a better and better idea.

Policies consistent with these new attitudes emerged. They included an increased willingness to revoke probation and parole, and also the "three strikes" approach. The latter makes a lengthy prison term mandatory if a defendant is convicted of a felony for a third time. Legislators also grew enamored with requiring minimum prison sentences for certain crimes, with fixing the length of sentences rather than allowing them to be decided by judges in individual cases, and with "truth in sentencing," which exposes how short prison terms might be and in turn generally leads to longer terms.

All of these policies would arguably prevent large numbers of criminals from slipping through the net of the criminal justice system. In fact, huge numbers of people are caught in the net and then dumped into prison or jail, sometimes for sentences that strike commentators in other parts of the world as extraordinarily lengthy.[75]

The "get-tough" attitude and policies acquired a razor-sharp animus during the 1980s. The Reagan administration led the way, eliminating the federal parole system, reinstating the federal death penalty, and deepening the relationship between the military and prison officials.[76] More importantly, the Reagan administration's determination to crack down on drug use and sales deposited unprecedented numbers of men and women into the prisons. Some readers of this work might remember First Lady Nancy Reagan's obtuse "Just Say No" campaign, but in reality most of the $900 million allocated by Congress for the campaign went for enhanced intelligence gathering, tactical drug-enforcement units, and surveillance helicopters.[77]

The subsequent Bush administration eagerly continued to wage the "War on Drugs," and state and local elected officials simultaneously fought smaller skirmishes of their own. The war-making continued into the Clinton years and into the second Bush administration. Then, well into his second term, President Obama issued a 104-page report announcing that the War on Drugs had ended.[78] The report insisted that "we cannot incarcerate our way out of the drug problem" and called for treating drug use and abuse as a public health issue rather than a criminal problem.[79] But unfortunately, resumption of the war-making seems likely during the Trump presidency, what with its determination to reverse many of the steps taken by the Obama administration. President Trump and Attorney General Sessions have instructed federal prosecutors to seek maximum sentences for even nonviolent drug offenders.[80]

The growth of the private prison industry also contributed to the mass incarceration of drug offenders. The federal and state governments began turning to private companies to design, construct, and operate prisons in the 1980s, with Tennessee's 1984 agreement with the Corrections Corporation of America to begin operating a Shelby County prison launching the trend.[81] Most private prisons are located in the South and West, and the largest private prison, a facility located in Pecos, Texas, has a capacity of almost four thousand inmates. As the industry has grown in recent decades, Wall Street banks have taken note and invested heavily in the industry.[82]

While Pecos, Texas, is obviously not an urban center, most of the people serving time in private prisons come from Texas cities. A 2014 study by a doctoral student at the University of California, Berkeley found that minorities make up a greater percentage of inmates in private prisons than in public prisons.[83] Critics have also alleged that the federal private prisons are less safe and more punitive than public prisons.[84]

The standard justification for contractual agreements between government and prison companies is cost control, but the profit-making of private prison companies should not be overlooked. Stated simply, the construction and operation of private prisons is a highly profitable business. The private prison companies receive per diem or monthly payments for each prisoner, or at least for the space available in a private facility. Hence, the companies have a vested interest in larger and larger numbers of inmates and in spending as little on each one as is tolerable.

Time will tell if America comes to its senses about dumping large numbers of men and women into its public and private prisons for long periods of time, but at least the mainstream media have deplored the disproportionate number of African Americans in the prison population. Creative journalists are in fact constantly hunting for new ways to demonstrate this point. A quarter of all African American children fourteen or younger have a parent who is or who has been in prison.[85] The number of African American men incarcerated in the United States is greater than the total prison populations of India, Argentina, Canada, Lebanon, Japan, Germany, Finland, Israel, and England combined.[86] The racial disparities in the American prison population justify this crack following the election of Barack Obama to the presidency: "One black man in the White House, one million black men in the Big House."[87]

While the disproportionate number of African Americans in American prisons is in fact appalling, this problem derives from more than racism. The radical criminologist Loïc Wacquant has argued that the people targeted for imprisonment are identified not only by race but also by class and origin. Our bulging prison population, he argues, is drawn from African Americans of humble means who come from the ghetto, while the rest of society—including, most remarkably, middle-class and upper-class African Americans—is for the most part untouched.[88] One study found that incarcerated men and women had a pre-incarceration income 41 percent lower than non-incarcerated people of similar ages.[89]

Other scholars have even identified the specific poor inner-city neighborhoods most likely to produce inmates. The Crime Lab at the University of Chicago has identified fifteen home zip codes in which men have a one-in-two chance of being imprisoned in the course of their lives. The Crime Lab has also found 775 zip codes in which men have a one-in-three chance of imprisonment.[90] Nearly 50 percent of these inner-city inmates were unemployed before their sentencing, 65 percent had not completed high school, and 80 percent could not afford to hire an attorney.[91]

The removal and incarceration of large parts of their populations might make poor inner-city neighborhoods somewhat safer in the short term, but there is little proof that lengthy, mandatory prison sentences for large numbers of people do much to reduce these neighborhoods' drug problems. While the number of men and women imprisoned for drug-related offenses rose dramatically in recent decades, drug sales and drug use have continued to increase. In fact, some illegal drugs have become less expensive and easier to obtain because, according to one study, drug prices have fallen by a factor of five since 1980.[92] The War on Drugs has also done virtually nothing to prevent the development of newer drug-related problems such as opioid addiction. Commentators have often pointed out how opioid addiction is a special menace in rural areas and affluent suburbs, but opioid-related deaths among African Americans rose by 41 percent in 2016, a greater increase than for any other ethnic group.[93] Many of the urban poor are unemployed, and studies have shown that as the unemployment rate rises, so do suicides and deadly overdoses related to opioids.[94] The bottom line: the War on Drugs has created a behemoth of incarceration facilities that have done little to decrease the use of drugs or crime in general.[95]

The distinguished linguist and tireless social critic Noam Chomsky contends, "In the United States the drug war is basically a technique for controlling dangerous populations internal to the country and doesn't have much to do with drugs." The War on Drugs and especially the increased reliance on imprisonment could be seen primarily as a way to label, control, and remove the urban poor. Chomsky says it is an American variety of the "social cleansing" we were so eager to deplore in the Balkans, Rwanda, the Middle East, and elsewhere. "In a country like the United States, where you can't really send out the paramilitary forces to murder people, as they do more and more in the Third World, you rely more heavily on techniques of social control. That's basically what the drug war is all about."[96]

Chomsky might overstate the disingenuousness of our policymakers, but perhaps he does not. Regardless, it appears that the emergence of the recognizable socioeconomic sector known in the 1980s and 1990s as the "underclass," and the increased reliance on warehouse-style prisons are parallel historical phenomena. As I noted in the introduction, deindustrialization in the decades following World War II and especially during the 1960s and 1970s led to the growth of a semipermanent impoverished population living in inner-city neighborhoods.[97] The middle and upper classes came to see this population as criminal and dangerous, and imprisonment struck many as an important variety of social control. Members of the urban poor might be rightly arrested and convicted. Judges might conscientiously follow sentencing guidelines and give impoverished men and women appropriate prison sentences. But still, there is a larger collective reality: We, as a society, have spawned extremely large prison populations consisting primarily of the urban poor.

To make matters worse, most inmates complete their terms in extraordinarily unhealthy facilities and then return to their home communities bringing maladies and harmful traits along with them. The prevalence of infectious diseases in prisons is four to ten times greater than it is in the general population, and the disparity in chronic diseases is even greater.[98] Overcrowding, poor ventilation, and limited medical care have led to the pronounced spread of tuberculosis and HIV infections in prison populations, and a surprising percentage of men and women return to their home communities without knowing their HIV serostatus.[99]

Furthermore, many inmates grow hardened and increasingly violent while serving their terms. They return home not only with diseases but also an "attitude." Recently released men are sometimes demanding in their relationships with women. They are anxious to have sex and reckless in their sexual conduct.

This in turn contributes to higher rates of teenage pregnancy and the spread of sexually transmitted diseases such as syphilis and gonorrhea.

Prospects for the former inmate are bleak. Having acquired the new label of "ex-con," he or she, for starters, has fewer rights and entitlements than the rest of the population. Almost all states deny inmates their voting rights during imprisonment, and ten states also continue to deny voting rights to former inmates after they have left prison. In addition, thirty-two states prohibit felons on parole from voting.[100] Twenty-five states restrict the rights of felons to hold political office, and former inmates are routinely denied the right to own guns as well as government benefits, including but not limited to access to student loans, driver's licenses, welfare, food stamps, and places in public housing. Former inmates who are not citizens are increasingly deported after serving their sentences.[101]

The American Bar Association has taken on the rather daunting task of counting up all the rights and entitlements lost by felons who have served their time. A treatise titled *Collateral Consequences of Criminal Convictions: Law, Policy and Practice* has resulted, as has a collateral-consequences website, where former inmates and, perhaps, their attorneys can look up the lost rights and entitlements by type of offense and by state jurisdiction. Researchers undertaking this project had by 2013 surveyed seventeen jurisdictions and identified 17,000 collateral consequences. The best guess is that 50,000 collateral consequences will have been identified by the time the survey is complete.[102]

The former inmate also encounters terrible bias if he or she seeks employment. Time in prison marks a person, and the "ex-con" label is especially devastating in the labor market. One survey of employers in five cities found that 65 percent would not knowingly hire a person who had been in prison, regardless of the crime that prompted the prison sentence.[103] This discrimination obviously contributes to the economic marginalization of the urban poor. Former inmates make up a large group of people who may never be able to find anything better in the job market than an unskilled, minimum-wage job at Taco Bell or Burger King. The lack of job prospects often leads recently released inmates to commit new crimes, sometimes to obtain cash and valuable goods and more frequently out of frustration and alienation. Lives without meaningful work tend to be, among other things, incredibly boring and monotonous. Risky, thrill-seeking criminal conduct relieves the tedium, and members of the former inmates' families and communities are the leading candidates for victimization.

Families and communities also suffer in more subtle and collective ways when large numbers of people leave and return from prison. Scholars have spoken of this movement as a variety of "coercive mobility," in that people sent to prison have no choice in the matter.[104] Furthermore, most people released from prison pretty much have to take up residence in the inner city. The magnitude of the movement should not be underestimated: more than a half million people are released from prison and return to their families and communities annually.[105]

This constant, large-scale movement of people in and out of impoverished inner-city neighborhoods is harmful to the already deficient social capital. Poor urban communities routinely have weak and limited social networks and do not easily compensate for the loss of large numbers of young adults who could be valuable in these networks. In addition, when these neighborhoods accommodate large numbers of reentering former inmates, what exists in the way of networks and social arrangements is insufficient, especially given the styles and attitudes inmates develop and refine while in prison. Those who have been imprisoned have often come to see social relationships in terms of power and domination, and this perspective hinders the successful deployment and utilization of social capital. Former inmates also sometimes supplant older community members, ministers, and others as the most respected and influential figures. In short, the communities that can least afford reductions in, or harm to, their social capital see that social capital diminished because they are home for the lion's share of former inmates.

During just the past few years, some policymakers have fortunately begun to recognize the huge toll mass incarceration extracts from inmates, their families, and their communities. During his final years in the White House, President Obama endorsed reducing prison sentences for nonviolent lawbreakers. He also issued more commutations of convicted felons "than the number issued by the prior 11 presidents combined."[106] In 2014, the United States Sentencing Commission showed it shared Obama's views when it invited

64,000 inmates in federal prisons to apply for early release if they thought their sentences were excessive.[107] A handful of Republicans also backed off the ideas of aggressive prosecutions and lengthy sentences in warehouse-style prisons, and some variety of two-party agreement has at least appeared on the horizon of possibilities.[108] Will the attempts to reduce the size of the prison population continue? President Trump and his attorney general Jeff Sessions have called for increased federal spending on prisons.[109]

Regardless of what happens during the Trump administration, mass incarceration has been harmful to the urban poor. The prison population has swelled like a giant, ugly, and badly shaped balloon.[110] Despite having only 4.4 percent of the world's population, the United States is responsible for 22 percent of the world's prison population.[111] The War on Drugs, in particular, has deposited huge numbers of the urban poor in prison. According to one estimate, one in three males from the urban poor ultimately do time.[112] People are labeled as "inmates" while they are in prison and as "ex-cons" when they get out. Over two-thirds of those who have worn these labels are destined to reclaim them, as the recidivism rate in the contemporary United States is 67.5 percent.[113]

Criminalizing the Urban Poor

The labeling of individual criminals can lead to a broader and even more disturbing criminalization. The repeated arresting, convicting, and imprisoning of countless poor men and women contributes to a belief that the urban poor are in general criminal. Mainstream society unreflectively takes the urban poor to be prone to crime and violence and therefore largely irredeemable. This has the effect of making the urban poor outcasts in the very society they call home. Loïc Wacquant has suggested the criminalized urban poor have become a "pariah group" that is "alien to the national body."[114]

The plight of poor individuals in the criminal justice system is troubling enough, but this general condemnation of the urban poor as criminal demands especially rigorous criticism. Yes, the urban poor commit a large percentage of reported crimes. And yes, some members of the urban poor should be arrested, prosecuted, and imprisoned. However, most of the urban poor are not criminals. They obey the laws and actually, on average, are more worried about crime than are members of the middle and upper classes. The urban poor, after all, are the most likely to be victims of crime. They also watch the criminal justice system constantly remove friends and loved ones from their homes and families. While the urban poor are unlikely to use the phrase "social capital," they see clearly the harm the movement of large numbers of people from the community to prison and back does to their communities.

Our times exacerbate the deleterious effects of the criminalization process. Society's impression that the urban poor are criminal has taken hold during a time in which concern with crime has acquired a large and central role in the culture as a whole. We live in an era of exaggerated, overwhelming, and almost desperate reports on and portrayals of crime. In the eyes of some observers, it seems sometimes that Americans are absolutely fixated on crime.[115]

This fixation on crime is most obvious in political discourse, but it is also important elsewhere. In *Governing through Crime: How the War on Crime Transformed American Democracy and Created a Culture of Fear*, Jonathan Simon suggests that thoughts about crime often trump other concerns—civil rights, poverty, the sexual revolution, armed conflict—and that the victim of crime has become the "idealized subject" for legislation.[116] In addition, newspapers, television, and internet sites devote large amounts of attention to crime. Given the pervasiveness of this thinking about crime, it is surprising that block watches, alarm systems, and transport services in university areas and elsewhere are not more common than they already are.

Since in the present a concern with crime plays such an important role in how contemporary Americans understand their society, the criminalization of the urban poor is especially consequential. Taking the urban poor to be criminal not only makes them outsiders in American life but also becomes a central premise in the entire framework of sociopolitical thought. The urban poor, as the ultimate "outsider group," register on most members of the middle and upper classes as a "problem" that must be addressed, often through law. In addition to using "get-tough-on-crime" measures as well as mass incarceration for individual members of the urban poor, the law invites Americans to turn away from the urban poor in general rather than incorporate them into American life. The men on the towering billboards I mentioned at the beginning of this chapter do not realize it, but they are the poster children for a social group that society cruelly criminalizes. The criminalization of the urban poor is a fundamental part of their oppression.

CHAPTER TWO

No Place to Call Home

Several years ago, one of my students told me of the ingenious way her mother came to visit. Using a combination of highways, belt roads, and bypasses, "Mom" was able to get from a home in an outlying suburb to her daughter's downtown dormitory without driving through anything in between! Her mother's chief goal, my student reported, was to avoid the neighborhoods and the kind of people that made her feel uneasy.

A more adventuresome and open-minded visitor could actually have used the drive to tour the range of metropolitan housing. Occasional homes and even neighborhoods might seem misplaced, but in general a pattern would appear. On the outer edge of the metropolitan area, new single-family homes and condo complexes would dominate, usually surrounded by the type of green space best maintained with a power mower. In the suburbs closer to the center of the metropolitan area, the homes would become heftier and sturdier, but the green space surrounding those homes would tend, although smaller, to remain bright and attractive. The housing in some of the still older suburbs, meanwhile, might show a bit of its age, needing a paint job here and there and perhaps a new roof. Then, in the inner city, the housing would decline precipitously. Consisting of older wood-frame homes and duplexes, small brick apartment buildings, aging housing projects, and stores curtained on the first floors and serving as residences, the housing would register as shabby and in need of repair. The most noticeable green space would now take the form of trash-littered vacant lots where other housing had collapsed or burned down.

The urban poor live chiefly in the latter area, and their housing is troubling on many levels. Truly acceptable housing, after all, needs to be safe, habitable, and affordable. Only then might housing serve the fundamental human needs for personal space and privacy. Only then might housing serve as a gathering place and be a physical base for supporting and empowering communities. Without acceptable housing, the urban poor are limited and in some cases psychologically disabled.

Problems with the urban poor's housing are numerous and also intertwined. The nation's public housing program has stagnated. The remaining projects can accommodate only a small percentage of the urban poor, and the newer, government-supported mixed-income housing developments are also insufficient. As a result, most of the urban poor turn to unsafe rental housing, which is itself deteriorating. This housing falls under the purview of local housing codes, but the codes go largely unenforced. For their part, the suburbs offer little relief, as many use zoning laws and other legal restrictions to exclude the urban poor. This has the effect of semipermanently consigning the urban poor to their current housing and neighborhoods.

Calls for law reform that would improve the housing of the urban poor have largely fallen on deaf ears. Many members of the middle and upper classes, including perhaps my student's skittish mother, are ignorant of the overall situation or—even worse—comfortable with it. They are not bothered by the state of the urban poor's housing or by the way law helps create and maintain housing problems for the poor.

Public Housing

In some countries, the state provides abundant housing for the poor, but in the United States the public housing program is deficient. While it began with great compassion and a genuinely cooperative ardor, the actual construction of federally funded public housing declined precipitously in the final decades of the twentieth century and has today virtually stopped. A federally funded voucher program cannot accommodate demand. For better or worse, the preferred options for the urban poor have become "affordable housing" in mixed-income developments, an approach to housing the poor championed by neoliberal politicians. With good reason, the urban poor no longer necessarily look to the government for a place to live. Many circle aimlessly, fully aware that their society is not really prepared to house them.

Public housing in the United States dates back to the Great Depression and the early years of Franklin D. Roosevelt's administration. In the spring of 1934, Harold Ickes, director of the newly established Public Works Administration, ordered the construction of public housing for the needy, and during the next three years, the Housing Division under the leadership of Colonel Horatio B. Hackett did in fact construct fifty-two housing projects. The first to open was the Techwood Homes in Atlanta. Like other early public housing projects, Techwood Homes was a one-race project, with the race of the project's population dictated by the race of the surrounding neighborhood population. The resulting segregation notwithstanding, these early public housing projects did include people with a range of incomes and had relatively high design and construction standards.[1]

In 1937, Congress's passage of the Wagner-Steagall Housing Act further helped increase public housing.[2] The act established the United States Housing Authority, which provided subsidies to local governments and their housing authorities to build and run public housing projects. Local authorities took eagerly to the task, and new public housing projects often received enthusiastic support from the labor movement and charitable organizations. An amazing 50,000 units became available during just 1939.[3] One key to the rapid expansion and general success of the early public housing program was the pervasive sense that the housing was for average Americans down on their luck. Only later in time would the public come to see the nation's public housing as a residential dumping ground for society's least fortunate and least respected.

During and immediately after World War II, the funding and developing of public housing largely targeted enlisted men and their families, but the

Housing Act of 1949 created public housing for other parts of the population. The act established an impressive goal of 810,000 units of new public housing. President Harry Truman seemed imbued with some of the same spirit that had invigorated public housing advocates in the midst of the Great Depression. This nation, he told the press, "wanted decent homes in wholesome surroundings for low-income families now living in the squalor of the slums."[4]

Enthusiasm for public housing continued into the 1960s, especially in the context of the War on Poverty. The Housing and Urban Development Act of 1965 created the Department of Housing and Urban Development (HUD), and the head of HUD assumed a position in the Cabinet. Public housing continued to suggest a social contract of a sort, in which the better-off accepted some degree of social responsibility for the housing of the less fortunate. Indeed, some of the new public housing from the 1960s embodied a belief that "architecture in itself could engender meaningful social change" and manifested a "sense of exuberant experimentalism."[5]

Unfortunately, the problems of urban poverty eventually overwhelmed public housing. While during public housing's earliest decades policymakers and housing authority administrators hoped to serve a "submerged middle class," another socioeconomic group was knocking on the doors and pushing the elevator buttons of public housing.[6] The increasingly numerous and predominantly African American urban poor—the group sociologist William Julius Wilson and others originally labeled the "underclass"—needed places to live. Administrators began giving preference on the public-housing waiting lists to severely disadvantaged applicants, especially the homeless and unemployed. Income limits settled into place and assured that places in public housing would go only to "the least well-off segments of society."[7] People who owned a car or could make the down payment for a mortgage eagerly moved out of public housing, and the projects became known for crime and drug problems.

As the residents of public housing changed, the general public became less and less sanguine about the endeavor. During the era when tenants were still perceived as average Americans down on their luck, the general public was sympathetic. When the group that Stanford historian Lawrence Friedman calls "the real poor" began to take up residence, attitudes regarding public housing shifted. As Friedman observes soberly, "The standard reaction to these members of the poor is exile and rage."[8]

While every president between Franklin Delano Roosevelt and Jimmy Carter increased federal housing assistance, the Reagan and Bush administrations of the late-twentieth century played to the growing public sense that the poor were receiving too many handouts by reducing the budget for public housing.[9] President William Clinton caved in to the anti–public housing forces to an even greater extent. Clinton had been elected in 1992 with only 43 percent of the national vote, and then, in 1994, Republicans won a sizable majority in the Congress. Their leadership threatened to eliminate HUD and public housing in general. In order to save HUD, and perhaps because of his only limited enthusiasm for public housing, Clinton further reduced funding for the nation's public housing program.

In the years since Clinton, in effect, sold out on public housing, no administration has been willing to reverse the decision, and construction of new public housing in the United States has largely ceased. The overall budget for HUD has dropped to less than half of what it was in 1976, and in just the six years between 1999 and 2005 the actual funding for public housing declined by 25 percent.[10] According to the Center on Budget and Policy Priorities, the number of public housing units dropped by 211,000 between 1995 and 2012.[11] To the extent that federal funds remained available, state and local housing authorities used them primarily to rehabilitate distressed public housing.[12]

This "rehabilitation" has sometimes included the elimination of housing units for the poor, a development that has been especially well documented and critiqued in Chicago due to the dismantling of the huge and infamous Cabrini-Green housing project. Chicago was once the home to the nation's second-largest stock of public housing, with 43,000 units housing literally hundreds of thousands of people. Then, responding to signals from Washington, DC, the Chicago Housing Authority tore down tower after tower until only 15,000 family units and another 10,000 senior-citizen units remained. Trying to slip into more attractive figurative garb, the Chicago Housing Authority announced it would henceforth be not the manager of the city's public housing but rather the "facilitator of housing opportunities."[13]

New York City has somewhat surprisingly eschewed tearing down public housing complexes and made the greatest effort of any major city to preserve its public housing stock. The stock includes 270 buildings that are at least thirty years old, and the projected cost of fully rehabilitating these aging buildings is truly staggering. In hopes of raising money for rehabilitation, city officials announced in early 2015 that they would invite private developers to build in open spaces within the public housing complexes. If the developers take the bait, courtyards originally designed as "breathing room" for the urban poor would disappear. What's more, luxury high-rises would assume locations next to housing projects and in some cases loom over them just as castle towers loomed over peasant huts. Would well-to-do New Yorkers want to live near public housing? Developers seem to think potential residents care more about height than location, and some tentatively envision "gated communities in the sky."[14]

One alternative for the urban poor who cannot find or do not want places in housing projects is the venerable Housing Choice Voucher Program, known in the inner city as "Section 8." The program was established in 1974, and it enables some low-income households to rent housing that already exists in the private market. Would-be tenants apply for rental housing that has qualified with the local housing authority and sign a lease with the landlord for at least a year. The government then subsidizes the rent, and the renting family contributes a percentage of monthly adjusted income, if any. As is the case with traditional public housing, the voucher program allows the tenant to renew the lease unless somebody can show cause for terminating the rental arrangement.

In 2015, the Housing Choice Voucher Program served 2.2 million households with more than 5 million people.[15] Yet while the program is popular with the urban poor, it has severe limitations. Many landlords are leery of the paperwork and extra obligations that are required by the program, and other landlords simply do not trust voucher holders. As a result, the supply of voucher units does not match the demand. In some cities waiting lists are closed, and eligible poor families cannot even apply.[16] In addition, potential tenants often assume that the available units are going to be dirty, rundown, or dangerous. The assumption is unfair to some landlords, who do their best to keep up their properties, but one can hardly blame the urban poor for being skeptical of government programs. And, furthermore, it bears repeating that voucher units are not always "free." If renters have income, they routinely pay 30 percent of that income before HUD pays the landlord the remainder of the rent.

The current favorite among policymakers for housing the urban poor is neither traditional public housing nor vouchers, but rather so-called affordable housing in mixed-income housing developments.[17] The latter program is another example of neoliberalism's infatuation with markets, and confidence that private transactions will allocate resources more efficiently than government agencies. Like the private, for-profit prisons I critiqued in the previous chapter, "affordable housing" affects the freedom and well-being of the urban poor in fundamental, problematic ways.

The affordable housing program revolves around federal tax credits, which private developers receive and then routinely sell in order to raise money for apartment complexes. In return, the developers agree to hold 10–25 percent of a complex's units out of the general market and to rent these units to people with income below an area's average. If a tenant moves out before the lease runs out, he or she forfeits any claim to a rent subsidy. This option, in other words, is project-based, but unlike the traditional housing projects, the poor in mixed-income developments are not concentrated. The poor in middle-income mixed housing developments routinely have middle-class neighbors, and a few of the neighbors might even be wealthy. Members of Congress thought this approach would reduce the crime and drug problems that plagued older public housing and, more generally, lead to better housing for the urban poor.

Some critics doubt the altruism of the program. Voices on the left say that, against the backdrop of surging neoliberalism, government leaders are turning responsibility for housing the poor over to the private sector. The move to affordable housing units in mixed-income developments is, in this sense, part of an attempt to privatize public housing.

The scholar John Arena reached this conclusion with regard to developments in New Orleans. He called the nonprofit organizations that supported the changeover "wolves in sheep's clothing" and characterized the demolition and privatization of public housing, stretching from President George W. Bush and New Orleans Mayor Ray Nagin through President Barack Obama and New Orleans Mayor Mitch Landrieu, as an "insider's game."[18]

Unfortunately, the units in mixed-income developments do not begin to replace the number of units lost through the demolition of public housing projects, in part because developers are not necessarily eager to include low-income units in their new apartment and condominium complexes. Some cities attempt to move them in that direction. Chicago, for example, enacted the Affordable Requirements Ordinance, which requires builders developing a complex on land rezoned for residential use to designate at least 20 percent of the units as low-income housing and to rent them for below-market rates. If they do not include these units, they must instead make payments for each potential affordable unit into the City's Housing Opportunity Fund. The amounts of the donations, intriguingly, reflect an awareness of the special problems in redeveloping concentrated-poverty neighborhoods. The developers in general have to donate $100,000 in lieu of an affordable unit, but, in hopes of encouraging redevelopment in the poorest areas, the required in-lieu donation drops to $50,000 if the development is in a concentrated-poverty neighborhood.[19]

In the mixed-income developments with affordable units, owners are always delighted to find tenants who are technically within the income limits but are not really the urban poor. University students—especially white, middle-class students—are common picks. Then, too, actual poor people who might claim units theoretically designed for them in the first place sometimes find different rules for their units and conduct than for middle-class units and their tenants.

An embarrassing incident in New York City in 2014 illustrated that the urban poor were not really equal residents of mixed-income developments. A huge mixed-income development went up on the western edge of Manhattan, with 20 percent of the units designated as "affordable" and therefore available to the urban poor. However, it turned out that the developer had grouped all of the affordable units in one area and also given those units a separate entrance. When the mayor's office learned of this "design flaw," red-faced city officials hastily retracted their approval of a high-rise with a separate entrance for low-income residents. Others were left shaking their heads that a development boasting of its racial and socioeconomic diversity in reality had a "poor door."[20]

Since the "poor door" incident, New York City has paid a great deal more attention to developments purportedly combining affordable and market-rate housing, but I wonder how much socioeconomic integration will result. New York City officials have, for example, approved another large mixed-income development at 1 West End Avenue, and although it is envisioned that everyone will have access to a roof deck and courtyard, the swimming pool will not be available to poor tenants.[21] Overall, the urban poor who manage to secure an apartment in a mixed-income development might be less like fish out of water than like an invasive species nobody really wants around.

Overall, less than one-third of the urban poor who are eligible for federal assistance for housing actually receive it. Subsidized housing for the poor looks to some like more of a lottery than an entitlement.[22] If anyone truly benefits from recent developments, it is the developers, who can use tax credits to turn a profit, and banks, which seek the tax credits. The middle- and upper-class public pays little attention to these matters. Many quite simply take public housing to be another of those "handouts" that the lazy ones among us receive. Few take to heart any responsibility to house the poor, or any sense that housing the poor would be good for society as a whole.

The Ineffectiveness of Housing Codes

About three-quarters of the people eligible for publicly supported housing are unable or unwilling to receive it.[23] Almost all of them rent inexpensive housing from private landlords in the inner city. Some have enough money from part-time jobs or illegal activities to pay the rent. Others live with or off friends and relatives who have jobs, usually on the lower rungs of the labor market. So many low-income urbanites are eager to rent that the supply of inexpensive rental units is insufficient. No county in the United States has a large enough supply of housing to meet the demand among "extremely low-income households," the latter being defined as families making no more than 30 percent of an area's median household income. In some counties the shortfall is immense. The Dallas–Fort Worth metropolitan area, for example, has only 8 inexpensive rental units for every 100 low-income families.[24]

The rental housing that exists tends to be rundown and getting worse, spinning downward in what some commentators call a "deterioration spiral."[25]

Observers became aware of the deterioration in the 1950s and then increasingly alarmed by it in the 1960s. My goodness, American cities had neighborhoods that were not only poor but also falling apart right before our eyes.

These neighborhoods had long been called "ghettos" and "slums," but the neighborhoods now struck many as "blighted."[26] In an earlier usage, "blight" had referred to some sort of plant disease that could spread rapidly and cause vegetation to wither and decay. Ramshackle housing, the thinking was, could strike a neighborhood, spread, and cause the rest of the housing stock to wither and decay. Calling an inner city blighted, a cynic might say, employs an organic metaphor to obscure the socioeconomic factors that forced the majority of the urban poor to live compacted together in dilapidated housing.

Blighted housing, of course, is often dangerous. Furnaces can be ancient, and electrical lines can spark and ignite, while gas lines leak and sometimes explode. The housing's wooden frames, doors, and windows from which the lead-based paint falls are old, dried out, and highly flammable. A month rarely goes by in the inner city of an American metropolitan area without an inner-city house burning down.

Earlier in the twentieth century, many of these now-decrepit homes were occupied by working-class or perhaps middle-class Americans, and the homes and the people who lived in them were the foundation of stable, thriving neighborhoods. However, African Americans who migrated from the rural American South or the poor from foreign countries carved out parts of the neighborhoods, and as the poor families grew and welcomed other poor families, working- and middle-class residents gradually moved elsewhere. The housing once occupied by people with more assets came to be occupied by poorer people. In language preferred by city planners, the housing "filtered down." And, indeed, "the bulk of conventional housing occupied by low-income people is filtered rather than newly constructed."[27]

Many of the departing working- and middle-class residents had title to their own homes, and the more prosperous among them had often lived in the best unit in the duplexes and small apartment buildings they owned. During the post–World War II decades, individuals and real estate companies purchased the homes and apartment buildings, becoming proverbial absentee landlords and—even worse—"slumlords." The new owners' upkeep of these income properties was often minimal, but that did not mean rents went down. The National Low Rent Housing Coalition suggests that only 30 percent of income can be prudently devoted to rent, but rents in the inner city routinely exceed that percentage for people earning the minimum wage. In addition, the coalition found that rent for modest housing was "two to three times the minimum wage in 92 metropolitan areas and 63 non-metropolitan counties, and more than triple the minimum wage in 24 metro areas and 12 non-metro areas."[28]

The biggest impetus for addressing the shoddy and deteriorating rental housing for the poor came from the federal government. As I noted in the introduction, the self-styled belligerents who launched the federal War on Poverty had a special interest in the living conditions of the nation's urban poor and wanted to see those conditions improve. Hence, in the Housing Act of 1964 and the Housing and Urban Development Act of 1965, the Congress, with the urging of President Lyndon Johnson, required that any officials seeking federal support for local public housing or urban renewal have in place a workable program addressing the deterioration of the housing stock in the inner city. Shortly thereafter, the federal government tightened the statutes to require a "minimum standards housing code related but not limited to health, sanitation, and occupancy requirements" and "an effective program of enforcement to achieve compliance with such code."[29]

The federal government, in other words, took local housing codes to be devices that could be used to stop the blight from spreading, and local governments were not about to turn their backs on the federal money they could obtain by going along with this plan. While as late as 1956 only 56 towns and municipalities had such codes, by 1968 the number had skyrocketed to 4,904. In little over a decade, 85 percent of the cities with populations over fifty thousand had concluded that a properly drafted and vigorously enforced housing code could help stop the deterioration of the housing for the urban poor and address the blight in the neighborhoods in which the poor lived.[30]

The codes themselves still exist and, without a doubt, have grown more numerous and much longer. They address everything from what constitutes a working toilet to the location of a light socket in a particular room, from the type of shingles on your roof to the correct type of smoke detector. The language and standards in the code vary from city to city, but if local housing measured up to all the provisions in a code, the poor living in the city with that code would live in safe, clean, and proper houses and apartments.

For various reasons the housing does not come close to what the codes implicitly envision. In inner-city neighborhoods, a majority of landlords approach their properties less with love and care and more with thoughts of the bottom line and crude cost-benefit analyses. Against the backdrop of what are likely to be relatively stable property values, landlords' costs include taxes, mortgage payments, and investment in repairs and upkeep, while their benefits are chiefly rent payments. Full compliance with the housing codes would increase costs appreciably, and as a result, landlords customarily avoid whatever repairs and improvements they can in order to increase the likelihood of turning a profit. At best, landlords tend faithfully to code violations that make living in their properties truly dangerous; missing fire exits and faulty furnaces, for example, are ominous for even the most dastardly of slumlords. Cosmetic matters such as peeling paint, or security concerns such as window locks are less likely to spur a landlord to action. If, to use familiar language from landlord circles, the "costs of bringing a property up to code" become too great, a landlord might decide to cut his or her losses and abandon the property. Such abandonment is common, and boarded-up, abandoned houses are everywhere in the inner city, serving as stark and sobering reminders of what used to be. Abandoned houses are also frequently sites for crime, drug use, and prostitution, and, in the words of one scholar, abandonment is "contagious."[31]

Faced with the obvious lack of code compliance, tenants can fight back. They can contact the compliance office in city hall, list the problems in their housing, and ask that an inspector come to the site to confirm their tales of woe. But tenants are unlikely to complain. Some are unfamiliar with housing codes and code enforcement offices, and even more are leery of getting on the proverbial "wrong side" of their landlords. Most of the urban poor live where they do because it is the best they can afford and not because they like the places in which they live. If their landlords actually made the repairs called for by the code, rents would go up, potentially to a level outside the reach of current tenants.

Tenants also cannot just pack up their things and move to comparable housing because the vacancy rate in inexpensive housing is at its lowest level in decades.[32] According to the Joint Center for Housing Studies of Harvard University, "In 2001, the 9.9 million renters in the bottom income quintile outnumbered the supply of the lowest-cost units by fully 2 million. Reducing the pool even further, higher-income households occupied 2.7 million of 7.9 million lowest-cost units."[33]

Furthermore, tenants are unlikely to complain to the authorities because they know complainers have a way of getting evicted when landlords conclude they are "troublemakers." The most common reason for eviction is failure to pay the rent, but tenants fear so-called retaliatory evictions. The latter are illegal in most cities, but cases invalidating retaliatory evictions are more common in law-school textbooks than in the actual courts.

Evictions are, technically speaking, legal proceedings and so common among the urban poor as to be "part of the texture of life."[34] One study found that landlords evict one in fourteen African American households each year, and African Americans are on average among the poorest of Americans. What's more, formally evicted households do not include households that move because a disgruntled landlord has turned off the electricity or water. If one adds these types of "involuntary displacements" to the formal evictions, one in eight households leaves unwillingly each year.[35] These evictions and involuntary displacements can have a domino effect. When forced out of the places they had been renting, the urban poor move in with friends and relatives, who can in turn be booted out of their places for having too many occupants.[36] Ever since the mortgage foreclosure crisis during the first decade of the twenty-first century, authorities have kept tabs on the number of mortgage foreclosures, but authorities have not as successfully kept tabs on evictions, which are much more worrisome than foreclosures for the urban poor.

Champions of the urban poor might hope that enforcement officials would step in on their own, point out the requirements of the code, and thereby reduce the abandonments, evictions, and social disruptions, but that is only wishful thinking. A study of housing-code enforcement in Baltimore, Boston, and Buffalo made clear that housing codes are woefully underenforced.[37] Inspectors are for the most part neither inept nor corrupt, but the inspectors rely on their own informal standards when it comes to enforcement. They tend to "go easy" on landlords with only one property who might themselves be struggling to pay their bills, and then, too, inspectors give landlords who appear to be making some repairs greater leeway. Some of the inspectors might even realize that "vigorous and literal enforcement of the housing code might fail to improve, and even worsen the condition of low-income neighborhoods."[38] Most inspectors would nod in agreement at the words of the historian Lawrence M. Friedman: "No housing code ever created a single unit of decent, affordable housing. Actual enforcement, arguably, would have the opposite effect: it would reduce the supply of places where the poor could find a roof over their heads."[39]

If the codes accomplish anything, it might be to deflect attention from the sorry realities of housing for the urban poor. In the present, landlords try to maximize their profit by holding down expenses and then, if necessary, abandon their investments. The urban poor have no choice but to reside in lousy, rundown rental housing in the inner city, and the unattractive shabbiness of this housing is only the beginning of the problem. As already noted, much of the housing is a fire hazard. Sanitary problems also abound. More subtly, the lousy rental housing of the urban poor contributes to their stress and alienation, and this, in turn, hurts school attendance and workplace productivity. Substandard housing for the urban poor, in other words, has serious social and economic consequences.[40] The miserable state and ongoing decline of the housing stock in our inner cities would be unthinkable in other developed countries.[41]

The United Nations would agree with this judgment. In 2000, it established the position of "special rapporteur on adequate housing" and charged the person in that position with, among other things, investigating housing and measuring respect for housing rights in member nations. One would expect, perhaps, that the rapporteur would investigate the hovels and shacks in the world's developing countries, and investigations of this sort have occurred. However, the rapporteur has also made visits to the United States, stopping in, among other places, Chicago and New Orleans. Reports and condemnations followed, but, surprisingly, nobody in the United States seemed particularly embarrassed that the rapporteur deplored the state of rental housing for the American urban poor.[42]

Zoning Out the Urban Poor

As I acknowledged in the introduction, some of the urban poor have in recent years moved to older suburbs adjacent or close to the inner city, but the "suburbanization of poverty," as some call it, has not lifted the urban poor out of poverty. In most cases, the physical appearance and social norms of the older suburbs that have become home for the urban poor begin to resemble what one would find in the inner city. The urban poor have, in effect, extended their poverty into new neighborhoods and communities.

Why do the urban poor move in the direction they do? Why do they even more frequently remain in the inner city, dealing with dilapidated housing and coping with crime and other social pathologies? After all, many readers of this book have in recent decades relocated and found new places they consider culturally and socially appealing. Technological advances and modern mobility have supposedly enabled many Americans to choose their preferred neighborhoods and communities.[43]

Various factors explain why the urban poor tend to stay put. For some, their neighborhoods, as rundown as they might be, have been "home" for generations now, and once a person—rich or poor—comes to feel truly attached to a community, he or she is loath to leave. In addition, moving is time-consuming and expensive, and the urban poor often lack the economic wherewithal to move to the suburbs. Most importantly, the urban poor in general do not have many housing options in the newer, more affluent suburbs. Obtuse and/or spiteful middle- and upper-class suburbanites have used zoning laws to prevent the development of inexpensive rental housing that the urban poor might be able to afford.

Zoning is a variety of lawmaking undertaken largely at the local level. City and county legislative bodies enact zoning ordinances that indicate what varieties of buildings and land usages are anticipated in different areas. Assorted zoning boards, administrative agencies, and planning bodies hear appeals related to the zoning for individual parcels and also sometimes amend and alter the original zoning ordinances. The process caught on in the United States in the years immediately following World War I. New York City claimed to have enacted the first comprehensive zoning ordinance, but even more influential was a model zoning act distributed by secretary of commerce Herbert Hoover in 1922 and 1923. By the end of 1923, some 208 municipalities and 40 percent of the nation's urban population had zoning.[44]

One reason for the remarkably rapid acceptance and spread of zoning was that it afforded an effective way to control not only building sizes and land usages but also socioeconomic sectors of the population and where the people in those sectors might live. When metropolitan areas burgeoned in the middle decades of the twentieth century, the use of zoning to control socioeconomic sectors of the population grew even more important, and one need look no further than the earliest important zoning controversies for an awareness that zoning was about people as well as buildings.

In the case of *Miller v. Board of Public Works* from the early 1920s, for example, the California Supreme Court considered a Los Angeles zoning ordinance making it unlawful to construct or alter buildings in certain districts so that the buildings could house more than two families. A local resident named George Miller had sought a court order compelling the issuance of a building permit so that he could construct a four-unit structure in the regulated area. In upholding a lower court's denial of Miller's request, the California Supreme Court held that Los Angeles's ordinance was not a denial of constitutional guarantees, and also that a municipality could through its zoning banish dangerous or unappealing housing from certain districts. More specifically, the California Supreme Court thought that the creation of districts limited to single-family homes and duplexes made sense as a way to protect the venerable American home. "It is axiomatic," the court stated, "that the welfare, and the very existence of a nation depends upon the character and caliber of its citizenry. The character and quality of manhood and womanhood are in a large measure the result of the home environment."[45] Realizing, perhaps, that the linkage of character to single-family housing could be seen as impugning the character of those who lived in other kinds of housing, the court quickly added a series of awkward qualifications that served only to underscore its biases:

> We do not wish to unduly emphasize the single family resident as a means of perpetuating the home life of a people. There are many persons, who, by reason of circumstances, find apartment, flat, or hotel life necessary or preferable.

Undoubtedly many families do maintain ideal home life in apartments, flats and hotels; and it is also undoubtedly true that in many single family dwellings there is much of dissension and discord.[46]

The concerns expressed by the California Supreme Court were hardly unusual, and the location of apartment buildings was central in early debates regarding zoning. According to a scholar who has conducted a detailed study of zoning in New Haven, Connecticut, during the 1920s, not only had apartments by this point in time differentiated themselves from "tenements," the established home of poor immigrants, but apartments had also become suspect in general. "Apartments incited a variety of often-passionate arguments by judges, city planners, and city residents concerned with both the constitutionality of zoning ordinances creating single-family residential districts and the wisdom of allowing apartment buildings in specific residential areas."[47] The key, of course, was not the actual apartment buildings, but rather the people who might conceivably live in them. If apartment buildings "were portrayed as a threat to the very heart of the country," it was because apartment dwellers were thought by many to be an undesirable lot.[48]

In 1926, the Supreme Court of the United States gave its general stamp of approval to zoning law in the famous case of *Village of Euclid v. Ambler Realty Company*. The case involved the zoning ordinance from a suburb of Cleveland named Euclid that separated residential districts from commercial and industrial districts and also differentiated among residential districts, separating them into single-family and multifamily areas. The Ambler Realty Company sought to invalidate the ordinance largely because the ordinance precluded commercial and industrial development on large portions of Ambler's land, but the Supreme Court rejected Ambler's argument. The Supreme Court also went on to discuss the connections among zoning, housing types, and the people living in each housing type. Speaking for the Supreme Court, Justice Sutherland analogized zoning to nuisance law, which was already well established. He cast apartment buildings as a type of quasi-nuisance comparable to certain businesses and industries, all of which could be harmful to a neighborhood. Sutherland then described at length how apartment buildings can destroy a neighborhood, casting apartment buildings as nothing less than parasitical.[49]

Concerns about apartment buildings and apartment dwellers lived on into more recent times, and, more generally, the biases embedded in zoning acquired a sharper edge in the context of the accelerating suburbanization of the post–World War II decades.[50] Suburbs existed prior to then, but during the first half of the twentieth century, Americans in general saw the cities and their suburbs as complementary. In the post–World War II decades, by contrast, many Americans came to see cities and suburbs as antagonistic. By the 1960s, some even "concluded that cities and suburbs represented completely different, and conflicting, cultural values." It became increasingly common to speak of "an 'urban culture' and a 'suburban culture' as represented by distinct outlooks and ways of life."[51]

The intensity of what became the suburbanites' attitudes regarding the inner city should not be underestimated. Some suburbanites came to perceive the needs of the inner city—better schools, extended support programs, and enlightened law enforcement—as terribly expensive and did not want to tax themselves in order to address these needs. Many suburbanites began to fear that "when poor people move next door, crime, drugs, blight, bad public schools and higher taxes inevitably follow. They worried that the value of their homes will fall and the image of their towns would suffer."[52]

On a deeper level, many suburbanites, especially those in the so-called edge cities that constitute the outer ring of suburbs, continue to see themselves as "normal, decent, and under siege."[53] These suburbanites construct their identities at least in part with reference to their communities' houses, streets, parks, and undeveloped land, and this "seemingly innocent appreciation of landscapes and desire to protect local history and nature can act as subtle but highly effective mechanisms of exclusion and reaffirmation of class identity."[54] Furthermore, the construction of identity is aided immensely if there is a "constitutive outside."[55] Law professor Gerald Frug argued that suburbs require central cities as a constituent part of their identity.[56] He noted that "in the resulting, socially polarized metropolitan landscape, representations of cities as 'landscapes of fear' and their residents as inherently threatening flourished."[57]

Zoning is the major type of law used by contemporary American suburbs to keep the urban poor, the rental housing in which they live, and "the city" in general out of their communities. As late as World War I, local officials used zoning to discriminate against African Americans, as in the example of a notorious Louisville ordinance that forbade whites on blocks where a majority of the renters and owners were white to rent or sell their properties to African Americans. Fortunately, the Supreme Court of the United States invalidated the ordinance, saying that zoning based on race was "in direct violation of the fundamental law enacted in the Fourteenth Amendment."[58]

Today, socioeconomic considerations rather than race are the primary basis of exclusionary zoning. If one uses zoning to exclude the poor, this would adversely affect African Americans, who are disproportionately overrepresented among the poor, but the law requires drafters of zoning ordinances to speak in socioeconomic terms rather than through race. The much-cited political scientist Robert Putnam has said this approach is responsible for "a kind of incipient class apartheid."[59]

Perhaps needless to add, zoning ordinances do not mention the urban poor themselves. Instead, the zoning ordinances use designations related to building locations, types, and sizes to indirectly address who might be able to live in certain areas or municipalities. This approach is both more politically copacetic and less susceptible to legal challenge, but the approach is hardly secret or clandestine. The major techniques of exclusionary zoning include zoning for nonresidential uses only, or, in residential areas, using minimum lot size, minimum street frontage, and minimum square-footage requirements. The standard legal guidebooks for planners and zoning boards shamelessly describe how to use these techniques without running into trouble.[60]

The zoning techniques work in predictable ways. If the ordinance excludes all residential use in a given area and designates that area for commerce or industry, the ordinance thereby precludes housing for the poor as well as anybody else. With the zoning involving lot size, frontage, and square footage, the goal is to promote the development of large, expensive homes and to deter the development of inexpensive rental housing. The urban poor are rarely in a position to purchase even the smallest of single-family homes; inexpensive rental housing is necessary if the urban poor are to take up residence in a suburb.

Much remains to be said regarding challenges to exclusionary zoning using constitutional law, but note for now that as early as 1974 the United States Court of Appeals for the Ninth Circuit made clear that exclusive large-lot zoning would not be vulnerable to challenges mounted by the poor. Two individuals and the Confederación de la Raza Unida challenged the zoning ordinance of Los Altos, California, which provided that all housing lots in Los Altos consist of not less than one acre and contain no more than one primary structure. This zoning kept out the poor and reinforced the exclusivity of the community. The court ruled that the zoning could stand since it was "rationally related to preserving the town's rural environment." Low-cost housing was available in other parts of the county, and the court ruled that while California law did require a town to have housing for its residents, the law "does not require it to provide housing for non-residents, even though the non-residents may live in the broader urban community of which the town is a part."[61]

State courts have also accepted large-lot zoning for even larger minimum lot sizes than Los Altos required. In Massachusetts, for example, plaintiffs challenged a zoning ordinance that required all lots in about one-half of Edgartown to be at least three acres in size. The zoning seemed clearly designed to fortify the socioeconomic exclusiveness of Martha's Vineyard, but the court chose to emphasize that the large-lot zoning would help protect the swampy Edgartown Great Pond and, as a result, found the ordinance tolerable.[62] Indeed, it seems, the more exclusive a suburb aspires to be, the larger its lots will be. In the town of New Bedford, New York, for example, 80 percent of the land has a four-acre minimum, and some communities in Marin County, just across the Bay from San Francisco, have five-acre zoning.[63]

One aspect of zoning law that is especially revealing involves mobile homes and the negative reactions of suburbanites to them. Mobile homes to some extent evolved from the trailer homes that first came to the public's attention during the 1930s. These trailer homes grew in popularity during World War II and the late 1940s, but during the 1950s trailer homes started to grow larger, boxier, and flimsier. In addition, the owners of this new breed of trailers were increasingly likely to plant them permanently in their lots. The very wheels on their trailers shrunk and then disappeared completely. Much to the chagrin of sellers and buyers alike, the public continues to refer to "trailers" and "trailer parks," while the preferred usage has become "mobile homes" and "mobile home parks."[64]

The mobile home is a variety of housing that is within the reach of the urban poor. They might buy a used three-bedroom mobile home for $15,000 and then have as long as ten years to pay for it. In addition to making the monthly payments, the owner of a mobile home also has to pay $250–$300 per month in what is often called "dirt rent," that is, a fee for using the ground on which the mobile home sits. However, many mobile-home park proprietors allow owners to deduct half of the "dirt rent" from the installment payments. In the final accounting, the percentage of household income going to housing is often smaller than it is for public housing.[65]

Despite the great potential of mobile homes to reduce the shortage of inexpensive housing, "no other type of housing in America has been more broadly vilified."[66] Why is that? One could honestly complain that mobile homes are mass-produced, standardized, and not particularly appealing to the eye. Those hostile to mobile homes could also argue that mobile homes deteriorate rapidly and that they are especially vulnerable to tornadoes, hurricanes, and other storms. In fact, mobile homes depreciate in value over time more like motor vehicles than single-family homes. That relatively rapid depreciation could wreak havoc with a suburban tax base.

In reality, though, excluding mobile homes from one's suburb relates less to the type of housing in and of itself than to the type of people thought most likely to occupy that housing. Almost as soon as the mobile home market shifted in the late 1950s to a less-affluent and less-educated population, mobile homes came to register among middle- and upper-class Americans as "low-class." As early as the 1950s, residents of mobile home parks came to be seen as "trailer trash," and mobile home parks struck some "as a new kind of slum."[67] The negative attitude regarding the presumably lower-class residents of the mobile home parks remained dominant in subsequent decades and even surfaced in comments by an influential member of the national executive branch. In 1996, Paula Jones alleged that President Bill Clinton had sexually harassed her while he was governor of Arkansas. When inner-circle Clinton adviser James Carville responded to the allegations by Jones, he attempted to discredit her by playing on the widespread bias against those who live in mobile homes. "Drag $100 bills through trailer parks," Carville said, "and there's no telling what you'll find."[68] Everyone appreciated that the comment was intended as an insult to

Jones. Perhaps some realized the insult extended to the poor and working-class people who live in mobile home parks.

Suburbs can and do exclude mobile homes and mobile home parks or restrict them to designated areas.[69] In fact, sometimes the areas designated for mobile home parks do not really exist. One Pennsylvania town, for example, restricted mobile home parks to commercial areas, knowing in advance that no land for future parks was available in those areas. A court declined to find this approach unfair or arbitrary and allowed it to continue.[70] The courts have also upheld a zoning ordinance that allowed mobile home parks only in restricted planned-development districts with special application procedures.[71] An estimated 12 million people currently live in mobile home parks, but given these restrictive zoning laws, supply is static even as demand for inexpensive places to live is growing.[72]

Short of direct exclusion, suburbs might also enact guidelines and regulations for mobile homes that are equally effective in keeping the urban poor out. These hostile enactments might go to height/length ratios, minimum floor areas, foundation requirements, exterior siding quality, window sizes, and even roof pitch.[73] One survey found that these types of regulations for mobile home placements were most likely in wealthy communities that spent heavily on their schools and were growing rapidly.[74] Outlying suburbs are perfect examples of communities with these characteristics.

Excluding mobile homes from the suburbs in hopes of keeping out poor people is a further illustration of how zoning and housing regulations are about not only property but also people. Zoning, the distinguished cultural anthropologist Constance Perin once noted, can be "a short-hand for unstated rules regarding what are widely regarded as correct social categories and relationships, that is, not only how land uses should be arranged but how land users, as a social category, are to be related to one another."[75] Like apartment dwellers in the 1920s, the contemporary urban poor are held in low esteem. They are unwelcome in middle- and upper-class suburbs, and many zoning boards, planning commissions, and local officials have successfully zoned the urban poor out of their communities.

Constitutional Challenges to Exclusionary Zoning

If suburban councils and zoning boards have demonstrated their determination to exclude the urban poor whenever possible, an optimistic soul might hope the courts would put a stop to such obviously discriminatory practices. That is, given one body of law and one set of legal institutions' biases against the urban poor, other bodies of law and other legal institutions might conceivably eliminate the bias. The function of law related to the poor is not simply an unabated crushing of the poor. The law might contain and condemn the urban poor, but law, as an immense and complicated discourse, is nothing if not fluid, contested, and even contradicted.

To a limited extent, the type of legal "correcting" regarding the exclusion of the urban poor has indeed occurred, although primarily in the state courts and especially in New Jersey. In the late 1970s and early 1980s, the NAACP and others sued the Township of Mount Laurel, New Jersey, and on two occasions lower-court decisions involving Mount Laurel were appealed to the New Jersey Supreme Court.

Mount Laurel is exactly the kind of outlying suburban community most likely to engage in exclusionary zoning. It is located on the eastern edge of the sprawling metropolitan area that includes Philadelphia and its suburbs to the west of the Delaware River in Pennsylvania, and Camden and other suburbs and small municipalities to the east of the Delaware River in New Jersey. Philadelphia and Camden in particular are home to many poor people. Some of the urban poor in Philadelphia and Camden might have liked to move to an outlying area of the metropolitan area such as Mount Laurel in order to escape the problems of their inner-city neighborhoods. Mount Laurel, meanwhile, decided to zone in ways that squelched this plan.

The first of the appeals to the New Jersey Supreme Court involving Mount Laurel dates from 1975. The court concluded that the Township of Mount Laurel had excluded low- and moderate-income people by, in effect, overzoning for industry in the remaining swaths of undeveloped land in the township. The court quoted with approval the lower court's statement that the Township of Mount Laurel "through its zoning ordinances has exhibited economic discrimination in that the poor have been deprived of adequate housing and the opportunity to secure the construction of subsidized housing."[76] The Township of Mount Laurel, in the court's view, had overlooked the obligation of New Jersey municipalities located in or near metropolitan areas to assume their "fair share of the present and prospective regional need" to house the urban poor.[77]

Eight years later, the New Jersey Supreme Court revisited and reaffirmed matters in a decision commonly known as "Mount Laurel II." By this point in time, the court had grown irritated with the Township of Mount Laurel's piddling efforts to abide by what now had become known as "Mount Laurel I." In the words of the court,

> The *Mount Laurel* case threatens to become infamous. After all this time, ten years after the trial court's initial order invalidating the zoning ordinance, Mount Laurel remains afflicted with a blatantly exclusionary ordinance. Papered over with studies, rationalized by hired experts, the ordinance at its core is true to nothing but Mount Laurel's determination to exclude the poor.[78]

The court was also angry that other New Jersey suburbs had engaged in the same kind of exclusionary zoning as Mount Laurel, and the court in fact combined its review of the Mount Laurel ordinance with reviews of ordinances from five other New Jersey municipalities: the Townships of Mahwah, Franklin, Chester, and Clinton and the Borough of Carteret. Detectably upset by what the New Jersey suburbs were doing, the court paused to contemplate what New Jersey would look like if such action continued: "Poor people forever zoned out of substantial areas of the state, not because housing could not be built for them but because they are not wanted; poor people forced to live in urban slums forever not because suburbia, developing rural areas, fully developed residential sections, seashore resorts, and other attractive locations could not accommodate them, but simply because they are not wanted."[79]

The court in "Mount Laurel II" tried both to stop the suburban resistance to "Mount Laurel I" and also to get municipalities and developers to actually build inexpensive, multifamily housing that the urban poor might be able to rent. Non-lawyers sometimes fail to appreciate it, but a court has limited powers and would be hard-pressed to simply order inclusion, much less equality. Yet the New Jersey Supreme Court showed an unusual degree of judicial determination and listed the kinds of inclusionary steps that could and should be taken: density bonuses for developers who provide for low- and moderate-income families, mandatory set-asides for low- and moderate-income housing, over-zoning for low- and moderate-income housing, and acceptance of mobile homes and mobile home parks.[80]

So, here's a toast to the New Jersey courts for perceiving the problem and trying to rectify it; but what about the federal courts? They, in general, have more clout and garner more respect and prestige than the state courts. Most state court judges would surely take an appointment to the federal bench to be a step up in the world. Then, too, the federal courts have at their disposal the constitutional law of the United States, and the Fourteenth Amendment, in particular, on the surface offers great promise. Local governments of the sort that enact and amend zoning ordinances are political subdivisions of the state, and the Fourteenth Amendment's guarantees of due process and equal protection could, therefore, plausibly apply. Yet despite great promise and potential, the federal courts and constitutional law have done almost nothing to alleviate the problem of zoning that excludes the urban poor. In a string of important decisions from the 1970s, the Supreme Court of the United States closed the door to effective challenges to exclusionary suburban zoning based on socioeconomic standing, and nobody has ever succeeded in reopening that door.

If the urban poor hoped to prevail in a challenge to suburban exclusion under federal constitutional law, they would want to hitch their challenge to a supercharged wagon. In conventional legal language, the urban poor would want the federal courts to see their complaints as ones that required "height-ened scrutiny." The plaintiffs' best hope would involve either demonstrating that their fundamental rights had been taken away without due process, or showing they had been denied the equal protection of the law as members of a suspect class.[81]

As for the first possibility, the federal courts in some areas have found government action to violate fundamental rights of the poor. For example, the Supreme Court of the United States has strictly scrutinized limitations on the rights of the poor with regard to voting and with regard to criminal trials and appellate processes.[82] However, the federal courts take rights and protections in these areas to be more important from a constitutional perspective than rights and protections related to housing.

The most important case in this area is *Lindsey v. Normet* from 1972. In the case, tenants in Portland, Oregon, took a stand against their landlord. They withheld their rent after the local government declared their building unfit for habitation and their landlord refused to make the necessary repairs. In keeping with what is often done to unhappy tenants who withhold the rent, the landlord then initiated eviction proceedings against them and had at his disposal the "Oregon Forcible Entry and Wrongful Detention Statute." The latter required, among other things, that (1) the trial, if any, be held no later than six days after notification of the eviction proceeding, (2) the trial, if any, could consider only the tenant's failure to pay the rent and could not get into complaints about the landlord, and (3) a bond of twice the amount of accrued rent would be required to appeal a decision from the trial. All of these requirements, the tenants felt, must surely deny them their fundamental housing rights without due process of law. How could they possibly win if they had to fight the eviction so quickly and without being able to point out the landlord's failings? And if the tenants lost in the trial court, how could they be expected to post the bond needed for any appeal?

The tenants challenged the very constitutionality of the Oregon statute, winning on some points and losing on others. However, when the case finally wended its way to the Supreme Court of the United States, a majority of the justices were largely unsympathetic to the tenants' appeal. Speaking for the majority, Justice White said,

> We are unable to perceive [in the United States Constitution] any constitutional guarantee of access to dwellings of a particular quality, or any recognition of the right of a tenant to occupy the real property of his landlord beyond the term of his lease without payment of rent or otherwise contrary to the terms of the relevant agreement. Absent constitutional mandate, the assurance of adequate housing and the definition of landlord-tenant relationships are legislative, not judicial, functions. Nor should we forget that the Constitution expressly protects against confiscation of private property or the income therefrom.[83]

In short, no recognizable fundamental right to housing exists in the United States, and as a result, a state could regulate housing and landlord-tenant relations without being concerned that due process be scrupulously observed. Sounding more than a bit irritated, Justice White's opinion in *Lindsey v. Normet* reminds us that "the Constitution does not provide judicial remedies for every social and economic ill."[84]

With regard to an equal protection claim, the Fourteenth Amendment of the United States Constitution guarantees that no state shall "deny to any person within its jurisdiction the equal protection of the laws."[85] One might think that suburban zoning designed to keep out the urban poor would surely deny them equal protection of the law, but a major problem lurks. Namely, the federal courts have made clear that socioeconomic class distinctions are not a suspect condition of the sort that would subject suburban zoning to heightened scrutiny.

In the case of *James v. Valtierra* from 1971, the Supreme Court considered claims involving a provision of the California state constitution providing that low-rent housing projects for the poor could not be developed in a given community until the majority of people living there approved. Not surprisingly, when low-rent housing projects were proposed in several communities, the voters rejected them in referenda. Citizens in the City of San Jose and also in San Mateo County then sued, alleging, among other things, that the provision in the state constitution denied the poor equal protection of the law. After all, there was no need for a referendum if somebody proposed a high-rent housing project or a big new subdivision. Only the poor faced the extra burden of an approval referendum. A three-judge federal district panel agreed with the plaintiffs, but the Supreme Court of the United States reversed.

In his opinion for the Supreme Court in the case, Justice Black carefully distinguished between laws that were based on racial considerations and those related to socioeconomic concerns. The former would certainly be unconstitutional. In Black's mind, the California referendum requirement did not apply only to low-rent housing that would necessarily be occupied by members of a racial minority group.[86] He also observed that the actual record "would not support any claim that a law seemingly neutral on its face is in fact aimed at a racial minority."[87] Obviously, the provision in the California constitution placed a special burden on those seeking to develop low-rent housing and, by extension, on poor people seeking low-rent housing. But according to Black, "a lawmaking procedure that 'disadvantages' a particular group does not always deny equal protection."[88]

It made no difference in the ultimate disposition of the case, but the Supreme Court's liberal wing filed a vigorous dissent in the case. Justice Marshall, joined by Justices Brennan and Blackmun, thought the California constitutional provision clearly singled out low-income persons and on its face constituted invidious discrimination, which the Equal Protection Clause of the Fourteenth Amendment prohibited. Justice Marshall, himself an African American who had labored long and hard for racial equality while counsel for the NAACP, made clear that he did not think the equal protection guarantees of the Fourteenth Amendment were limited to race. "It is far too late in the day to contend that the Fourteenth Amendment prohibits only racial discrimination; and, to me, singling out the poor to bear a burden not placed on any other class of citizens tramples the values that the Fourteenth Amendment was designed to protect."[89]

Without the argument that housing is their fundamental right or that they have been denied equal protection of the law, the urban poor find themselves in a nearly impossible legal position. They would have to show that suburban zoning is arbitrary or capricious, but as I have suggested, courts have traditionally taken zoning classifications to be reasonable. A strong presumption of constitutionality attaches to zoning ordinances, and without "heightened scrutiny" being brought to bear, zoning ordinances are extraordinarily difficult to topple.

Overall, then, the urban poor have little reason to hope they could successfully challenge exclusionary zoning in the august and sometimes self-impressed federal courts. "One should not be optimistic of the chances for success in the federal courts in a case challenging exclusionary zoning because it is economically discriminatory."[90] Suburban zoning in American metropolitan areas effectively prevents the urban poor from living in the suburbs and thereby confines them to the inner city. When the urban poor have challenged this as exclusionary, the courts have for the most part refused to accept their constitutional arguments. Law, in the form of zoning, seals off areas in which the urban poor cannot live, and law, in the form of constitutional doctrine, refuses to end the exclusion.

What Does Exclusionary Zoning Accomplish?

Any discussion of patterns in a large socio-legal phenomenon such as exclusionary zoning should acknowledge exceptions and counterexamples. As already mentioned, certain suburbs exist in which the urban poor have been able to find low-cost rental housing.[91] These suburbs are likely to be older communities located immediately adjacent to the inner city, but some of the communities that the urban poor call home are in the outer ring.[92] In addition, as I have noted, some state courts, most notably those in New Jersey, have ruled that cities and towns must plan for a variety of housing, including inexpensive rental housing, and take on their fair share of the latter.[93] Most generally, commentators and critics have suggested how "inclusionary" as opposed to exclusionary zoning might work.[94]

But exceptions, counterexamples, and pleas for reform notwithstanding, the core story involving zoning and the urban poor remains sobering. Many middle- and upper-class Americans do not want the urban poor nearby, and outlying suburbs in general have used zoning ordinances to make it difficult if not impossible for the urban poor to relocate to those suburbs. The federal courts, in turn, have been unreceptive to constitutional challenges to this variety of exclusionary zoning. As a result, the urban poor often stay put, dealing with urban decay and encountering difficulty finding, getting to, or even caring about jobs.

Suburbanites sometimes reflect on their reasons for keeping the urban poor out of their communities, and sometimes they do not. The most conscious and shaped resistance is fiscal in nature. A large part of school funding, for example, comes from the local property tax, and if a suburb were to house the poor and their children, that could mean higher taxes to support more schools and expensive special programs in the schools.[95] Then, too, housing the poor might mean increased expenditures for law enforcement and for social welfare programs. Beyond fiscal concerns, an unreflective, gut fear of what urban poverty supposedly includes—dysfunctional families, crime, drug use, and "the city" in general—spawns the efforts to exclude the poor.

Are these fears supported by facts? A study of the impact of 140 units of affordable housing in none other than Mount Laurel, New Jersey, suggests there is nothing to fear. A decade after the suburb lost its fight to keep out the poor *and* after countless meetings of local government boards and committees and commissions, Mount Laurel finally agreed in 1999 to allow the development of a housing complex for the poor. Some predicted that the complex and the people who lived in it would drag down Mount Laurel, but *Climbing Mount Laurel*, a study undertaken by a group of Princeton sociologists, found that has not taken place.[96] Middle- and upper-class residents of Mount Laurel have been unaffected. Mount Laurel's property values have gone up, crime rates have dropped, and tax rates have even fallen. Any changes in Mount Laurel are totally comparable with those in demographically similar suburbs adjacent to Mount Laurel.[97]

In my opinion, suburban racism is widespread and especially ugly, but suburban exclusionary zoning is not only a matter of race. Professionals and business executives who belong to minority groups can and do purchase appealing single-family residences in the suburbs. Luxury condominiums are one option, but those with families might prefer sprawling homes on newly plotted twisty lanes and cul-de-sacs. White suburbanites usually welcome these new residents, and some might even boast of "the black doctor down the street" or "the Puerto Rican CEO a block over." The urban poor, by contrast, are often unable to find low-rent housing in the suburbs regardless of their race.

If you keep the urban poor out of the suburbs, meanwhile, you also, for the most part, keep them in the inner city, and there are reasons for doing this as well. The goals here are less intentional and more a matter of usefulness. Legislative studies do not call for them. Master plans do not address them. Nevertheless, keeping the urban poor in inner-city neighborhoods does contain a "problem population" in what are considered undesirable areas. Furthermore, these neighborhoods in which the poor are concentrated can be useful to middle- and upper-class Americans in concrete, specific ways.

Two examples involve the location of vice activities and assorted rehabilitation facilities. Inner-city neighborhoods can and do serve as marketplaces for prostitution and illegal drugs—that is, for services and goods some members of the middle and upper classes might want to purchase but not in their own neighborhoods and communities. Also, poor neighborhoods can "be used for facilities other neighborhoods reject, from homeless shelters and halfway houses for AIDS patients and rehabilitated drug abusers to toxic and other dumps."[98] All metropolitan areas need "stigmatized areas" of this sort in which unwanted activities can continue, but the concentration and further development of such facilities in the inner city "help ensure that underclass communities are perceived as dysfunctional and dangerous communities."[99]

"Stigmatized areas," of course, are undesirable places to live, especially because of the housing. Dangerous neighborhoods with rundown housing are difficult to call home. But alas, these areas are in fact where one might expect America's urban poor to live, and their residence in the inner city with its fundamentally unacceptable housing is a major aspect of what can be seen as the urban poor's oppression. As I have illustrated, law contributes in myriad ways to the problem.

CHAPTER THREE

Channeling Family Life

y oldest daughter teaches bilingual English in an inner-city public high school, and her reports on pregnancies and approaches to parenthood among her students are disconcerting. At any given point, 10 percent of the girls might be pregnant, and for some expecting students, their pregnancies are not their first ones. A majority of the pregnant girls have no particular plans to marry the fathers of their children, and some are unsure who those fathers might be. High school graduation might eventually fall by the wayside, but the girls optimistically and even buoyantly carry on. Their hope is that biological fathers, mothers, grandmothers, and siblings—themselves poor and unmarried—will help them raise their offspring. And who knows? Maybe the fathers of some of the children will make support payments or at least regularly stop by with birthday gifts and bags of groceries. The high school girls' extended, loosely structured families will perhaps successfully nurture most of the children.

Few middle- or upper-class Americans are aware of the family lives these teenagers are experiencing *and* plan to continue experiencing, but those who are aware might be appalled. My goodness, more prosperous Americans might think, the urban poor do not respect the institution of marriage, take seriously their responsibility to financially support their children, or build the sturdy, tightly knit families in which the children are more likely to thrive.

Law and legal institutions might offer ways to channel the urban poor in a more conventional direction. Laws could direct not only teenagers but also the urban poor in general toward what are considered better choices and behavior. Officials charged with enforcing these laws might also castigate and penalize those who do not conduct themselves in the preferred ways. Champions of the approach could even understand it as benevolent. In his now-classic discussion of the channeling function in family law, Professor Carl E. Schneider, for example, suggested that using law this way was not the same thing as coercion. Channeling could be misused in heavy-handed ways, but in Schneider's opinion, "It is also one of the ways we try to soften the harshness of life."[1]

But, unfortunately, plans to direct and channel the urban poor into different styles of family life do not always "soften." They are not necessarily benevolent. In reviewing the plans, one can hear those with sociopolitical clout expressing their biases, preferences, and disapproval. Many do not care for how the urban poor behave in the private family sphere of their lives, and they would like to see a greater commitment to marriage, the faithful payment of child support, and more attentive, conventional child-rearing. Many members of the middle and upper classes, it seems to me, think the urban poor should have family lives like the ones they have.[2]

The Promotion of Marriage

Laws regarding the meanings and ramifications of marriage are frequently discussed in middle- and upper-class circles. Who should or should not be allowed to legally marry? To what extent should we limit the negotiating and drafting of prenuptial agreements, that is, agreements for distributing assets if a marriage ends with a divorce or a spouse's death? How much alimony or maintenance might a divorced spouse hope to receive after a marriage ends?

These mainstream questions—and many more similar to them—have less urgency for the urban poor. The chief reason is that the urban poor do not seek to marry, or actually marry as frequently, as members of the middle and upper classes. While throughout most of the twentieth century Americans of all classes married at roughly the same rate, the decline of marriage among the urban poor became evident in the 1970s.[3] By the end of the 1980s, poor women were only three-quarters as likely to marry as middle- and upper-class women. During the first fifteen years of the twenty-first century, the contrast has grown even more striking, and in the present, poor men and women are only one-half as likely to marry as men and women with incomes three times greater than the poverty level.[4]

Variations of course exist according to region, ethnicity, and race, but the emerging gulf is primarily socioeconomic. We have on our hands "what demographers, sociologists, and those who study often depressing statistics about the wedded state call a 'marriage gap' between the well-off and the less so."[5] Thinking of the way the well-to-do continue to marry while the poor increasingly decline to do so, the journalist Andrew Yarrow has said, "There's a growing danger that marriage, with all its advantages for stability, income, and child well-being will look like a gated community for the baccalaureate class."[6]

Why are the urban poor less likely to marry? A large number of social scientists and demographers have attempted to answer this question. As early as 1981, for example, Gary S. Becker argued that, with women's increased entry into the labor force and the rise in their income relative to men's income, women no longer needed to marry and could remain single if they wished.[7] In contemporary metropolitan areas, poor women are more likely to be employed than poor men, and even their borderline financial independence makes it more likely that they will choose to live without husbands.[8] William Julius Wilson, whose sociological thinking has been highlighted at several earlier points in this book, emphasized that the number of "marriageable" men in the inner city is declining. He argued that "the sharp increase in black male joblessness since 1970 accounts in large measure for the rise in the rate of single-parent families, and that because jobless rates are highest in the inner-city, rates of single parenthood are also highest there."[9] Wilson's theory is that, against the backdrop of deindustrialization, inner-city men have declining or nonexistent wages, and inner-city women have less interest in drawing from the pool of potential but unemployed husbands.[10] In addition, and as I previously lamented, large numbers of poor urban men are behind bars. It is obviously difficult to marry or to be married to a man doing time, and when a man completes his sentence, he may not strike women as a particularly desirable mate. Not only employers but also potential spouses have difficulty taking to men who carry the label "ex-con."

These observations suggest that the urban poor, and especially women among the urban poor, know what they are doing when they choose not to marry. The women realize, social critic Barbara Ehrenreich has suggested in her distinctively lively manner, that a large percentage of inner-city men are more likely to be "bread-eaters" than "bread-winners."[11] "Particularly for women who are on welfare or are employed in low-wage jobs marriage to a man with no income makes little sense, and most women are unwilling to bear the financial responsibility."[12]

Christina M. Gibson-Davis, Kathryn Edin, and Sara McLanahan conducted what is probably the most revealing recent study of the urban poor's low marriage rates. They began with data from the *Fragile Families and Child Well-being Study*, a nationally representative study of 3,700 unmarried couples with newborns and a comparison sample of 1,200 married couples with newborns. They then extended the data with their *Time, Love, Cash, Caring and Children Study*, an embedded, qualitative, interview-based study of forty-nine "fragile families" and twenty-six married couples. The "fragile family" sample was limited to English-speaking parents whose household incomes were less than $30,000 or who used Medicaid to pay for the birth of their children.[13]

Gibson-Davis, Edin, and McLanahan concluded that financial instability was by far the most common barrier to marriage. The overwhelming number of interviewed people said they wanted to get their finances in order before getting married. This included the ability to regularly make ends meet, the acquisition of suitable semipermanent assets, the development of prudent asset-management skills, and the accumulation of enough savings to have a proper wedding.[14]

The latter goal, although not necessarily the key financial concern, suggests that while the urban poor may not marry as frequently as more prosperous Americans, the urban poor *do* respect marriage and consider it an important and desirable undertaking. The urban poor could modestly and quickly marry before magistrates and justices of the peace, but, like most Americans, the urban poor want something fancier and more elaborate. They would like members of the wedding party to wear gowns and tuxedos. They would like to ride to the church and reception hall in limousines. After they say "I do" and toss their bridal bouquets into the air, they would like honeymoons in distant, romantic places.

All of this costs money. According to a survey conducted by the XO Group, the parent company of the online wedding planner "The Knot," the average cost of a wedding in the United States in 2016 was $35,329. The figure includes charges for rings, a photographer, the venue, and food and drink, but it excludes charges for the honeymoon.[15] Weddings of this sort are impractical for the urban poor, but the urban poor would still like to have them. Gibson-Davis, Edin, and McLanahan argue that the poor's expectations "reflect the idea among low-income parents that getting married should signal that a couple has 'arrived' in a financial sense."[16]

The urban poor's actual respect for marriage seems to be lost on some religious and pro-family groups. These groups worry that the urban poor do not appreciate marriage as the bedrock of Western civilization. The groups argue that the urban poor do not understand that marriage, especially in and through a church, demonstrates a commitment to a moral code and constitutes an important milestone on the journey of life. The groups believe that getting the urban poor to marry should be an important part of the "moral crusade against those evils of promiscuity, illegitimacy, single mother–headed households, and so on."[17] Believers in marriage, and especially those with a sense that the institution of marriage is in jeopardy, are numerous, and in the context of the ongoing skirmishes in the culture wars, no shortage of political figures are eager to have the support of traditional religious and pro-family voters.

In addition, condemnation of the urban poor for declining to marry reflects fiscal concerns. Some think married people would be better able to support themselves and their children than would unmarried people. In particular, a mother would be better able to pay the bills if a legal husband, especially one with a job and a paycheck, were around to help. This would, in turn, reduce the amount of support expected from the state and from the taxpayers who routinely understand themselves as the foundation of the state. Politicians do not put it as explicitly as certain conservative policymakers, but some of the latter, imbued no doubt with a neoliberal animus, think getting the poor to marry could be a valuable part of the effort "to privatize poor women and children's dependency."[18]

The promotion of marriage by political figures began in a sense in 1992 with the complaints and pronouncements of much-maligned Vice President Dan Quayle. In a speech to the Commonwealth Club of California, Quayle cited unwed motherhood as a contributing factor to the riots that occurred in Los Angeles earlier in the year.[19] More surprisingly, he criticized the sitcom character Murphy Brown, a fictional news anchorwoman played by the actress Candice Bergen. In one of the sitcom's many narrative twists, Brown wanted to have a baby but also remain single. Quayle complained: "It doesn't help matters when prime-time TV has Murphy Brown—a character who supposedly epitomizes today's intelligent, highly paid, professional woman—mocking the importance of fathers, by bearing a child alone, and calling it just another 'lifestyle choice.'"[20] Instead of delivering messages of this sort, Quayle thought, we should be promoting marriage and teaching Americans how to sustain their marriages.

The media ridiculed Quayle for picking a fight with a fictional character,[21] and he and his running mate George H. W. Bush lost their bid for reelection, albeit for unrelated reasons. Still, marriage promotion remained available as something politicians of many stripes could champion. In the mid-1990s, for example, Congress approved and President William Clinton signed into law massive changes in the welfare system. The new welfare-reform statute began with ten congressional findings, and the first two concern marriage. Right at the beginning, the statute tells us directly that "Marriage is the foundation of a successful society" and also that "Marriage is an essential institution of a successful society which promotes the interests of children."[22] This endorsement had obvious appeal for members of pro-family and religious groups. It also implied that certain Americans were neither contributing to the well-being of their society nor tending to the raising of their children.

When George W. Bush moved into the White House in 2001, he wanted to project the image of a "compassionate conservative," and he appreciated that marriage promotion could be coordinated with that imagery.[23] President Bush also made more specific the link between the supposed immorality of living "outside of wedlock" and reducing budget expenditures that had attracted attention in the prior administrations of his father and William Clinton. If people married, they would follow the traditional path *and* could more easily be removed from the welfare rolls. Newly married, one-time welfare recipients could become productive members of society and achieve financial security.[24]

The Deficit Reduction Act of 2005 created "The Healthy Marriage Initiative" and made funding of $150 million available for each of the fiscal years 2006 through 2010 for marriage promotion programs and activities.[25] What from the Bush administration's perspective was a "healthy marriage"? According to information provided by the Department of Health and Human Services, "There are at least two characteristics that all healthy marriages have in common. First, they are mutually enriching, and second, both spouses have a deep respect for each other."[26] "We don't want to come in with a heavy hand," said Dr. Wade F. Horn, assistant secretary of Health and Human Services for Children and Families. "We want to help couples, especially low-income couples, manage conflict in healthy ways."[27]

The federal "Healthy Marriage Initiative" buttressed programs that had preceded it in individual states. Oklahoma, for example, had mounted programs even before the federal initiative, and the so-called Oklahoma Marriage Initiative had become the nation's first statewide initiative.[28] Oklahoma then used $10 million in additional federal monies to create a marriage resource center and to mount youth outreach campaigns, school-based programs, and community workshops.[29]

Most of the marriage promotion organizations operate locally, but the national organizations are particularly aggressive and ambitious. They include, but are not limited to, the African American Healthy Marriage Initiative, the Hispanic Healthy Marriage Initiative, and the Native American Healthy Marriage Initiative.[30] All serve members of minority groups regardless of where they live, and the African American Healthy Marriage Initiative is the largest. It has ten regional offices, and each of its regional offices makes subgrants to local organizations.

One especially intriguing effort of the African American Healthy Marriage Initiative involves distributing the *Jump the Broom* video. It recalls the noble determination of some slaves to marry even though the law of the Antebellum South precluded it. In some areas, slaves unofficially married by jumping over a broom.[31] The modern video is a one-act play directed by Thomas Melon and presented by Truth Theater of Houston. It features a series of vignettes challenging popular marriage-related beliefs such as: relinquishing your virginity to a man proves your love for him, abstaining from premarital sex is corny and old-fashioned, and building a happy marriage if your own parents were unmarried is impossible. In its own way, *Jump the Broom* tries to get viewers to think about what might lead to a healthy marriage.[32]

Given the realities of "marriage gap," the marriage promotion organizations are especially focused on the urban poor, and some of the organizations have realized that programs designed with white, middle-class, well-educated couples in mind might not work as well for those in poverty. Hence, programs exist that are consciously designed for poor people. One example is "Loving Couples Loving Children," which uses a television "talk show" format and features couples discussing their relationships in front of a lively audience.[33] Fortunately, the tone is closer to *Oprah* than to *Jerry Springer*. "Love's Cradle," another marriage promotion program designed for the urban poor, self-consciously "dumbs down" the presentation. It pitches to a fifth-grade educational level, apparently never stopping to realize this might be insulting to even poorly educated people.[34]

Anticipating criticism, advocates of marriage promotion denied any sinister motives or conniving agendas. Forcefully routing people into marriages or into certain kinds of marriages, after all, would hint of the marriage-arranging and marriage-dictating found in certain traditional societies. When pushed on the matter, Assistant Secretary Wade F. Horn, for example, insisted that assorted marriage initiatives would not force anyone to get or stay married.[35]

Beyond the original federal "Healthy Marriage Initiative" funding, additional funds continue to become available. Some states continue to fund marriage initiatives, and nonprofit foundations such as the New Hope Foundation and the National Christian Association are also funders of marriage promotion programs for the urban poor.[36] Most importantly, acting with the encouragement of the Obama administration, Congress extended the federal "Healthy Marriage Initiative" by amending the original Bush-era federal statute.[37]

Before applying for funding, meanwhile, pro-marriage groups and organizations might note that existing marriage-promotion programs have not found much success. For starters, "Very little research exists to show that marriage promotion programs are effective in creating marriages among low-income families."[38] Then, too, according to the Council for Contemporary Families, a nonpartisan, nonprofit family research organization based at the University of Miami, evaluations of federally funded programs indicate that most programs did not strengthen the quality and stability of marriages among the poor.[39] An author of a magazine article captured the results of marriage promotion laws more playfully: "Uncle Sam tends to make a poor Cupid."[40]

Religious and pro-family groups, government officials, and the middle and upper classes in general have not, to recall a notion introduced at the beginning of this chapter, effectively "channeled" the urban poor into marriage using marriage promotion laws. Marriage promotion laws have not to date routed the urban poor to an institution the middle and upper classes consider desirable.

Delinquent Child Support

American parents have a troubling record when it comes to paying child support. Customarily, child-support payments do not go directly to children but rather pass through the hands of their custodial parents. In 2011, only 43.4 percent of the country's 14.4 million custodial parents entitled to receive child-support payments received the full amount. Since almost 92 percent of the custodial parents are the mothers of the children, the problems largely involve the failure of fathers to faithfully pay their child support.[41]

The problems are even more pronounced among those living below the poverty line. Many of the poor, and especially poor fathers, do not have the ability to make the anticipated payments. Unemployment within this group is high, and assets are small. Impoverished custodial parents as a result routinely receive nothing, and many have quite simply given up hope for child-support payments. Nationally, poor fathers are responsible for 70 percent of the officially delinquent child support.[42] In the words of a lengthy report in the

New York Times, "The vast majority of unpaid child support is owed by the very poor."[43]

Beyond the basic lack of jobs and funds, is there anything in the nature of the urban poor's marriages, divorces, and relationships that might further explain the low rate of child-support payment? For starters, marriages are especially prone to disruption in communities with significant male unemployment, lower median family income, greater poverty, and higher receipt of welfare, and "the divorce rate among those who live below the poverty line is just about double that of the general population."[44] Then, too, the majority of divorces among the urban poor are pro se proceedings, that is, they go forward without lawyers. They resemble speedy, informal administrative hearings, and a good chance exists that one or even both of the divorcing spouses will not be present at the finalization hearing. This means, at least arguably, that commitments and arrangements involving child support are less likely to lock into place psychologically.

In addition, since the urban poor tend not to marry in the first place, their children are not in most instances born or raised in the context of marriage. Mothers have custody of the great majority of children born out of wedlock, and never-married mothers might truly welcome the faithful payment of child support by their children's fathers. But when child-support calculations and payments do not take place against the backdrop of a marriage, fathers are less likely to recognize, much less internalize, their support obligations.

For decades, state welfare systems have stumbled along trying to address the child-support delinquency problem. In all of the states, delinquent payers can be prosecuted for failure to pay child support or, in extreme cases, for desertion of their children. All of the states have also enacted some form of the Uniform Reciprocal Enforcement of Support Act, known colloquially as "The Runaway Papa Act."[45] It provides a process to thwart fathers who flee to another state in hopes of avoiding child support. The states also have a range of measures at their disposal for establishing paternity, locating fugitive fathers, and enforcing child-support orders through civil actions for attachment and garnishment.[46] If a petition for attachment is successful, the judge will order the sheriff to seize assets and properties of the father. With garnishment, the indebted father sees part of his wages sent directly to his children's mother.

The usefulness of an attachment or a garnishment, of course, depends on the availability of assets or wages, and the urban poor are unlikely to have much of either.

Even though these methods of collecting child support were in place *and* were being used, the pursuit of delinquent fathers acquired a new urgency during the 1980s. The notion of a "deadbeat dad" took hold with pejorative connotations even greater than those attached earlier to the "welfare mom." Sporting an alliterative lilt, the phrase "deadbeat dad" suggested indolent, shiftless, and duplicitous men who probably should not have fathered children in the first place. State and local governments began distributing lists and photos of the "Ten Worst Deadbeats," and some called for a national "most wanted deadbeats list."[47] Police departments conducted predawn raids and roundups and in some cases led delinquent fathers away in handcuffs while television crews eagerly captured the moment.[48] Bounty hunters paid with federal money set out after delinquent fathers on the run.[49]

Prosecutors and judges in the criminal courts also became more inclined toward punitive treatment of delinquent payers. They usually cloaked their unapologetic attempts to punish with claims that this punishment would not only sting prosecuted delinquents but also catch the eye of other fathers who were delinquent in their payments. Some prosecutors and judges were sure these other delinquents, fearing they would eventually be prosecuted, would become more likely to make their child-support payments on time and in full.[50]

An especially noteworthy example of prosecutors and judges striking out aggressively against a delinquent father occurred in Manitowoc County, Wisconsin, along the western shore of Lake Michigan. The biggest cities in the area are Sheboygan and Manitowoc, and neither is an idyllic country town. Once the home of ship- and submarine-building, Sheboygan and Manitowoc have in their own way undergone the deindustrialization so common in the Midwestern "Rust Belt." David Oakley was one of many individuals in the area who could not find or hold onto regular employment. He was known as a charmer among some women in the county, and Cheri Pasdo, who gave birth to one of Oakley's children but never married him, said, "He could talk an Eskimo into buying an ice cube."[51] By the time he turned thirty-four, Oakley had fathered nine children by four women and also fallen hopelessly behind in his child-support payments.

Eventually, local prosecutors and judges had enough of Oakley. The district attorney charged him with intentional refusal to pay child support and struck a deal in which Oakley would plead guilty in return for a reduced sentence. However, Manitowoc County judge Fred Hazelwood disregarded the plea bargain and sentenced Oakley to three years in prison with probation on the condition that Oakley father no more children until he demonstrated that he could support them and that he was supporting the nine children he already had. Given Oakley's financial situation, this amounted to an order to stop having children. "If you think I'm trampling over your constitutional rights," Hazelwood told Oakley at sentencing, "so be it."[52]

Critics took the terms of Oakley's probation to jeopardize a fundamental right to procreate, but when Oakley appealed his case, the Wisconsin Supreme Court upheld Judge Hazelwood's sentencing decision in a 4–3 vote.[53] While the court split regarding the constitutionality of Oakley's terms of probation, the justices were in agreement about what to make of Oakley and his conduct. From one end of the bench to the other, the justices said they found Oakley's conduct and, indeed, Oakley himself deplorable. Justice Jon P. Wilcox, one of the four justices in the majority, consciously segued from considerations of Oakley to questions of social policy:

> Inadequate child support is a direct contributor to childhood poverty. And childhood poverty is all too pervasive in our society. . . . There is little doubt that the payment of child support benefits poverty-stricken children the most. Enforcing child support orders thus has surfaced as a major policy directive in our society.[54]

Justice Ann Walsh Bradley, a member of the three-justice minority, struck a similar tone: "As the majority amply demonstrates, the lack of adequate support for children affects not only the lives of individual children, but also has created a widespread societal problem."[55] Nobody was sympathetic because of Oakley's unemployment or dismal prospects in life. Instead, the justices felt the Oakleys among us were causes of poverty. With their chests puffed up for the world (or, at least, Wisconsin) to see, the majority of the justices on the Wisconsin Supreme Court were sure the time had come to get tough on "deadbeat dads."

Although an occasional physician or architect might serve as a convenient poster child for the "deadbeat dad" population, underemployed and unemployed men like Oakley are the most likely to be delinquent in their child-support payments. These delinquent and irresponsible fathers, the argument goes, are agents of poverty. What about the fathers who were themselves born into poverty and are still living in poverty? The building outrage about "deadbeat dads" obscured that complicating possibility.

One ambitious politician who latched onto the notion that "deadbeat dads" were causing poverty was Joseph Lieberman, later a member of the United States Senate and a vice-presidential candidate, but earlier in time the attorney general of Connecticut. In 1986, he hurried into print a screed on the need to collect delinquent child support and the ways to do it. Lieberman asserted that the "failure of delinquent fathers to pay child support is the major reason why more than half the American families that are headed by a woman live below the poverty level."[56] One chapter in the book discussed "the legal weapons available to mothers."[57] Lest he seem too warlike, Lieberman also sappily invoked the loving memory of his father, Henry Lieberman: "It is altogether fitting that this book about what can be done to force delinquent fathers to support their children be dedicated to a man who was the embodiment of what a responsible father should be."[58]

Judge Hazelwood, Connecticut attorney general Joseph Lieberman, and others were state and local officials, but national figures also cast impoverished fathers as disreputable agents of poverty. Party affiliations seemed not to matter, and the criticism of "deadbeat dads" was heard on both sides of the congressional aisle. Occupants of the White House—including Republican presidents Ronald Reagan, George H. W. Bush, and George W. Bush, as well as Democratic presidents William Clinton and Barack Obama—sharply criticized the seemingly ubiquitous "deadbeats" who were impoverishing American mothers and children. All of these figures also perceived a link between the payment of child support and the need for welfare. If fathers would only pay their child support, the state could reduce expenditures for welfare.

The magnitude and range of federal child-support legislation enacted since the mid-1980s are striking, especially because family law has traditionally been a state concern rather than a federal matter. In 1984, Congress enacted a new round of amendments to Title IV-D of the Social Security Act. Designed to get delinquents to pay up, the amendments directed states to enhance efforts to collect child support by making available employer withholding, liens against property, and deductions from tax refunds.[59]

In 1992, the federal government took even bolder steps to address the problem of unpaid child support. Political leaders in both parties—Republican congressman Henry Hyde and Democratic congressman Charles Schumer, for example—spearheaded the effort to enact the Child Support Recovery Act (CSRA).[60] The only opponents of the act were members of the nascent fathers' rights movement. Some of them questioned the assumption that child-support delinquency caused poverty and argued that most of the impoverished families headed by unmarried mothers would not be lifted out of poverty even if the delinquent fathers were somehow able to pay their child support.[61] Having found a convenient whipping boy in the "deadbeat dad," Congress ignored the argument.

The CSRA itself authorized fines and imprisonment for noncustodial parents who owed child support in one state but lived in another. However, prosecutions under the CSRA suggested the uselessness of the legislation with regard to obtaining child support from the urban poor. Between October 1992 and February 1999, federal prosecutions resulted in only 105 convictions. Most notably, "None of the CSRA cases brought to trial involve[d] debts owed to single-mother households where the family was 'poor' before the father left the household."[62] In other words, even though the CSRA could theoretically be used to address problems of delinquent child support in all walks of life, it was not. The great majority of convictions involved well-to-do fathers who were divorced from the mothers of their children and owed large amounts of child support. Poor fathers, most of whom had never married the mothers of their children and who had no substantial assets, never really became candidates for prosecution.

Congress might have taken note of the small number of prosecutions and the CSRA's obvious ineffectiveness as a poverty-reducing measure. Instead, Congress decided to stiffen the penalties for offenders who lived in one state and owed child support in another, and in 1998 President Clinton signed into law the menacingly named Deadbeat Parents Punishment Act (DPPA).[63] The DPPA amended the CSRA and made offenses under the latter into felonies and provided that certain offenders could be imprisoned for up to two years. The DPPA also created the rather remarkable legal presumption, at least for the urban poor, that a delinquent payer is able to pay child support.

The changes in the welfare laws in the 1990s also included measures designed to improve child-support collection. President Clinton made his now-legendary promise to "end welfare as we know it,"[64] and he shepherded the Personal Responsibility and Work Opportunity Reconciliation Act (PRWORA) through Congress in 1996.[65] PRWORA replaced the prior entitlement named Aid to Families with Dependent Children (AFDC) with a program known as Temporary Assistance for Needy Families (TANF). In Clinton's mind, the welfare changes related to child-support collection. "For a lot of women and children," according to Clinton, "the only reason they're on welfare today—the only reason—is that the father up and walked away when he could have made a contribution to the welfare of the children."[66]

PRWORA itself required that the states take measures to increase child-support collection in order to qualify for federal block grants. The measures include, but are not limited to, in-hospital paternity determination, faster courtroom paternity proceedings, statewide registration of delinquent payers, and the denial of licenses to drive, hunt, and engage in assorted occupations and professional practices.[67] According to the author of a law review article published at the time Clinton signed PRWORA into law, the new legislation was supposed to make the collection of child support "automatic and inescapable—like death and taxes."[68]

Have the more aggressive child-support collection measures enacted and undertaken since the mid-1980s helped reduce the child-support delinquency problem? On the one hand, some progress has been made, and the lives of some custodial mothers and their children have grown easier due to the welcome payment of child support. Law, in this sense, has functioned to bring some parents the payments to which, on behalf of their children, they are entitled. On the other hand, almost all of the success has been with middle- and upper-class families and not among the urban poor.

Lacking significant effectiveness among the poor, the "deadbeat dad" laws have had only a negligible impact on poverty. The collection of child support, assuming it even occurs, does not eliminate poverty.[69] Furthermore, some have also argued that the aggressive pursuit of delinquent parents and especially the incarceration of supposed "deadbeats" actually increases poverty. Incarcerated parents have no income from which to make payments, and when incarcerated parents have served their three or six months, they still owe a large amount of money. Unable to pay, a delinquent parent might find himself "tossed right back into the county jail."[70] Punitive policies related to child-support delinquency, some assert, help make poverty permanent. Unemployment and debt lead to punishment and jail, which lead to more unemployment and debt.

None of this means that child-support collection laws and processes have ceased to be "law" for the urban poor. As was the case with the pro-marriage legislation and initiatives, middle- and upper-class Americans continue to put laws on the books, and other middle- and upper-class Americans attempt to enforce these laws. The call to do something when certain types of people fail to satisfactorily support their children resonates with most Americans. Barack Obama, who grew up without his father being present, made "the epidemic of fatherlessness" among poor African Americans his major theme when he spoke at one of inner-city Chicago's largest African American churches in 2008.[71] "There are a lot of men out there," Obama has asserted, "who need to stop acting like boys, who need to realize that responsibility does not end at conception, who need to know that what makes you a man is not the ability to have a child but the courage to raise one."[72]

Child Welfare

The uninformed might assume that governmental programs promoting "child welfare" would chiefly revolve around educational opportunities, nutritional food, and cash benefits for children in need. In reality, the most heavily funded "child welfare" agencies and programs concentrate on neglect and abuse in what are taken to be dysfunctional families, with neglect being a much more common concern than abuse.[73] In the average year, the child welfare system has approximately a half million children in its care, and the great majority of these children are poor.[74]

The child welfare system's handling of children has several stages. At the start, the system dispatches agents to determine if suspect parents are abusing or neglecting particular children. This approach, in the words of one critic, is based on the idea of a "guilty parent." Identifying a "guilty parent" enables the system to ignore the complex of familial and community factors that lead to the supposed child mistreatment.[75] If the system finds abuse or neglect, the system transfers the children to relatives or short-term foster parents. The legal parents enter counseling and rehabilitation programs. A majority successfully complete their case plans, and the children then return to their original homes. Those parents who are unable to demonstrate that they can provide care and safety for their children, meanwhile, lose those children to long-term foster care, which is called "permanent custody" in some states.

At this point, the termination of the parents' rights might occur, and the children might be adopted. This development depends on the availability of adults willing to adopt the children, but if would-be adoptive parents are available, caring for the welfare of the children shifts from the state to private parties.[76] More frequently, children in long-term foster care ride out their youths in uncertain, unstable situations. Each year in the United States, roughly twenty thousand children "age out" of long-term foster care without ever being adopted or settling into a secure family arrangement.[77]

Not surprisingly, the clientele of the child welfare system does not consist of happy adults and thriving children. Many of the parents who relinquish control of their children are unmarried and unemployed. If fortunate, these parents might be receiving welfare payments and/or child-support payments. But as I noted earlier, modern-day welfare is paltry, and child support is hardly certain. In our era of mass incarceration, a significant number of the parents reviewed by the child welfare system are in fact imprisoned.[78] Most of the children in the system have deprived socioeconomic backgrounds. As the tireless crusader for children's rights Dorothy E. Roberts has bluntly observed, "The public welfare system is populated almost exclusively by poor children."[79]

The reasons poor children are disproportionately overrepresented in the child welfare system include the debilitating effects of poverty, systemic bias against the poor, and the manner in which the child welfare system is funded. On the first score, various studies have found that poor children are at higher risk of abuse and neglect, with one eager researcher of the 1990s concluding that poor children were forty-four times more likely to be neglected than middle- and upper-class children.[80] The risk of abuse and neglect, the argument goes, is understandable given neighborhoods with high crime rates and rampant substance abuse, deficient social capital, and parents forever busing back and forth from prison.

Poverty is certainly stressful and alienating enough to contribute to the rougher, less attentive treatment of children, or anyone else for that matter, but it also seems likely that many caseworkers, foster parents, and administrators are biased. "Black families are . . . disproportionately affected by the seemingly arbitrary decisions that the child-protection system inflicts on low-income parents."[81] Even when poor, African American parents fight off the child welfare system, they have "suffered the indignity of having children yanked away from them."[82] The child welfare system often assumes that race, poverty, and poor parenting, especially by single mothers, go hand in hand. The most frequently cited evidence of neglect is rundown and unsafe housing,[83] but as I noted in an earlier discussion of inner-city housing, rundown and unsafe housing is pretty much what the urban poor call home.

The definitions of abuse and neglect tend to be vague and open-ended, and the law leaves caseworkers ample opportunity to equate urban poverty with abuse and neglect. The problem is in fact so severe that several states have even created so-called poverty exemptions to guard against it. These states are a distinct minority, but they say, in essence, that a child cannot be deemed abused or neglected because their parents are poor. How plausible is it to expect enforcement of these exemptions? It is easy to imagine child welfare officials who want to remove a child from a home pointing to conditions and conduct that do not on the surface relate to poverty. How about a bedbug infestation? Would moldy food or sour milk in the refrigerator suffice?

The funding of child welfare, meanwhile, creates an incentive to find and bring children into the system. These programs themselves operate on the state and local levels, but federal legislation provides for funding. This funding is greater if more children are deemed abused and neglected. Federal funders require reporting on child abuse and neglect, and lengthier reports with larger numbers in them can result in bigger grants. One researcher has said this amounts to a "huge fundraiser" for child protective services.[84]

If an agency wants to beef up its reports in hopes of increased funding, the urban poor are especially useful resources. Low-income parents are good candidates for being investigated and being brought into the system just as young African American and Latino men are "good collars" for the criminal justice system. The children of the urban poor, for reasons already noted, might easily be perceived as needing protective services and could therefore bolster grant applications, assuming these children are numerous enough.

Regardless of the reasons for the urban poor's overrepresentation in the child welfare system, everyone agrees that inclusion in the system is customarily harmful for the children. Some children stabilize their environments due to the efforts of nurturing, committed foster parents, but more frequently children in the system "float" from one home to another, never knowing how long their new home will last. Indeed, some children might be anxious to move to new foster parents, given the reports of widespread abuse and neglect *by* foster parents.[85]

The term "outcomes" seems particularly inhumane in this context, but the "outcomes" for the child welfare system are sobering. Numerous studies have shown that children who have been in kinship and foster care had more than their share of school delinquency, teenage births, and mental health difficulties. Those who "age out" experience substance abuse, incarceration, and welfare dependency to a much greater extent than those who have never been in the system.[86] The child welfare system is especially likely to draw children from poor families, and the system seems to guarantee that most of these children will become poor adults.

Haves Adopting Have-Nots

As previously noted, adults seeking a child sometimes adopt from long-term foster care. These adults and also those who adopt through private adoption agencies are generally happy with their adoptions. Most adopted children as well welcome their new homes and are pleased with their new families. However, adoption as a whole has a way of moving children from one set of cultural values to another, with the process inevitably assuming the new cultural values are superior to the old ones.

There is a long and often offensive history of this. In the late nineteenth century, for example, government officials and representatives of some religious groups loaded thousands of immigrant children from eastern cities onto so-called orphan trains and transported them to Midwestern farms, where they were adopted and expected to develop an appreciation of hard work and a taste for self-advancement. Well into the twentieth century, distant, state-sponsored boarding schools enrolled Native American children, removing them in the process from their parents' custody and hoping the children would assimilate to their conquerors' way of doing things. And in more recent decades, courts ordered the removal of non-Mexican or half-Mexican children from Mexican homes into which they had been placed in hopes of insulating these children from improper values and practices. Child-welfare workers and courts invariably insisted these programs and undertakings were in the "best interests of the children," but it is also clear the system wanted children from selected ethnic and racial groups to develop preferred middle- and upper-class white identities.[87]

Modern-day adoption is less offensive than the orphan trains or so-called Indian schools, but when it is complete and finished, adoption leads most adopted children, natural outbursts of child rebellion notwithstanding, to take on the values of their adoptive parents. Parents, after all, are customarily the most important transmitters of language, culture, and values to their children. This is not sinister or conspiratorial, but it is inevitable. Adoptive parents are no exception. They transmit the language, culture, and values they hold dear and take to be normal to the children they have adopted.[88]

Furthermore, this transmission involves a simple but crucial socioeconomic reality: in adoption, "have-nots" relinquish children to "haves." In the great majority of adoptions, the biological parents are poor, and the children leave the homes of these biological parents to become the children of middle- and upper-class parents. This transfer is perhaps most obvious in international adoptions, but it is standard in domestic adoptions as well.

The class imbalance in adoption helps explain why adoptive parents and biological parents often experience and recall adoption so differently. For those who adopt, adoption is usually a wonderful development, and adoptive parents commonly feel proud and enriched. Impoverished biological parents, by contrast, sense a lack of agency and a silencing of their voices. They express feelings of helplessness, and they often recall the adoption experience with regret and a sense of loss.[89] "It is hard to believe," the impoverished biological parent might reflect, "but I was not financially stable enough to hold onto my own flesh and blood"—with "flesh and blood" sometimes standing metaphorically for lifestyles as well as genetic makeup. Other biological parents are more clear-headed when placing children for adoption, but they might feel guilty that they chose to place children for adoption in order to avoid exacerbating their own poverty or becoming dependent on their children's fathers.[90]

The role of the urban poor as the most important "suppliers" of adoptable children became clear during the post–World War II decades—that is, at roughly the same time the contemporary urban poor settled into place and came to be thought of as an underclass. Between the end of World War II and 1970, the number of American adoptions jumped more than threefold, from approximately 50,000 to 175,000 annually.[91] Although in earlier eras the most sought-after adoptees might have been young adults who could perform work on family farms or in family businesses, infants and toddlers became the preferred adoptees during the adoption boom. Adoptive parents had the money—and were willing to expend it—for healthy youngsters. Writing in the period during which adoptions were surging, the sociologist Viviana Zelizer noted the "sentimentalization of adoption," and she spoke of the often poignant efforts of middle- and upper-class Americans to find "the priceless child."[92]

As the demand for adoptees came to exceed the number of available children, earlier attempts to "match" the ethnicity or race of the child with the ethnicity or race of the adoptive parents fell by the wayside. It no longer seemed like much of a problem if Norwegian-looking parents adopted a Greek-looking infant. It also became common for whites to adopt African American children, especially those who were poor.[93]

Defenders liked to cast these adoptions as matters of racial harmony and also to underscore that African American children adopted by white and middle- and upper-class parents would live "better" lives in their new homes. Harvard law professor Elizabeth Bartholet was the most prominent of the defenders, and she snidely reminded anyone who would listen that "we should not romanticize what it is like to live on the social and economic margins of society."[94] However, a bevy of scholars and commentators remained uneasy with transracial adoption.[95] The adoption of African American children from the inner city by whites from the suburbs uncomfortably reminded some of race-related power and dominance.

What's more, adoption law facilitates cross-class and transracial adoption due to its longstanding tilt in favor of adoptive parents. People who teach Family Law in a university setting often present adoption as "triangular," with three types of people—adoptive parents, biological parents, and children—positioned on the three points of the triangle. This is easy to capture and convey with a Family Law PowerPoint, and the triangular conceptualization suggests, if nothing else, the different interests that are present and perhaps in tension in adoption. Law supposedly balances the interests. In reality, adoptive parents hold the upper hand, and courts and legislatures have done little to equalize the three sets of interests suggested by the theoretical diagram. If adoptive parents are at the top of the triangle, their weight is likely to tip over the whole thing.

The relative power of the adoptive parents in the process is neither new nor surprising, but what might be noteworthy is that during the second half of the twentieth century, courts and legislatures refined adoption law to further facilitate adoptions by those with assets and incomes. The law and legal procedures, in the process, revealed a willingness bordering on an eagerness to route poor children to the homes of wealthier adoptive parents.[96]

To be more specific, when attorneys file adoption petitions on behalf of their middle- and upper-class clients with the appropriate court, the standard proceedings include obtaining consent from the biological parents and a judicial decree that the adoption is in the best interests of the child. With regard to both of these matters, those seeking to adopt have substantial advantages. The controlling approaches and standards help adoptions move forward toward finalization. American law, in a sense, wants to send children from poor families to new, more prosperous ones.

The law's approach to consent from the biological parents is especially revealing. Adoption agencies and courts obtain consents somewhat routinely from biological mothers, and the consents are difficult to challenge at a later point in time even if the poor and poorly educated mothers consented hastily. Courts usually require traditional varieties of fraud or duress before they are willing to invalidate a biological mother's consent. That is, the biological mother would have to convince the court that the adoptive parents or representatives of adoption agencies tricked or forced her into consenting to the adoption. Consent prompted by immaturity, financial desperation, or pressure from parents and lovers does not constitute fraud or duress.

Consents from poor biological fathers, meanwhile, can be difficult to obtain. As already noted in this chapter, these fathers are in many cases not married to the mothers of the children placed for adoption. Frequently, the fathers do not live with the biological mothers of their children, and the whereabouts of some biological fathers are simply unknown. How might adoptive parents and their lawyers obtain consent from these men? States routinely authorize constructive notice to these fathers in legal publications with which the fathers could not possibly be familiar. Most states have also established so-called putative fathers' registries. Men who know or suspect they have fathered a child may place their names in the registries and be notified if and when the child they think is theirs is placed for adoption. However, if a man fails to register, he waives his rights to notice, hearing, and consent. Many poor fathers, of course, lack the means, mobility, and confidence to register, and most are simply unaware of the registries.[97]

The adoption finalization decree, couched with reference to "the best interests of the child," also favors the adoption of children from poor families. "Best interests" in the context of adoption is not the same as "best interests" when two parents are battling for child custody at the time of divorce. In the latter, the judge might weigh the strengths and weaknesses of one parent against those of the other in hopes of placing the child in the most nurturing home. In the adoption context, by contrast, the judge is not really choosing between options but rather simply concluding that would-be adoptive parents have what it takes to parent. Indeed, courts have ruled that a child may simply be sent off to foster care with the hope that well-suited adoptive parents will ultimately come along.[98]

The workings of the "best interests of the child" legal standard in the adoption context, in short, make it easy for middle- and upper-class parents to finalize adoptions. The biological parent or parents have voluntarily or involuntarily relinquished parental rights, a caseworker has studied the files and the home of the adoptive parents, and a government department or nonprofit agency has lent its support. The determination at this point in the process that the adoption is in "the best interests of the child" is, for all intents and purposes, a foregone conclusion. Poor parents or, in most cases, poor, unmarried mothers cannot successfully argue at finalization that they should keep their children or that this would be in the children's "best interests."

How might one rationalize the frequent and routine adoption of children by members of the middle and upper classes and the bias in favor of the latter in the standard legal proceeding? In answering that question, it is worth remembering how a rationalization works. Basically, it is a defense mechanism that casts ragged behavior or processes in more acceptable terms. A rationalization puts a seemingly rational or logical spin on something that is irrational or illogical. A rationalization is not an expression of thoughtful public policy or even good thinking. Perhaps needless to add, rationalizations should always be taken with grains, if not whole shakers, of salt.

One prominent rationalizer of how adoption law favors middle- and upper-class adoptive parents is the crusty and outspoken "law and economics" scholar and former federal appellate judge Richard Posner. In one of his earlier and most controversial articles, Posner perceived his beloved market economy attempting to assert itself. In fact, he urged that the market be cut loose even further in order to get babies whose parents were willing to place them for adoption into the hands of those who want to adopt them.[99] There's no particular reason to think Posner's love affair with markets and the market economy is phony, but his proposal would of course benefit those with greater resources. Middle- and upper-class would-be adoptive parents would more easily find the children they wanted when they wanted them. In addition, one suspects only a small part of the payments by adoptive parents would make its way to the biological mothers who place their children for adoption.

When critics accused Posner of endorsing "baby selling,"[100] he insisted in a typically prickly retort that he had proposed only that selected adoption agencies use a part of their fees to pay women to forego abortions, have their babies, and place them for adoption. People who criticized him for proposing a market for baby sales, Posner thought, were the kind of "people who feel free to criticize an article without having read it." His article, he insisted, was "addressed to those willing to think about possible solutions in a rational manner."[101]

While Posner's rationalization failed to take hold, a more forceful rationalization for the biases in adoption law in favor of the middle and upper classes involved a deep-seated disrespect for the urban poor's approach to family life. The process of American adoption incorporates a clear preference for the middle- and upper-class nuclear family. The law takes poor families to be inferior, and "under nuclear family–based adoption policy, the law terminates the birth parents' rights before it engrafts parental rights on the adoptive parents."[102] When children move to middle- and upper-class nuclear families, this can be rationalized by the claim that the children will benefit from better parenting.

To a large extent, these preferences grow out of a larger set of assumptions regarding mothering. Most members of the middle and upper classes hold dear a model of exclusive mothering. This intense style of mothering first appeared in Europe, and Freud critiqued it as early as the turn of the twentieth century.[103] Exclusive mothering and a related normative attitude regarding it appeared in the United States in the 1950s and 1960s, and despite the many changes in women's socioeconomic condition since then, the model still has sway.[104] Even though the majority of middle- and upper-class mothers now work outside the home, many middle- and upper-class mothers' sense of what is required for good mothering remains traditional. The proverbial "supermom" somehow finds a way to devote extraordinary amounts of time to her children.

In her groundbreaking feminist scholarship, Nancy Chodorow pointed out that the intense, exclusive style of mothering accepted by middle- and upper-class Americans derives from "a socially and historically specific mother-child relationship."[105] For the urban poor, by contrast, financial necessities and subcultural norms lead parents to share child-rearing responsibilities with others, often within extended families.[106] Rayna Rapp studied mothering styles and family structures among the poor in American cities and found "there is a tremendous sharing of the children themselves."[107]

Raising children in extended families is perhaps most common among poor African Americans. Even though slavery was in general terribly harmful to family makeup and cohesion, slaves often found a way to collectively raise children, with slaves unofficially adopting the parentless children in their midst. Child-rearing in extended families became a source of pride in slave communities, and to some extent the tradition lives on in the African American parts of the modern inner city. Necessity plays a role, but so does custom, as siblings, aunties, grandparents, and others take responsibility for raising children temporarily or on a permanent basis.[108]

This, for the most part, is invisible to those raising children within intact nuclear families. They are imbued with what law professor Annette R. Appell calls the "platonic idea of mother."[109] This type of mother does not have too many children, and she surely is not an active grandmother at the same time she is actively mothering. This type of mother is also not a part of an extended family and does not have responsibilities related to children other than the ones to whom she gave birth.

Similar attitudes are found in adoption agencies and courts. Certain they are "correct" about parenting, they give the urban poor low scores as parents. They deplore the ways the urban poor raise their children. This, then, sets the stage for the transfer of the children. Law professor Twila Perry has noted that "children transferred from devalued women to valued women are deemed to have received a lucky break."[110] Adopting children usually seems an altruistic, even noble undertaking. Friends and relatives of adoptive parents often praise them for "saving" poor children, and some adoptive parents proudly think of themselves as child-rescuers.

Attitudes of this sort dwell not only within adoption law but also within the culture as a whole, and bias against the parenting of the urban poor parent can be found in a wide range of cultural forms and media. Print journalism, for example, is rife with superficially sympathetic reports on the urban poor's attempts to protect their children and, against all odds, get them out of the trouble they all too frequently have found. The evening television news abounds with accounts of co-sleeping deaths, domestic abuse, child abandonment, and house fires, many of which identify the urban poor as innocent victims and even more so as irresponsible victimizers. These accounts, of course, almost never explore socioeconomic class, preferring to dwell on individual tales of woe. However, the badges of poverty are worn for all to see, and members of the middle and upper classes can head to bed feeling lucky and, perhaps, a bit superior.

Not only journalists but also the marketers of selected consumer goods have subtly deplored the parenting of the urban poor. These marketers are aware that a surprising number of consumers will choose one brand of a product over another if they approve of a company's "purpose-driven activities," and some promote adoption as one such activity. The Wendy's hamburger chain has long led the way in this regard. Dave Thomas, its founder, was adopted, and taking the adoption to be the big break in his life, Thomas established the Dave Thomas Foundation for Adoption. Since Thomas's death in 2002, Wendy's has continued to promote adoption, launching a national ad campaign touting adoption and also placing an adoption hub on the company website. When defending the ad campaign and hub, Michael Towell, a publicist for Wendy's, slyly pointed at poor parenting when he said, "There's a big difference between being a child and having a childhood." Jockey International has followed Wendy's lead in promoting and supporting adoption as a presumably appealing "purpose-driven activity."[111]

Even Hollywood has deplored child-rearing among the urban poor and offered its support for the adoption of poor children by the middle and upper classes. The much-acclaimed film *Precious* (2009), for example, dramatizes the nightmarish struggles of Precious Jones, played by Gabourey Sidibe, in an impoverished part of Harlem. Precious is an obese, HIV-positive, forlorn six-teen-year-old with two very young children, one of whom has Down syndrome. Would it be possible to imagine a life with a larger Dead End sign on it?

If a single person can be identified as the cause of Precious's woes, it is without a doubt her mother, Mary Jones, played with savage vigor by the actress Mo'Nique. Precious's mother physically and verbally abuses Precious and shamelessly connives to keep her at home in order to continue receiving welfare. Precious's mother also fails to object when her lover and Precious's father incestuously rapes and impregnates Precious.

This, supposedly, is child-rearing among the urban poor, and the filmmak-ers tell Precious's story in a self-consciously "realist" style. They want viewers to believe the portrayal as they go about enjoying it. Such an over-the-top portrayal of family life could not possibly work if the characters belonged to a white, middle-class nuclear family, but *Precious* becomes plausible because it plays off negative assumptions regarding parenting among the urban poor. More than one reviewer said *Precious* was an example of "poverty porn"—a representation of family life among the urban poor that is somehow titillating for the middle- and upper-class viewers.[112]

Losing Isaiah (1995), another Hollywood film, also indicts parenting among the urban poor and goes further to suggest that the children of the urban poor should be adopted by middle-class whites. One scholar has criticized the film's negative portrayal of African American mothering,[113] but Khaila Richards, the film's biological mother, is poor as well as African American. Her race serves as a convenient marker for socioeconomic class.

The Richards character, played by Halle Berry, conceived Isaiah during sex-for-drugs intercourse, but she is unprepared to be his mother. Young, addicted, and looking for more drugs, she leaves Isaiah on a trash can. Fortunately, sanitation workers find him and race him to the hospital. At the hospital, a social worker named Margaret Lewin, played by Jessica Lange, helps Isaiah through his crack-related difficulties, and then she and her husband Charles, played by David Straithairn, adopt him. But alas, a rehabilitated Richards appears, wanting her son back. A series of unpleasant personal exchanges among the characters follow, as do wrenching courtroom proceedings.

Through it all, viewers are invited to side with the Lewins and to oppose Richards's attempts to regain her son. We are horrified when the judge grants Richards custody. We flinch when Richards tries to get Isaiah to eat French fries, gives him a baseball cap he can wear backwards, and leaves him in a noisy daycare facility. And we understand when Isaiah pitches a fit and cries for his "Mommy," that is, Margaret Lewin. Toward the end of the film, Richards's frustrations drive her to the brink of child abuse, and the audience is immensely relieved when she turns to Margaret Lewin for help. It has been implied in almost every new scene that the middle-class Lewin would be a better parent than the impoverished Richards.

Whenever middle- or upper-class parents are available and willing to adopt, law, journalism, advertising, movies, and the dominant culture in general tell us the children should be moved to these new homes. According to reigning thought, children of the urban poor are poised on the junk heap of life. Their families are unstable and perhaps unhealthy, and their biological parents do an inferior job of parenting. The children will have a better chance to thrive if they move from their scrambled, impoverished families to stable, middle-class families typical of what is taken to be the American mainstream.

Channeling and Disapproval

At first glance, family law regarding marriage, child support, child welfare, and adoption is the same for the middle and upper classes as it is for the urban poor, but when one considers this family law more critically, one realizes it has a different thrust for the urban poor. Often, family law tries to channel the urban poor toward such things as marriage and the regular payment of child support. The legal definitions and procedures used by the child welfare system are designed to protect children, yet the "protection" most commonly involves removing poor children from the homes of their poor parents. Adoptions are finalized in court, and the laws for the courtroom proceedings facilitate the transfer of the urban poor's children to middle- and upper-class families.

Sometimes the law accomplishes what it sets out to do, and other times attaining goals is difficult. Through it all, the laws and the application of the laws reflect middle- and upper-class preferences, and the urban poor themselves have very little to say about things. The middle and upper classes, imbued with a sense of social superiority, are quite prepared to route the urban poor toward certain kinds of behavior, relationships, and living arrangements.

These attempts to channel the urban poor through law involve not only an effort to direct the urban poor toward something taken to be superior but also an effort to direct them away from something taken to be inferior. Channeling, in this sense, has a pronounced normativity to it. While parents are supposed to love their children equally, they often tip their hands as to which children they love the most. While the law is supposed to honor all families equally, the law tips its hand regarding the types of family life it prefers.

In addition, channeling through family law implicitly and, in some instances, explicitly censures the urban poor for the way they conduct their private lives. The urban poor's failure to marry strikes the middle and upper classes as disrespectful of the very institution of marriage and also disdainful of a way to avoid welfare and achieve economic success. From the perspective of lawmaking elites, the failure on the part of poor men to faithfully pay child support not only ignores the resulting plight of their children and the mothers of those children but also actually contributes mightily to their poverty. Poor parenting, it seems, leaves the children of the urban poor staring down the tunnel of empty lives, and only the luckiest of poor children get adopted by middle- and upper-class parents.

The law's complaining and pontificating regarding the family life of the urban poor supplements the attempts to channel. With an almost audible huff, the law voices its disapproval of the ways the urban poor behave in the private, domestic spheres of their lives. Family law for the urban poor suggests the urban poor's values and conduct—and not the denial of meaningful employment, educational opportunity, and residential stability—explain the urban poor's plight. Most generally, family law for the urban poor casts the urban poor as a problem in and of themselves rather than a sector of the population unjustly deprived of the material and social sustenance their society provides to others.

CHAPTER FOUR

Marketplace Exploitation

A s is the case in other metropolitan areas, the proverbial "marketplace" in my hometown consists of various sectors serving different groups of people. No walls or formal borders exist between the sectors, but the comparative prices, quality of goods, and financing options vary tremendously from one sector to another.

In my own middle-class sector, most people shop in relatively nearby drugstores, hardware stores, supermarkets, or suburban malls and tend to do their banking in branch banks. Destinations are easy to reach by car or SUV, parking is ample, and the stores are bright and clean. The clerks and tellers have a schooled politeness about them and wear distinctive clothing and name tags. Customers are also well-groomed, albeit in a casual way. Aside from occasional complaints to the sales clerks or store managers and inevitable arguments in the parking lots, customers are a peaceful, congenial lot. Some of them even offer clipped greetings to one another as they pass in the stores' aisles. Overall, middle- and upper-class ventures into the marketplace are blandly pleasant.

By contrast, my city's urban poor shop in cramped neighborhood shops, small groceries and bodegas, and understaffed box stores if they are accessible. Clutter is common in these neighborhood shops, and sales clerks are bored and, perhaps as a result, often have an "attitude." Most of the customers are African American, Latino, or Hmong, and they do not interact much while shopping. Sometimes the poor turn to rent-to-own outlets for larger household goods. Without savings or assets that can serve as collateral, the urban poor cannot use the services of local branch banks, but they can and do obtain financing from payday lenders and title pawns. Their borrowing of money, not surprisingly, is a hurried, stressful affair.

With the question of the urban poor's "oppression" on the table, the rent-to-owns, payday lenders, and title pawns will receive special attention in this chapter. These businesses are sprinkled about the suburbs, rural areas, and even on Indian reservations, but the concentration of rent-to-owns, payday lenders, and title pawns in poor African American and Latino inner-city neighborhoods is unrivaled. Indeed, these types of businesses aggressively feast on the urban poor. Their garish signs, flashing lights, and extended hours entice the impoverished people of our inner cities. Once the urban poor enter their stores, rent-to-owns, payday lenders, and title pawns often ensnare them in terribly disadvantageous financial arrangements.

The business practices of the rent-to-owns, payday lenders, and title pawns are especially troubling because they involve exploitation of the urban poor *as* poor people. These businesses anticipate that the poor will frequently be unable to pay on time and in full, and the businesses profit to a greater extent when the poor become trapped by debt obligations involving the goods they are purchasing or the monies they are borrowing. As I will detail later in this chapter, these businesses not only exacerbate poverty but also help to perpetuate it.

Law, lawmakers, and legal institutions are accomplices in this tawdry process. The contracts at the heart of these business operations are legally binding, and the businesses can turn to law enforcement, the courts, and other legal institutions to enforce them. Then, too, when well-intentioned but often naive law reformers have attempted to rein in these businesses, their efforts have been largely ineffective. The business models and contractual agreements of rent-to-owns, payday lenders, and title pawns are so sophisticated and adjustable as to make the businesses virtually impossible to control. Law and legal institutions do not limit the impoverishment that takes place in and through the marketplace as much as they facilitate and legitimate it.

The Poor Shop for Basics

One reason many members of the middle and upper classes are fond of the market economy is that they are managers, store owners, and entrepreneurs, or can at least imagine themselves in those roles. Despite bromides about the customers always being right, these are the superior positions in the marketplace. Small numbers of the urban poor are also able to imagine themselves as managers, store owners, and entrepreneurs, and some in fact *are* sellers in illegal and often dangerous black markets. For the most part, though, the urban poor participate in the marketplace as consumers, a decidedly inferior position.

In fact, the urban poor can sometimes be especially avid consumers. Poverty, after all, is relative rather than absolute, and the urban poor are quite prepared, even eager, to use their resources to buy goods and services and to obtain financing for their purchases. Their lives are often less than fulfilling, and they might as a result be more likely to long for goods that, we have been told, bring contentment and happiness to those who possess them. The urban poor are not without consumer goods to begin with, but, looking around their towns and neighborhoods, they might experience feelings of relative deprivation, a condition one commentator describes as "a process of social comparison whereby individuals feel deprived in relative evaluation with another group in society."[1]

Basically, it hurts when you look around and see people who are better off and happier than you are. It *really* hurts if you realize you are stuck among oppressed people and unlikely to ever reach the socioeconomic class you take to be the happiest. The acquisition of consumer goods is a way to ease the pain and claim some degree of status.

In addition, the urban poor as a group rely less on social relations and institutions as the building blocks of their identities than do the middle and upper classes, and as a result, they are more likely to turn to what Robert G.

Dunn calls "the mediated forms of signification derived from consumer goods, telecommunications, and informational technology" to craft personal identity.[2] Lacking satisfactory amounts of social capital and deprived of strong, supportive organizations and institutions, the urban poor might seek existential sustenance through consumer goods.

The plight of these consumers is exacerbated because they must on average pay more for their purchases than middle- and upper-class consumers pay for comparable purchases. For fifty years now, observers have deplored the way the urban poor are overcharged for their consumer goods."[3] Higher prices are the norm for everything from snack foods to refrigerators, and some journalists have taken to calling the price differential a "ghetto tax."[4] The phrase is misleading, but at least it suggests the extra financial burdens and complications that come with being poor. One scholar doggedly studied the price differential encountered by poor consumers in the metropolitan Buffalo area and found that it was 10–15 percent for everyday grocery items.[5]

The typical stores in the inner city, not surprisingly, welcome hearty consumption. The box stores have large parking lots in front of them, as do the box stores in suburbs and small towns, but many customers at inner-city box stores walk to the stores from their homes or from the nearest bus stops. Inside, everything from candy to computers and from scarves to sound systems are for sale. The wide aisles and high ceilings create a certain "openness," but the interior features of the box stores cut against any intimacy or congeniality. Customers feverishly pile whatever they want in their shopping carts, but the customers had best heed the direct and indirect warnings regarding theft. The bathrooms have menacing signs about the consequences of shoplifting, and all Xbox and PlayStation goods are displayed in securely locked cases.

Small neighborhood stores are far more numerous than box stores. These neighborhood stores are compact, and many are literally "corner stores." The stores offer a selection of dairy products, prepackaged breads, canned goods, frozen dinners, soft drinks, condiments, paper products, and pet food. Snack foods—or what some have taken to calling "junk food"—tend to have the best display places near the entrance and cash register. The stores also offer cigarettes, batteries, and hair-coloring products, although these goods are usually on the sales clerk's side of the counter, behind the bulletproof glass. Depending on the state, the stores might be able to sell beer and wine and lottery tickets, and the clerk can direct the customers to a portable ATM, one that is likely outside familiar bank networks.

Some argue that the proprietors of the corner stores are biased against their customers and ready and able to gouge them. These merchants, the argument goes, are often white, do not come from the neighborhood, and do not care about the general well-being of their customers. While certain proprietors surely feel this way, I think it is best *not* to cast inner-city shopkeepers as simply a sinister band of racist gougers. Business considerations and not personal biases are probably the most important reasons for the high pricing. The corner stores, after all, have limited shelf space and smaller inventory turnovers; therefore, they charge more to achieve their desired return.

In addition to dealing with higher prices in neighborhood stores, the urban poor are limited in how far they can realistically travel to shop. Many do not have motor vehicles, and the idea of transporting large or numerous purchases back home on the bus or subway is daunting. More affluent shoppers sometimes smirk when they see a poor person leaving a supermarket via cab, but for many poor residents of the inner city, a cab is actually a rational and cost-effective option for getting home after a weekly shop.

Given the difficulty of traveling any substantial distance to shop, the urban poor do not engage in as much price searching and comparative shopping as members of the middle and upper classes. In the study of the price differential for groceries in Buffalo that I just mentioned, for example, researchers found that households without a motor vehicle were only 26 percent as likely to engage in active price searching as households with a motor vehicle. Indeed, the researchers concluded that the overall price differential encountered by the urban poor derives less from the high prices in the neighborhood stores of the inner city and more from the shortage of motor vehicles among the urban poor. "The poor's typical advantage of low opportunity cost of search is negated by a severe limitation on their mobility, making them effectively the highest search cost group of consumers."[6]

While it is disturbing that the urban poor pay more for food, clothing, and basic goods than do members of the middle and upper classes, the pricing and selling of consumer goods in the inner city's box stores and neighborhood stores are fully legal. The urban poor have the financial resources to participate in the marketplace as consumers. They can and do have the resources to buy things, especially if they are for everyday use. For their part, the storekeepers have the proper licenses to sell what they do, and they operate out of buildings zoned for business. For the most part, inner-city businesses can sell their goods at higher prices if they want. Local and state governments tally up the sales taxes without much attention to where they have been paid. Other, more troubling varieties of buying and selling remain to be critiqued and are, perhaps, more susceptible to reform, but what happens in the box stores and neighborhood stores and bodegas of the inner city seems likely to continue as is. When it comes to acquiring basic goods, the urban poor's marketplace participation is a matter of "business as usual."

Rent-to-Own

The rent-to-own business first surfaced in the United States during the 1960s and then grew rapidly during the 1970s and 1980s as independent "mom and pop" rent-to-own stores and regional outlets gave way to large national chains. Two national chains, Rent-A-Center and Rent-Way, came to own half the rent-to-own stores in the country, and during the 1990s both of those chains doubled in size. In the present, Rent-A-Center is easily the nation's largest rent-to-own company in what has become a $20 billion a year industry.[7] As do its rent-to-own competitors, Rent-A-Center employs a business model well suited to exploit those members of the urban poor seeking relatively expensive household goods, with the ten most commonly acquired goods being, in order, televisions, sofas, washers, VCRs, stereos, beds, dryers, refrigerators, chairs, and dining room tables.[8]

The rent-to-own business is a resourceful participant and facilitator in the process known in the academic literature by the lumbering term "commodification."[9] The term refers to the way, in the context of consumer capitalism, things are forever being turned into "commodities." Household goods are perhaps what first spring to mind, but "commodities" need not necessarily be objects. Commodification can and does take place with services as well as with the news, educational offerings, political positions, and just about anything that can be offered and acquired. Even some of the adoptive parents discussed in the previous chapter approach their adoptive children as much sought-after human commodities, albeit ones they almost always come to love deeply.[10] Commodification is a central process in consumer capitalism, and as disconcerting as it might be, many spend large portions of their adult lives focused on the seeking and buying of commodities.

Commodification in the United States reached its mature stage in the 1920s, and advertising became its most reliable handmaiden.[11] Advertising's obvious goal is to influence the buying decisions of potential customers with regard to particular purchases, but this goal can be pursued in various ways. Advertising might attempt to persuade potential purchasers to buy one brand instead of another or even one type of consumer good instead of another. Advertising might motivate potential purchasers to buy immediately, perhaps by offering sales and discounts. Or advertising might encourage potential purchasers to buy goods in larger volume or more frequently. Then, too, advertising even reassures purchasers *after* they have made their purchases. The ads, after all, continue to appear and might help convince purchasers that they made the right choices. Advertising, in this sense, relieves the feeling sometimes known as "buyer's remorse." The latter psychological discomfort is especially common among the purchasers of expensive goods.

Just how effectively does advertising support commodification and consumption? Consumers are often heard to say they cannot remember a particular ad or associate an ad with specific goods or services. Even sellers sometimes lament that most of their advertising (and advertising expenditures) are wasted. But doubters should remember that advertising also pursues larger goals than the ones immediately at hand. Advertising's collective message is that the acquisition of goods and services makes one happier. The right type of car can make us prettier or more virile. A great refrigerator can lead to joyous entertaining and partying. And do not forget the new sofa. It can contribute to greater connectedness within a family and, of course, be the ideal place to enjoy watching whatever is playing on the new flat screen. Speaking generally, advertising holds out the buying of commodities as the pathway to contentment and a sense of well-being.

This message is most evident in, although certainly not limited to, the many ads that feature not the commodities themselves but rather the gleeful process of purchasing those commodities. Lighthearted, cute television ads for cars or smart phones, for example, emphasize how much fun it is to buy things. Shopping is like a party. Purchasing a high-priced commodity is free from stress and has no complications. If the ads are to be believed, buying transforms us in positive ways right on the spot.

Regardless of what happens to the sales of particular commodities, the collective message of advertising appears to work. Studies have shown a strong correlation between levels of exposure to advertising and levels of consumption.[12] In the words of historian and social critic Christopher Lasch, advertising and its promise of happiness for purchasers successfully promote "consumption as a way of life."[13]

Having realized that the rent-to-own industry might be especially able to profit from advertising and a concomitant commodity lust, the Federal Trade Commission (FTC) conducted a study of over 12,000 households in hopes of gauging the nature and extent of rent-to-own use. The study found, "Compared to survey respondents who had not used rent-to-own transactions, rent-to-own customers were more likely to be African American, younger, lower income, have children in the household, rent their residence, live in the South, and live in non-suburban areas."[14] Aside from rural southerners, rent-to-own customers, in other words, tend to be the urban poor. From the time the rent-to-own business burst on the scene, scholars have underscored that "many, if not most, rent-to-own customers are low-income, high credit-risk consumers."[15] "Rent-to-own agreements are typically entered into by customers who can neither afford to purchase the goods outright nor obtain credit."[16]

At the center of rent-to-own is a well-crafted, standardized agreement that controls all features of the transaction. It obligates the customer to make weekly or, in some cases, monthly payments for whatever commodities the customer has selected. The store is likely to deliver the commodities to the customer's home, and the customer then assumes responsibility for maintenance. However, under the terms of the agreement, the store remains in control of the commodities, and the weekly or monthly payments do not make the customer into an owner. Only if the customer makes all the payments set out in the agreement or manages to ante up a lump sum for some percentage of the remaining payments does the customer come to own the commodities.

The amount that might be paid to fully own a household commodity is higher than what would be paid if it was purchased at a standard retail outlet. In 2013, the Wisconsin Public Interest Research Group (WISPIRG) surveyed rent-to-own stores just across the state line in and around Rockford, Illinois. WISPIRG found that purchasing commodities at rent-to-own stores cost two to seven times as much as it would to purchase the same commodities at a major appliance store or electronics retailer. What's more, the rent-to-own commodities were often discontinued or even obsolete models. WISPIRG found that the effective APRs for these purchases were inevitably over 100 percent, or more than five times as much as much as prevailing APRs on credit cards.[17]

For obvious reasons, many customers fail in the end to make all of the payments, but most customers make their weekly or monthly payments for as long as they can. An estimated 85 percent of the customers drive or take the bus to the store and actually pay in person at the store. Each visit to the store in effect includes a new decision about whether to continue, because, after all, the option always exists to return the commodities and terminate the transaction. Business representatives argue that the "repetitive personal interaction" between store employees and customers "strengthen customer relationships."[18] That might be, but the repeat visits also present rent-to-own stores with an opportunity to encourage customers to rent more goods. And indeed, getting customers to acquire an ever-growing number of commodities is an important part of the rent-to-own business model. The FTC study of 12,000 households found that the average rent-to-own customer rented two-and-a-half items within the preceding five years. Thirteen percent of the customers, meanwhile, had rented at least four items, and 7 percent had rented more than five items.[19]

The stores also benefit from selling certain bundled services such as insurance against theft and damage, and the stores also offer a variety of so-called preferred customer options. The urban poor, who are eager to acquire commodities that make them feel better about themselves in the first place, seem to welcome the relatively rare opportunity to be "preferred." Industry representatives report that over half of the rent-to-own customers take a preferred customer option.[20]

Under the basic agreement, the stores also charge a range of fees if the customer does not comply with the original terms. These include late fees, reinstatement fees, and collection fees. The fees can be and are used as a threat for the customer whose ardor for a given commodity is waning. Make your weekly or monthly payment and hold onto the commodity, the store's salesman might say, or you will be charged for the payments you missed and lose the commodities anyway.

Overall, the rent-to-own business is an extremely profitable way to take advantage of the urban poor, and a standardized, legally binding agreement is at the very heart of it. A common question about this agreement has involved whether it is best understood as a lease or as an installment sales contract. Under a lease, the owner of the property grants to the renter the right to possess, use, and enjoy the property for a period of time in exchange for periodic payments. In an installment sales contract, by contrast, the customer is a buyer rather than renter. The original owner usually requires the buyer to make a down payment and then collects payment for the balance in installments paid over time. In return for accepting installment payments, the seller charges interest and penalty fees, and these help ensure that the sale is profitable once it is finally complete or even if it does not quite pan out.

The operator of a rent-to-own outlet is in a much better position if the outlet's agreement with the consumer is understood as a lease as opposed to an installment sales contract. With a lease, the business can simply reclaim the good if rental payments arc not madc in full, and thc customer is not awarded any of the value of the good. With an installment sale, by contrast, customers usually acquire a partial financial interest in the goods even if they are unable to make all of their installment payments for the goods. Customers might be given notice if the goods are being resold and have the chance to buy them back, or customers might simply get some money if the goods are sold for more than the customer owes on them. Furthermore, if the conditional sale includes interest payments, as is usually the case, state usury laws set limits on how much interest can be charged. A so-called usurious loan charges interest rates higher than what is allowed by state law and is an illegal loan than can be invalidated.

More remains to be said about whether rent-to-own transactions are leases or installment contracts, but suffice it to say for now that even if courts recognize that rent-to-own transactions are really installment sales, the rent-to-own business is hardly doomed. The business might become somewhat less profitable, but the business surely remains viable given the longing for commodities that has been cultivated among the urban poor. According to a Brooklyn consumer advocate, rent-to-own outlets are masters at "preying upon the financially illiterate in certain communities."[21] The local rent-to-loan outlet is a place at which the urban poor seek to satisfy their desire for relatively expensive consumer goods, and unfortunately for them, the setting is perfect for legally sanctioned exploitation.

Payday Lending

Should rent-to-own customers be dissatisfied with the selection available at the local Rent-A-Center or simply want to shop at the same stores as middle- and upper-class Americans, they can turn to businesses for cash to use for the purchase of commodities. Usually known as "payday lenders," these businesses are common in most inner-city neighborhoods. While the business did not even exist as recently as 1990, extraordinarily rapid growth has occurred during the past twenty-five years. The number of stores increased from 10,000 to 22,000 between 2000 and 2004, and there were as many as 25,000 outlets at the end of the Great Recession in 2009.[22] In 2013 alone, 2.5 million households obtained payday loans.[23]

Payday lenders have diversified in conjunction with the striking growth of the industry. Twenty years ago, almost all of the lenders were small local businesses, none of which were publicly traded. However, a set of national lenders recognized the lucrative nature of payday lending and became a larger part of the industry after the turn of the twenty-first century. These companies are often publicly traded and, basically, use the same signage, interior design, and procedures in as many of their neighborhood outlets as possible. Even more recently, internet-only payday lenders have appeared and are taking a larger and larger share of the lending market. One need only Google "payday loans" to obtain links to dozens of internet sites.[24]

Payday lenders of all these types are major players in contemporary society's extraordinary extension of credit. Even in the aftermath of the Great Recession, consumer borrowing has surged, reaching its highest peak in more than a decade in March 2012 and continuing to grow since then.[25] The recession, it appears, has made consumer borrowing even more likely. According to Millan Mulraine, a strategist at New York's TD Securities, "When the economy's not doing well, that's when you want the consumers to spend, and if it means borrowing to do that, then that certainly would be encouraged."[26]

Banks like to present themselves as totally respectable and standing apart from more tawdry extenders of credit such as payday lenders. In reality, banks are of great assistance to payday lenders, and the different types of lenders in the United States are interconnected. Payday lenders depend on major, highly regarded banks such as JPMorgan Chase, Bank of America, and Wells Fargo. These banks enable the payday lenders to withdraw payments automatically from their customers' checking accounts, even in those states that prohibit payday lending. The traditional banks say they are merely accommodating payday lenders whose customers have authorized them to withdraw money from their accounts to pay off loans. The banks' actions might seem trivial in the overall scheme of things, but the payday customers are often holding onto the edge of a financial cliff. The withdrawals can constitute overdrafts, for which substantial fees are charged. According to a report from the Pew Charitable Trust, "Roughly 27 percent of payday loan borrowers say that the loans caused them to overdraw their accounts."[27]

With the major banks fully aware of what is going on, payday lenders provide quick and easy loans for those strapped for cash. In general, a payday borrower need not necessarily have a job or a "payday." Basically, a would-be borrower need only have a checking account and be able to present some combination of the following: a driver's license, passport, relatively recent pay stub, bank statement, or telephone bill. Lenders do not conduct a credit check or ask for references, and, indeed, lenders routinely boast of how quickly they can process a loan application. Some lenders emphasize in their advertisements that borrowers can obtain their loans "in minutes."[28]

As is generally the case among the urban poor making their way in the contemporary marketplace, poor borrowers looking for a payday lender do not appear to shop around for the best deal. The urban poor of course have access to the previously mentioned internet-only payday lenders, but they are less likely to turn to these lenders than are members of the middle and upper classes, who tend to have greater computer savvy and internet access. The urban poor could also consider various payday lenders in their metropolitan area, perhaps finding better rates at one or another. But in reality, the urban poor usually choose a lender because of its convenient location. The urban poor routinely walk to the nearest payday lender; some use the closest bus line to get there. For the urban poor, the "best" payday lender is often the one that is easiest to reach.

Some have been tempted to call payday lending modern loan-sharking.[29] The latter flourished in American cities throughout the first three-quarters of the twentieth century. It took the form of private parties lending money at extremely high interest rates, and as the business evolved in the 1930s, loan sharks came increasingly to rely on the threat of violence to guarantee loans were paid back. Loan sharks sometimes used legal businesses as a front, but in most cases they met borrowers in their workplaces, in fraternal organizations, at sporting events, and—last but not least—in bars and taverns. Often, loan sharks had criminal records, and in fact organized crime increasingly made the loans and threatened severe harm if timely repayment was not forthcoming. Like gambling, bootlegging, and prostitution, loan-sharking became known as a "racket." Arnold Rothstein, one loan shark who seems to have attracted the public's attention, allegedly fixed the World Series in 1919, but his bread and butter was extending high-interest loans to gamblers who need extra credit.[30]

As troubling as the conduct of payday lenders might be, they are not racketeers demanding loans be promptly paid off. Payday lenders rely on a well-crafted, standardized contractual agreement rather than the threat of violence to make their business run. Under the terms of the loan agreement, a borrower provides a signed check for the amount of the loan he or she wants plus a stipulated fee. The fee is usually a percentage of the loan. The lender then agrees to hold onto the check, knowing in advance that it is highly unlikely that funds would be available in the borrower's checking account to cover the amount of the check.

Why, after all, would the borrower even turn to a payday lender if he or she could simply take the funds from an existing account? The borrowers in general do not have access to traditional forms of credit, much less fungible reserves. Many have maxed-out credit cards and been turned down for loans at local banks. They do not own their homes, have tarnished credit histories, and may even be in the mandatory waiting period before they can file for another bankruptcy. The fees in payday lending, as high as they may be, are the best legal option for financing that the urban poor have.[31]

The loan agreement also includes a maturity date a few weeks or perhaps a month subsequent to the date on which the agreement was signed. As of that date, the borrower has three options: (1) pay off the amount of the check with cash or a money order, (2) let the payday lender cash the check (usually through one of the previously mentioned established banks), or (3) pay just the fee and renew the loan by agreeing to pay another fee. Lenders have a strong preference for the third option, which in effect amounts to a refinancing of the loan at the same high rate that was officially stipulated.

Such refinancing is known in the business as a "rollover" and is standard. According to the Consumer Financial Protection Bureau, a federal agency, 80 percent of payday loans are rolled over or renewed within two weeks, and the average payday loan is refinanced eight times.[32] Rollovers are in fact the key to profit-making in payday lending's business model. It not only extends the period set for repayment under the original agreement but also can be done time and again. In the end, the refinancing totals routinely exceed the original loan amount. The Consumer Financial Protection Bureau's 2015 report estimated the average payday loan to be $350, but the average borrower then paid an additional $458 in fees associated with rollovers.[33] According to Nathalie Martin, a law professor at the University of New Mexico who has studied payday lending, "While the going rate is between 400 and 600% per annum, some payday loans exceed 1,000% per annum."[34]

Why would the urban poor refinance their loans time and again? Some borrowers lack sufficient self-control. Like the person who knows bacon will harden his arteries but cannot resist ordering a fourth and then a fifth strip, a borrower might realize more borrowing is imprudent but lacks the willpower to resist the lender and its enticing terms. Other borrowers might be of an especially optimistic sort, and their optimism contributes to their willingness to take on more borrowing. More specifically, payday borrowers might be optimistic that they will avoid another rollover fee because they expect their living expenses to go down, or that a sister or an uncle might finally get around to repaying a personal loan. Some borrowers are also so-called hyperbolic discounters. This is just a fancy phrase for people who mentally apply a higher discount rate to events in the near future and a lower discount rate to events that are further off. The problem is that the future becomes the present in the blink of an eye.[35]

Borrowing mistakes and the personal traits that might explain them are especially common among the urban poor, who want the loans and the commodities those loans can provide in order to enhance their status and self-respect. Lenders likely have not reflected on the urban poor's tendencies to underestimate the costs of future borrowing. But the lenders surely recognize the type of borrower who desperately wants their services, and know how to take advantage of that type of borrower.

In some instances, borrowers realize they can neither pay off the loan nor even afford to roll it over. At this point, the agreement authorizes the payday lender to turn to collection agencies and the small-claims courts. It appears that even against the backdrop of general collections practices, the tactics used to collect from payday borrowers are particularly tawdry. Routine practices include harassing customers' relatives, overstating possible damages, and threatening to destroy reputations, and, in fact, many loan agreements include clauses via which borrowers waive their rights to report and challenge certain aggressive collections practices.[36]

One reason borrowers might tolerate the distasteful collections practices is they are in the kind of perennial jam endemic to lives in poverty. They are not naive and inexperienced, and they deal with the manipulations of the marketplace on a day-to-day basis. Yet the notion of backup funding is only a dream, as the urban poor lack substantial savings. Then, too, the modern-day urban poor have limited social capital that could be of help in a pinch. The urban poor's social connections and linkages are often deficient, and most friends, relatives, and community organizations are unable to bail them out. When you make your way through life without backup funds and with limited social capital, you learn to stomach rude treatment from neighborhood merchants and from government officials. You come to take this for granted. If a collections agent complains about a deadbeat debtor to a borrower's relatives or threatens to report the debtor to the police, what else is new?

Payday lenders defend their targeting of the urban poor by saying it makes funds available for those who cannot turn to banks and traditional lenders. The defenders of payday lenders admit these borrowers are often impoverished and concentrated in minority neighborhoods, but according to the defenders of payday lending, these people should be as free as other Americans to consume to their hearts' content. It would be paternalistic, the argument goes, to take payday lending away from borrowers who have knowingly decided to pay huge amounts for the loans they need for their purchases.

This pitch has the support of neoliberal theorists and politicians. They sometimes argue that credit allows consumers to smooth out their spending over time, in effect borrowing from good times in the future to help make it through hard times in the present. Such "smoothing" is common, the argument goes, and we think little of it when students acquire loans to pay college bills, small business owners borrow to make improvements, or consumers use credit to buy motor vehicles. Yet when payday lenders make their loans, their conduct seems immoral and usurious. "While triple-digit interest rates may sound outrageous, borrowing against future paychecks at such a high APR can be worth it if consumers' marginal utility is raised sufficiently to outweigh the expenditure they will make on interest."[37]

Business spokesmen and neoliberal economists are often too busy with their rationalizations and economic abstractions to satisfactorily acknowledge that most payday lending targets the urban poor and is consciously geared to putting them into ever-larger debt as they struggle to pay their rollover fees and loans. Payday lending uses standardized loan agreements to drive borrowers into worse poverty by getting them onto what the scholars Lynn Drysdale and Kathleen E. Keest have described as "at best, a 'debt treadmill' or, at worst, a downward spiral."[38] Payday lenders know most borrowers will not be able to pay back their loans in a timely fashion. The borrowers ride the treadmill by borrowing again and then once again. Treadmills keep moving, but in the end they lead to nothing other than more profit for the payday lenders and more debt for the poor borrowers.

Title Pawns

Some of the urban poor have still another financing option for their commodity purchases: the title pawn. It might be located just down the block from the payday lender, and in fact, payday lenders also sometimes offer title loans. Regardless of location, title pawns are prepared to provide high-interest loans if would-be borrowers can produce the titles for motor vehicles. To say the title pawn business is thriving is an understatement. In Florida, a state in which title pawns are especially entrenched, they write an incredible $225 million in loans annually.[39]

As I noted earlier, a motor vehicle or, better put, the lack thereof is a major factor in the well-documented phenomenon of the poor paying more for goods and services. A motor vehicle is also crucial when it comes to finding and maintaining employment. Many of the urban poor are of course unemployed, but the most common jobs for those who manage to escape abject poverty and join the ranks of the working poor are as servers and cooks in fast-food restaurants and as janitors and maintenance people in office parks and consumer malls. These jobs for the most part are not within walking distance of where the urban poor live. According to the Brookings Institution's Metropolitan Policy Program, "In the nation's one hundred largest metropolitan areas, nearly half of all the jobs lie more than ten miles from the downtown core."[40] A second Brookings Institution study reveals that "the typical job in a major metro area is accessible to only twenty-seven percent of all working-age adults within an hour-and-a-half commute on public transportation."[41]

As if these figures are not troubling enough, the urban mass-transit systems to which the working poor might conceivably turn are in severe decline. For decades, public policy has prioritized automobiles at the expense of public transport, and this has undercut an important option for low-income Americans in urban areas. As a result, the working poor turn to motor vehicles to get to work. Workers who live in poorer households and have cars drive to work.[42]

In light of their reliance on cars to get to work, the working poor are making a risky move if they turn to title pawns to finance their commodity purchases. Such borrowing "clouds the title" of the working poor's most valuable asset *and* jeopardizes the working poor's employment. Title pawns are hardly the only reason why so many men and women from impoverished inner cities lose what were lousy jobs in the first place, but title pawns are a contributing factor to unemployment. They are partially responsible for some portion of the working poor becoming just poor. According to William White, senior vice president of Cash America International, "Somebody forfeits their VCR, life goes on. But you lose your car, that's a different ballgame. Now you're talking about somebody's livelihood."[43]

The distinction is surely lost on the average consumer, but the agreement at the center of the title pawn business is a variety of what the law calls a "security agreement." When entering into a security agreement, a person provides collateral to back up his or her promise to make payments that are becoming due or to pay off a loan. If the party does not pay in a timely manner, the lender can claim all or at least part of the collateral. The collateral is the source of the lender's so-called security.

A classic example of a security agreement is the one between a customer and a pawnbroker. A customer in need of quick cash can bring his or her valuable possessions to a pawnbroker, who lends money to the customer based on a percentage of the items' value. A study of pawnshops in Texas found that 49 percent of the pawned items were jewelry, with most of that jewelry being class and wedding rings. Other items frequently pawned in Texas include cameras, guns, musical instruments, and televisions.[44] The resulting loans are small, usually in the $75–$100 range, and if the customer pays off the loan with interest in the stipulated period of time (usually a few months), the customer gets the items back. According to the same study of Texas pawnshops, customers are most likely to pay off the loans if the pawned items have sentimental, personal meaning—rings and guns, for example, but not cameras and televisions.[45] If the customer does not make the payments and get the items out of hock, the pawnbroker has the option of selling the items to third parties.

In days gone by, some thought pawnbrokers dealt primarily in stolen goods, and this presumption, along with the image of desperate souls pleading for just a little more cash from the pawnbroker, tarnished the collective reputation of the business. The pawnbroker business declined and seemed on the verge of disappearing from the urban landscape.[46]

But then, in recent years, pawnbrokers found a new life. An estimated 7 percent of all households in the United States have turned at least once to a pawnbroker.[47] While there were only an estimated 6,400 pawnbrokers left in 2007, the number rose to over 10,000 by 2012. One key to this growth seems to be that pawnbrokers are revamping their images by offering a wider and wider range of financial services. Some cash checks, and some wire money. Some make loans, and some even accept payment for utility bills. Pawn America, a Minnesota-based chain, has created separate entrances for those hoping to hock a watch and for those seeking conventional financial services. Inside the latter entrance, the customer finds well-groomed tellers behind windows rather than the proverbial cigar-smoking men leaning forward over glass display cases.[48] Pawnbrokers have even developed something resembling a cachet for adventure. Although I personally cannot appreciate their appeal, such reality shows as "Pawn Stars" and "Hardcore Pawn," set, respectively, in Las Vegas and Detroit, have attracted devoted viewers.

Under the terms of a title pawn's security agreement, the borrower does not physically turn over a motor vehicle as the borrower might if there were pawnbrokers for cars and trucks. Instead, the title-pawn borrower uses the motor vehicle's title to secure the loan. Title to a piece of property is an indication that the title holder justly owns the property. Legally speaking, title to a motor vehicle is not merely the piece of paper issued by a state's department of motor vehicles, but rather the paramount ownership that piece of paper symbolizes. In addition to taking the title, or at least a copy of it, some title pawns require a set of keys for the motor vehicle in order to make things easier if they want to seize it.

More remains to be said about this possibility, but the loans are fraught with dubious features. The loans tend to be relatively small—$250 to $1,000—but they are large compared to borrowers' limited income and cash flow. The loans are based on the value of the motor vehicle offered as the de facto collateral rather than on the ability of borrowers to pay back the loans, and loans of this sort to financially stressed borrowers will be difficult and often impossible to pay back.[49]

If the typical borrower is unable to pay back the loan when it is due after a month or so, the title pawn offers an option comparable to that offered by a payday lender. To wit, the title pawn is only too happy to allow the loan to roll over for another month, charging a new fee for this option. In fact, unlike rent-to-own outlets, at which customers drop in to renew their transactions, some title pawns arrange for the agreement to renew automatically. The borrower does not even have to return to the lender's office to sign additional papers.

Rollovers can and do occur time and again, resulting in what amounts to an extraordinary interest rate as the borrower rides a "debt treadmill" into tighter and tighter financial straits. Surveys of borrowers from title pawns have found they routinely pay triple-digit interest rates, and many borrowers end up paying appreciably more in interest than they borrowed at the outset. Indeed, there are reported instances of borrowers paying over 800 percent in interest.[50] Should borrowers realize how outrageous the interest is, the borrowers might be hard-pressed to challenge things in court. Many resourceful title pawns insert binding mandatory arbitration clauses in the security agreement in order to prevent borrowers from suing. These clauses also deter the mounting of a "class action," a type of lawsuit available in federal court and most state courts through which one or more persons may seek a remedy on behalf of a large group of persons who are interested in the matter. A title pawn might be irked if an individual borrower sued, but a class action filed on behalf of a class of borrowers would be even more worrisome because of the much larger damages that might result.[51]

If the borrower cannot make the interest payments, or perhaps simply wants to get off his or her personal "debt treadmill," the security agreement enables the title pawn to take possession of the motor vehicle. To the dismay of many, these repossessions do in fact occur, with repossession rates varying among the states from 10 to 20 percent. Those figures may not sound high, but they are as much as ten times higher than the repossession rates for regular auto loans. The figures are also a dozen times higher than the national foreclosure rate for homes. Since the urban poor and working poor rarely own homes, their motor vehicles are likely to be their most valuable assets in raw dollars and cents. Furthermore, while many owners of foreclosed homes have no equity, almost all owners of repossessed motor vehicles do. When a title pawn repossesses, it pretty much amounts to a forfeiture on the borrower's part.[52]

According to data from Tennessee, 14–17 percent of borrowers are unable to make their interest payments, and title pawns take possession of roughly one-half of the motor vehicles to which they are entitled.[53] The vehicles can be routed to used car auctions or to used car lots, some of which are located next door to the title pawns. As for the other half of the motor vehicles, many have serious mechanical problems or structural damage. Some have been totaled or junked. Others quite simply were not worth that much at the outset of the borrowing process. In all of these cases, the title pawn makes the business decision that the cost of taking possession and trying to resell the motor vehicle is greater than what will be received through a resale.

As is the case with rent-to-own operators and payday lenders, title pawns have their neoliberal defenders. Some assert that without title pawns, borrowers would turn to "inferior forms of credit" and end up paying even more.[54] "If deprived access to title loans," the argument goes, "many consumers would substitute less-preferred sources of credit or risk losing access to credit altogether."[55] Another argument is that borrowers who turn to title pawns are not necessarily ensnared like unsuspecting animals in a trap. Informed borrowers are supposedly making intelligent, rational decisions to secure title loans in order to meet short-term liquidity crises, and others use title loans to finance small business operations.[56]

Defenders of the industry might like to believe some large portion of title pawns' customers belong to the middle class or perhaps are small businessmen, but in reality, most customers are the poor or belong to the working poor. One study in New Mexico found that the average borrower earned between $20,116 and $27,719 annually, amounts far below the state's median income. Data from other states also show borrowers' average income to be in the same range as in New Mexico.[57]

Why do the poor and working poor in effect hock their cars? Having enough money to make monthly mortgage payments on their homes is not the reason. An inner-city renter or resident of public housing, obviously, does not have to worry about a mortgage. Perhaps some use the money from a title pawn for utility bills or uninsured medical expenses. But when a poor borrower drives straight from the title pawn to Walmart or perhaps to Rent-A-Center, one suspects commodity lust is a motivating force.

The title pawns realize, of course, that their typical borrowers can ill afford such high-cost, short-term balloon loans. Poor borrowers are especially unlikely to be able to pay back the loans, and especially likely to incur the extraordinarily high interest charges. "Borrowers across the country find themselves sucked into a spiral of debt, paying more and more fees while the principal on the loan remains largely unchanged."[58] When an impoverished city dweller signs the dotted line of a security agreement at a title pawn, he or she has not found a way out of a financial pinch, but rather has begun a process by which the pinch will become more and more painful.

The Limits of Law Reform

The business practices of rent-to-owns, payday lenders, and title pawns have prompted concern. The businesses' legally enforceable agreements and their sophisticated use of collection agencies, police departments, and local courts clearly harm the urban poor. Maybe the courts could crack down on these businesses. Perhaps new laws could address exploitation in which the law in general is already implicated. We could hope at least that "law reform" could address what is being done to the urban poor. But, if one is realistic, it is difficult to meaningfully control successful businesses through law reform.

The primary sites for law reform are, of course, the courts and legislatures, and those who turn to these legal institutions tend not to be the urban poor themselves, but rather consumer advocates and community activists. In general, the reformers are imbued with optimism and a belief that legal institutions can and will make things better. We can use law to rein in the rent-to-own, payday lending, and title pawn businesses, the thinking goes, and the urban poor will be better off as a result. Unfortunately, though, the changes the reformers promote are smaller and have less impact than they anticipate.

The most important efforts in the courts have tended to involve just how we might legally conceptualize the rent-to-own, payday lending, and title pawn businesses. In the rent-to-own area, litigation involving Hilda Perez and a New Jersey rent-to-own outlet has attracted the most attention. In 2001 and 2002, Perez, a cook from Camden, shopped at the local Rent-A-Center five times. She acquired furniture, a washer-dryer, a DVD player, a computer, and a large television with cabinet, and she signed a standardized agreement for each acquisition. The forms required her to make weekly payments on the various goods, and she was also subject to penalty fees if payments were not made. At the top of each agreement a statement in capital letters read: "THIS IS A RENTAL AGREEMENT ONLY." Rent-A-Center repeated the statement at later points in the agreement, and lest anyone fail to appreciate the point, the agreement also said: "We own the property you are renting."

But was the core agreement best understood as a rental lease? Perez sued, arguing it was not. She lost in the trial court and the lower-level appellate court, but when the New Jersey Supreme Court made its final ruling in the case, Justice Virginia Long discussed at great length the manner in which the goods were sold and acquired. Together, all the consumer goods Perez supposedly had rented had a cash price of $9,301.72. That is roughly what a customer would have paid for them at the local Target. However, if Perez had somehow been able to make all her weekly payments on the goods at Rent-A-Center, she would have paid a total of $18,613.32—over 100 percent more than the cash price.[59] Perez stopped making payments well before she could claim to have purchased the goods, but one wonders if there was any chance that she could actually have "rented" the goods for a long enough time to ever "own" them.

Justice Long also relied on an actuary named James Hart to estimate what the "rental" payments would look like if considered as installment payments with interest. He calculated the annual interest rates on selected goods purchased by Perez as follows:

Washer-dryer	79.2%
Furniture	82.7%
DVD player	79.2% to 82.7%[60]

These figures were shocking for Justice Long and a majority of her Supreme Court brethren. They thought the agreement Perez had with Rent-A-Center really amounted to a high-interest installment sale. Perez's agreement with Rent-A-Center, they concluded, was covered by New Jersey's Retail Installment Act and also was in violation of the state's criminal usury statute because the interest was higher than the state allowed.

Decisions regarding payday lending and title pawns have not been as pointed as the *Perez* decision regarding the rent-to-own business, but payday-lending and title-pawn decisions have in their own way clarified just how it is we might conceptualize these businesses. The payday-lending decisions in general have rejected the claim of payday lenders that they should be seen merely as providers of check-cashing services rather than as lenders, a claim that would free the payday lenders from limits imposed by the previously mentioned state usury laws.[61] The United States District Court for the Eastern District of Kentucky, for example, found that payday lending was in fact a loan-making enterprise and subject to the state's usury laws, and in later litigation the Kentucky Supreme Court agreed with this interpretation.[62]

The courts have also for the most part rejected an argument from the title pawns that they are really no different than traditional pawnbrokers. The latter often have exemptions under state usury laws that limit interest rates on loans, and pawnbrokers can therefore impose larger interest charges. As mentioned earlier in this chapter, both pawnbrokers and title pawns rely on "security agreements." However, title pawns do not actually hold the personal property as collateral as pawnbrokers do. Title pawns hold only a motor vehicle's title, a piece of paper that only symbolizes the ownership of the actual motor vehicle. Hence, a number of courts have ruled that title pawns are best understood as lenders rather than as traditional pawnbrokers.[63]

State legislatures have also responded to demands from consumer advocates and community activists that the three types of businesses be carefully scrutinized. Admittedly, the legislatures are usually focused on "consumer affairs" rather than the exploitation of the poor and working poor, but perhaps we should not really expect mainstream American legislators to be particularly sensitive to the endemic, structural features of inequality. They are more inclined to tinker with the system rather than to make fundamental changes in it. The legislators' biggest hope is that mandatory disclosure of how rent-to-own outlets, payday lenders, and title pawns operate and are supposed to operate will aid the buyers and borrowers. Consumer laws in this area and in general do not deplore or even oppose consumption, but rather endorse and seek to facilitate informed consumption.

A bevy of legislative feints and stabs have resulted, and researchers Susan

Lorde Martin and Nancy White Huckins have provided a useful summary of what has been done. They report that most of the states now have laws requiring that rent-to-own outlets disclose the amount of each rent payment, the number of payments necessary to acquire a given commodity, and any fees that might be charged for delivery, late payments, and reinstatement of an agreement. A smaller number of laws also require outlets to provide, depending on the state, either the cash price if the commodities were bought at the standard retailer, or the fair market value of the commodity.[64]

The state legislatures have also attempted to make the operations of payday lenders more transparent. In fact, when Wisconsin enacted payday-lending legislation in 2010, it was actually the last state to do so.[65] Typically, states restrict the financing fees charged in conjunction with a loan, place a limit on loan amounts, and/or limit the number of rollovers within a given transaction. Some states have also explicitly brought payday lenders under state usury laws, thereby establishing ceilings on interest rates.

The states have not been as active in regulating title pawns as they have been in regulating payday lenders, but the regulations that do exist in the two areas are comparable. Oregon and Montana, for example, have amended their laws to impose a 36 percent interest cap on title loans.[66] The percentage on its surface might seem arbitrary and random, but it is something of an emerging, unofficial national standard for both title and payday lenders. A federal law that caps interest loans to active-duty military personnel at 36 percent appears to be the source of the 36-percent standard.[67]

A handful of states also limit the size of the loan that can be offered by a title pawn and/or restrict the number of rollovers. The simplest limit on the size of a loan is a fixed dollar amount that would apply to all loans regardless of the resale value of the motor vehicle for which the title is offered as collateral. A common amount in this regard is $2,500. With regard to rollovers, states might simply set a fixed number, or perhaps require that after a set number of rollovers, title pawns must begin reducing the loan's principal.[68]

The boldest but potentially most complicated reform would be a requirement that the title pawn look into the borrower's income, other indebtedness, and credit rating to gauge the borrower's overall financial wherewithal. Illinois, for example, has cut to the quick by barring any loans with a single payment exceeding 50 percent of the borrower's income. The federal Consumer Financial Protection Bureau also issued draft regulations in 2015 requiring that certain limits be imposed on payday lenders and title pawns nationally.[69] Most notably, the bureau proposed that payday lenders and title pawns be required to ensure that borrowers could repay their debt on schedule before they made the loans.[70]

Do the leading judicial decisions and most important state laws related to the rent-to-own, payday lending, and title pawn businesses shield the urban poor from exploitation? Do the decisions and laws have the potential to truly protect the urban poor? One thing to underscore at the outset is that the judicial decisions and new statutes are for the most part only operative in individual states. The Rent-A-Center decision of the New Jersey Supreme Court that rent-to-own transactions are really installment loans, for example, stands only in New Jersey. The great majority of states have no comparable judicial opinions, and rent-to-own outfits continue to conduct business as in the past. Statutes limiting how much interest a payday lender or title pawn might charge are also only state statutes.

Furthermore, opposition to these reforms abounds in the various states and also nationally. Lenders and their small business allies strongly oppose the reforms and have the ear of the Trump administration. The latter has in turn proposed eliminating the regulations affecting payday lenders and title pawns, and it also ordered the Consumer Financing Bureau to drop several suits that it had initiated against individual payday-lending companies. Indeed, the Trump administration has appointed a new director for the bureau who had previously called it "a joke."[71]

It also bears remembering that rent-to-own operations, payday lenders, and title pawns have sophisticated, adjustable business models and modify their core agreements in order to elude whatever limits well-intentioned judges and legislators place on them. Business law professor Todd J. Zywicki has outlined in this regard the ways businesses preying on the poor might get around the regulations. In Zywicki's opinion, law reform related to the consumer marketplace is routinely overwhelmed by crafty business adjustments. The businesses might engage in repricing, the process by which the businesses increase the price of unregulated parts of the transaction or on related products in order to offset what might be lost to usury limitations. A rent-to-own outlet, for example, is quite willing to bundle the core transaction with insurance sales. If usury caps limit what may be charged for an installment sale, the cost of insurance can easily be jacked up. "The final result," Zywicki argues, "will be to vitiate many of the extended benefits of the regulation by circumventing the intended effects of price controls. This would make consumers worse off as a group by encouraging a new pricing system that is less efficient and less transparent than that which would otherwise prevail."[72]

The businesses might also engage in product substitution in order to avoid rate caps. A payday lender, for example, could offer a rent-to-own arrangement or a title loan, or even operate as an old-fashioned pawnbroker, assuming the latter possibilities are unregulated. "Some commentators, in fact, have claimed that the growth of auto-title lending in some states resulted from laws that eliminated payday lending."[73] Then, too, payday lenders in Wisconsin shifted to what they call "installment loans," extremely high-interest, three-month loans that are not covered by the state's payday lending regulation. Some of these installment loans have annual interest rates of over 500 percent. An outside observer might think borrowers would realize these loans are as exploitative as payday loans, but many of the borrowers are poorly educated and unequipped to understand the ramifications of such loans. According to one disappointed Wisconsin legal services attorney, "This is an industry that just kind of morphs depending on the law to regulate them."[74]

In the end, and despite the much ballyhooed law reform, rent-to-own outlets, payday lenders, and title pawns are still doing business and still focusing on the urban poor more so than any other group. After its loss in the *Perez* litigation, Rent-A-Center agreed to pay class-action plaintiffs $109 million. The settlement was to reimburse New Jersey consumers who entered into agreements with Rent-A-Center between April 23, 1997, and March 16, 2007, for the amounts their payments exceeded what would have been allowable under New Jersey's usury limits. Even in light of the huge settlement, the company seemed genuinely nonplussed. For the first quarter of 2007, Rent-A-Center reported revenues of $755.3 million, and a company spokesman said Rent-A-Center could easily finance the settlement through its regular operating budget.[75]

Despite its losses in the courts and regulation from the state legislatures, payday lenders have continued to thrive. Since 2011, in fact, the number of American households with payday loans has grown by 19 percent.[76] Payday lenders have somewhat unbelievably come to outnumber the combined total of McDonald's, Burger King, Sears, J.C. Penney's, and Target stores; they also outnumber all of America's Starbucks.[77]

Obviously, the urban poor continue to rent from rent-to-owns and to borrow from payday lenders and title pawns. In addition, well-intentioned decisions by the courts and new statutes from assorted state legislatures have the effect of legitimating these businesses. Note the contrast in this regard with loan-sharking, the variety of unlicensed lending at very high rates for which the lenders use strong-armed enforcement to guarantee timely payment. Loan-sharking is illegitimate, and local police and district attorneys can arrest and prosecute loan sharks for criminal conduct. Graced with a veneer of legally required responsible operations, rent-to-owns, payday lenders, and title pawns are not susceptible to similar crackdowns. Indeed, some proprietors might belong to the Chamber of Commerce or proudly take their seat at the monthly meeting of the local Rotary Club.

Courts and legislatures do more than prescribe and proscribe. They also recognize and countenance. When it comes to rent-to-owns, payday lenders, and title pawns, courts and legislatures have provided not so much a stamp of approval as tacit acceptance under law. The middle-class and upper-class reformers who turned to the courts and legislatures surely did not have this as a goal when they launched their campaigns. But alas, the state has underscored the overarching right of the rent-to-owns, payday lenders, and title pawns to continue their operations. Their lights are flashing, and these businesses in poor African American and Latino neighborhoods are open well into the wee hours.

Exploitation and Subordination

On one level, the success and legitimacy of the rent-to-own, payday lending, and title pawn businesses make perfectly good sense. These businesses do not have a monopoly on using people and manipulating their hopes and dreams to turn a profit. They also are not the only ones charging the urban poor more. As I pointed out earlier, a sizable price differential exists between wealthy and poor Americans, with the poor routinely encountering higher prices in their parts of the marketplace. Selling commodities to the urban poor at high prices, or lending money to the urban poor at unbelievably high interest rates are viable and largely accepted American enterprises. After all, we have a market economy, don't we?

Neoliberal champions of the market economy take the workings of the market economy to be the key to a healthy society. However, certain of these champions are on edge about their beloved consumer markets. It seems they cannot believe that critics continue to question the value and fairness of these markets. James Livingston, to cite only one prominent defender of the market economy, is certain that consumer markets for the urban poor and in general are sources of personal freedom. In an earlier era of industrial capitalism, he admits, major industrialists and large corporations reaped profits by underpaying and otherwise taking advantage of their workers. But since the 1920s, things have changed. Workers and other Americans, Livingston maintains, now have high enough salaries and a range of government entitlements, and they are free to consume. Consumption, in his mind, is a welcome economic activity apart from work and brings great delight and satisfaction.[78]

The chief problem for Livingston and his ilk is that they assume that all markets are essentially the same and that they operate in similar ways for all sorts of consumers in all sorts of settings. In reality, markets operate in different ways and have different ramifications for different types of consumers. From the perspective of social justice as opposed to economic efficiency, some markets are unfair to the people who purchase in them, and some markets harm the society around them.

Debra Satz, professor of philosophy at Stanford University, has defined what she calls "noxious markets," and rent-to-own, payday lending, and title lending for the urban poor fit within this conceptualization. Some noxious markets take advantage of vulnerable consumers and also those whose consumption is dictated by necessity.[79] In addition, according to Satz, some markets are noxious because of those markets' "outcomes," that is, because of their impact on participants in the markets and/or on society as a whole. Consumers might, for example, be left destitute by their market transactions and then have to be carried by the society.[80]

A consideration of outcomes provides the greatest indictment of the deals rent-to-owns, payday lenders, and title pawns strike with the urban poor. These businesses craftily charge the urban poor a great deal for goods and loans, and this exploitation obviously drains the urban poor's limited resources. In addition, the rent-to-owns, payday lenders, and title pawns drive the poor deeper into poverty and, in effect, perpetuate that poverty. The poor are left with no choice but to be poor.

As I suggested at the beginning of this chapter, law and legal institutions are accomplices in these outcomes. When we scrutinize the exploitative perpetuation of poverty through the legal agreements used by rent-to-owns, payday lenders, and title pawns, we see the urban poor being consigned to an undesirable socioeconomic status. When we observe legal institutions and others policing and enforcing these disadvantageous agreements, we sense that the urban poor are likely to remain poor.

The manner in which rent-to-owns, payday lenders, and title pawns worsen and in effect perpetuate poverty illustrates that poverty is not just a status but also a process. It is not enough for oppressors to simply declare that certain people are members of a subaltern socioeconomic class. Oppressors must also ensure that the oppressed remain in that class. The marketplace creates possibilities for doing this to the urban poor. Rent-to-owns, payday lenders, and title pawns are especially nefarious because they drive the urban poor more deeply and permanently into debt. One critic has compared the urban poor's resulting condition to peonage, that is, the much discredited oppression in which subordinate people are held in servitude or partial slavery until they work off their debts.[81] That comparison seems apt.

CHAPTER FIVE

Health Inequity

am among those faculty members who whine and complain about the shortage of good places for lunch near our campus. In self-styled desperation, a few of us have even begun walking to the nearby inner-city hospital to eat in the hospital's cafeteria. The tuna casserole is tolerable, and it is difficult to wreck a salad bar. However, the scenes we see in and around the hospital are sobering: dazed teenage mothers and very young grandmothers awkwardly cradling newborns in the elevators, friends and family members in the emergency room's waiting area nervously hoping for news about loved ones' illness and injuries, and men and women in hospital gowns sneaking out the side door for a smoke in the hospital's "Peace Garden." Other than the small band of hungry professors, most of the people in and around the hospital are African American or Latino, poor or near-poor, and physically ill or emotionally distraught.

I am describing just one aging, inner-city hospital and the poor who come there for health care, but it is generally the case that the urban poor are unhealthier on average than most middle- and upper-class Americans. The bacteria, viruses, and toxins that make people sick are more prevalent in poor urban communities, and communicable diseases spread more easily. Chronic noninfectious conditions associated with poor diets and obesity and with drug, tobacco, and alcohol use are even more troublesome than the communicable diseases. Ischemic heart diseases, certain cancers, and type 2 diabetes not only disable the urban poor in large numbers but also result in shorter life expectancy. HIV/AIDS, now associated primarily with unprotected sexual intercourse and intravenous drug use, is also most highly concentrated among the urban poor. We should not mistake correlation for causation, but Scott Burris, director of the Center for Public Health Law Research at Temple University, accurately underscores "the tendency of positive health outcomes to line up on a steady slope from have-leasts to have-mosts."[1]

Policymakers as well as average citizens differ as to what they should make of the urban poor's health problems and health inequity vis-à-vis the middle and upper classes. Those more sympathetic to the plight of the urban poor often call for more doctors and better health-care facilities. Clinics should be available in the inner city, they say, and the urban poor should not have to rely on hospital emergency rooms for health care. Those unsympathetic to the urban poor point their fingers at the urban poor themselves and at the way they presumably choose to live their lives. The urban poor, the thinking might go, eat too much fried food and drink too many alcoholic beverages. And if diets high in fat and calories are not bad enough, the urban poor tend to use drugs and violently harm one another.

Neither those sympathetic to the urban poor nor those inclined to blame them for their own plight have a particularly insightful angle on the urban poor's health problems, but in recent decades medical and public-health professionals calling themselves "social epidemiologists" have offered a more valuable perspective.[2] While traditional epidemiologists study the causes and distribution of diseases and other health problems, the social epidemiologists ask why some societies or some sectors of a given society are healthier than other societies or other sectors of a given society. In answering those questions, the social epidemiologists insist we consider social context. They argue that "population health is shaped to a significant degree by fundamental social conditions."[3]

Employing nice metaphorical phrasing, the social epidemiologists urge us to intellectually "travel upstream" and consider living conditions, social arrangements, and structural realities such as wealth, share of income, and life prospects.[4] Located "upstream" for the urban poor are their neighborhoods and the lives they lead in those neighborhoods. Even further "upstream" are the urban poor's seemingly permanent poverty and the reasons for that poverty.

In the contemporary United States, law, legal institutions, and legal proceedings are of course crucial parts of what we find "upstream." We tend to overlook it, but law creates and stabilizes some of the very forces and phenomena that result in health problems. Law establishes, licenses, regulates, and otherwise legitimizes various pursuits that are detrimental to the urban poor's health, and various officials and institutions enforce and administer the law. From the perspective of the *Journal of Law, Medicine & Ethics*, "Law seeks to colonize everyday life and give it substance, to capture it, and hold it in its grasp, to attach itself to the solidity of the everyday, and, in so doing, to further solidify it."[5]

This does not mean it is impossible for creative and committed lawmakers to fashion laws that improve the collective health of the urban poor. However, using law to change social conditions in order to reduce the urban poor's health problems is even more difficult than using law to bridle profit-seeking rent-to-own outlets, payday lenders, and title pawns.

In the end, law's dominant function with regard to the health of the urban poor is clear. Rather than helping the poor lead healthier lives, law is more likely to leave the urban poor anxiously seeking short-term assistance in the type of aging, inner-city hospital at which I sometimes eat my lunch. Rather than prompting and inspiring better health among the urban poor, law is more likely to contain the urban poor in their unhealthy situation and to condemn them for their unhealthy attitudes and conduct.

Place Matters

When one looks "upstream" to the social conditions influencing the urban poor's health, one comes first to the neighborhoods of the inner city that I described in chapter 2. This environment likely has rundown public and private housing, large numbers of single-parent families, high crime rates, and no shortage of businesses prepared to take advantage of their customers' poverty. This is the "place" the urban poor call home, and "place matters" in the health of a sector of the population.[6]

The physical features and the social norms of the inner city intertwine, but I will initially address these two aspects of the urban poor's "place" separately. Turning first to the physical features, we can easily see how many of them present dangers and health risks. It is also evident that law and legal institutions often facilitate the dangerous and unhealthy physical features or, quite simply, fail to take them seriously enough.

Inner-city parks and recreation areas, for example, were usually small and ramshackle to begin with, but these parks and recreation areas are going from bad to worse.[7] The detectable decline began in the second half of the twentieth century, as cities began to deteriorate and middle- and upper-class Americans took their families and assets to the manicured suburbs.[8] When city governments faced severe economic problems in the 1990s, mayors and city lawmakers addressed budget woes by, among other things, cutting spending for the parks and recreation areas. Park maintenance became spotty, equipment and playing fields grew dangerous, and inadequate lighting often led people to avoid the parks and recreation areas after dark.

At one point in time, the federal government seemed to recognize the problems with urban parks. Congress established the Urban Park and Recreation Recovery Program, which authorized the Secretary of the Interior to assist economically distressed urban neighborhoods to improve their parks and recreation programs. Grants became available for park planning, the improvement of existing recreation programs, and the rehabilitation of parks that had fallen into disrepair. But alas, the program's annual funding shrank over time and then stopped altogether in 2002.[9] In most metropolitan areas, parks and recreation areas in the inner city quite simply do not provide the residents of the surrounding neighborhoods with as much fun and relaxation as they once did.[10]

Weedy, trash-strewn vacant lots where buildings have collapsed or burned down outnumber the inner-city parks and recreation areas. These vacant lots are eyesores if you drive past them, and they are even more troubling if you live near them. In fact, it makes a difference if vacant lots have been cleaned up and replanted. One study found that "in-view proximity to a greened vacant lot decreased heart rate compared with in-view proximity to a non-greened vacant lot."[11] Well-groomed vacant lots provide calm and peacefulness not only for people who use them for exercise and play but also for people who walk by these lots or just contemplate them.

The commercial fabric of the inner city is often as shabby as its green spaces. Alcohol outlets in the form of bars and liquor stores are numerous. Legally licensed, the alcohol outlets maintain long business hours and simultaneously facilitate and benefit from excessive alcohol consumption. Not only alcoholism but also liver problems can and do result. In addition, according to a study done in Boston, interpersonal violence increases in and around bars and liquor stores. Alcohol outlets, it appears, are both "producers" of violent behavior and "attractors" of potentially violent people. The greater the per capita number of alcohol outlets, the greater the per capita amount of violent crime. Poor urban neighborhoods lead the way in both calculations.[12]

Beyond the taverns and liquor stores, the range of shops in the inner city is limited. They include barbers, hair salons (some selling human hair), nail salons, discount tobacco outlets, cheap cell phone stores, and corner grocery stores and bodegas. Some are franchises with managers, but just as many are independently owned. The shops tend to be compact and cramped. Their signage is small, and some of it is handmade.

I underscored some of the pricing issues at the grocery stores and bodegas in the previous chapter, and the urban poor do indeed encounter inflated prices in these stores. Some of the goods for sale in these stores and bodegas can lead to or exacerbate health problems. Customers are most likely to purchase the snack food, soft drinks, and canned or frozen foods. All are prominently displayed. Customers are less likely to buy fresh fruit and vegetables, low-fat dairy products, or whole-grain breads and cereals.[13] The stores, of course, sell relatively little of the latter, and the urban poor do not routinely shop elsewhere.[14]

The inventory and practices of the inner-city grocery stores and bodegas are major factors in what has been called the "food desert" of the inner city.[15] According to the United States Department of Agriculture, almost 24 million people live in areas without ready access to fresh, healthy, and affordable food, and the great majority of people living in these "food deserts" are poor or have low incomes.[16] The immediate environs may not be quite as barren and windswept as the "food desert" metaphor connotes, but at the same time local food environments vary tremendously in quality. The one in the typical inner city is terrible and without a doubt affects the health and well-being of the urban poor.

The shortage of fresh fruit and vegetables, low-fat dairy products, and whole-grain breads increases the reliance on sugary and processed foods. This unhealthy diet, in turn, contributes to various chronic diseases and conditions. Diabetes in particular is especially common in neighborhoods with high concentrations of poverty. Living in high-poverty neighborhoods undeniably increases the odds of having diabetes.[17] African Americans are much more likely to live in high-poverty neighborhoods than others. This can create the impression that diabetes is linked to race, but poor Latinos and whites living in high-poverty neighborhoods also suffer disproportionately from diabetes.[18]

In the best of all worlds, the urban poor could harvest fresh fruit and vegetables from their gardens. With the rise of community gardens and urban farming, more of the urban poor could obtain fresh fruit and vegetables grown in their neighborhoods. However, a problem presents itself: inner-city neighborhoods are among the most polluted in the nation. In fact, the "dirtiest" zip code in the United States, as measured by the federal Environmental Protection Agency, is in poor, mostly African American, and intensely urban South Central Los Angeles.[19]

The sources of pollution and environmental hazards include private industry, power companies, incinerators, brownfields, and dumpsites, and toxic waste sites are especially problematic. A large literature scrutinizes the siting of these locally unwanted land uses, and the literature has even spawned the odd acronym "LULU." LULUs, it seems, are abundantly present in the neighborhoods in which the urban poor live.[20]

Since at least the time of the Love Canal scandal of the mid-1970s, in which a large swath of Niagara Falls, New York, was discovered to have been built on or near a toxic waste site, Americans have noisily opposed the siting of LULUs near where they live. However, it is worth remembering that "not in my backyard" campaigners tend not to object to the siting of LULUs in other people's neighborhoods. "Nimbys," as they are sometimes known, may not want a toxic waste site in their suburb, but they do not necessarily protest if the site is in the inner city. The residents of the inner city, meanwhile, often lack the social capital—the social organizations and connections—needed to build their own campaigns to oppose toxic waste sites.

When it came to light that the poor, both in the cities and elsewhere, were most likely to be near LULUs, a cry of "environmental justice" went up. Environmentalists and others decried the way the poor carried the heaviest load. Responding to these issues, President Bill Clinton in 1994 formally recognized the need to achieve greater environmental equity. He issued Executive Order 12898, which required all federal agencies to collect data about the health and environmental impact of their actions on low-income populations, and to develop strategies and programs to achieve environmental justice to the extent possible.[21]

But unfortunately, executive orders do not necessarily produce change—or, at least, enough of it. Barrels of data and long lists of strategies are available, but the successful use of this information to address the environmental problems of the inner city is hard to find. The urban poor themselves have almost no access to the data and know little about strategies for addressing structural and environmental inequity, something with which they live day in and day out. Overall, the siting of LULUs in the inner city continues, and LULUs extract a psychological as well as a physical toll on the urban poor.

A declining but still substantial percentage of people in the inner city live in public housing. As I pointed out in chapter 2, the construction of public housing began in the United States during the 1930s with great hope and enthusiasm. Americans of that era even had some rudimentary sense that the fortunate should help those who had fallen on hard times during the Great Depression. This sense of collective responsibility disappeared in the decades following World War II, and the "projects," as they came to be known, increasingly housed the poorest of the poor, the very sector of the population with which this book has been concerned. Furthermore, members of the middle and upper classes started to see public housing not as an entitlement for their fellow Americans but rather as a handout, as something more comparable to a welfare payment than to an abode providing security and a sense of connectedness for those who live or gather there.

During the Reagan presidency of the 1980s, with neoliberal thinking reigning supreme in the White House, public housing fell from favor. Federal funding declined, and Congress grew less and less enamored with constructing and renovating public housing, ultimately turning instead to low-income units in mixed-income developments. Given the shift in politics and change in governmental programs, public housing not surprisingly began to deteriorate. Repairs lagged, vandalism thrived, and accidents increased, including horrid instances of small children falling out of windows without screens on the higher floors of stifling project towers. Urban gangs also took up residence, and in addition to menacing one another and the residents of public housing, the gangs controlled and promoted the drug traffic. Sadly, the courtyards, a design feature in which public-housing architects had taken great pride, became ideal sites for drug-dealing because they were shielded from public view. As a result of the violence that spilled over from the drug sales, the courtyards became more dangerous than idyllic.[22]

In addition to the obvious physical dangers, other features of public housing have made the projects unhealthy. Cockroaches, rodents, and garbage were common. A Boston study also found dampness and heating problems that created concentrations of dust mites, fungi, and mold that caused or exacerbated asthma among the residents. Residents routinely requested transfers to other public housing complexes in order to avoid asthma "triggers."[23]

According to the *Journal of Urban Health*, "Research has shown that public housing residents have the worst health of any population in the USA."[24] And if the directness of that statement is not attention-grabbing enough, note that public housing is particularly unhealthy for children. On average, children in public housing have poorer health outcomes than other children living in the same neighborhoods and communities in which the public housing is located. Children in public housing have low immunization rates and high teenage pregnancy rates. The differences from other children in the same general neighborhoods are less pronounced for toddlers and preschoolers, but the differences increase for school-age children, that is, for children who most likely have lived in public housing for longer periods of time. The only encouraging thought is that children in public housing located in areas with middle-class populations rather than in areas with concentrations of poverty had better health and education outcomes. Public housing can provide a "place of residence," but public housing can be somewhat less dangerous and unhealthy if it is located in a better "place."[25]

Because of public housing's decline and the shortage of affordable units in mixed-income developments, the great majority of the urban poor rent in duplexes, triplexes, and small apartment buildings. Unfortunately this housing is almost as unhealthy as public housing. As noted in chapter 2, inner-city rental housing is old, and the upkeep is poor, as absentee landlords maneuver around the local housing codes in order to minimize costs associated with their properties. Corroded pipes and faulty heating systems can result in health problems. Bugs and rodents can bite, and those bites can become infected. If they are so unfortunate as to live in the worst of inner-city housing, the urban poor can experience living conditions approaching those of the developing world.

One particular danger in the urban poor's private rental housing is lead. It is in the dust and dirt, in pipes with lead solder, and especially in the house paint. Lead-based paint has not been sold in the United States since 1978, but it lurks in many older structures in the inner city, sometimes under more recent paint jobs. Chips from the lead-based paint appear on the floors, in the windowsills and jambs, and in the soil adjacent to the houses. The lead itself cannot be seen with the naked eye, but it can poison those who ingest or inhale paint chips and dust.

In the United States, the groups most at risk for lead exposure are impoverished city dwellers and recent immigrants, and the resulting lead-paint poisoning can cause serious illness.[26] Children in these groups are the most vulnerable since they sometimes eat paint chips and routinely put their fingers in their mouths. Researchers have in fact found that children living in high-poverty zip codes are more likely to have elevated lead levels in their blood than are children in more affluent zip codes.[27] These lead levels can increase over time and cause greater and greater problems for children's developing nervous systems and organs. Complications include but are not limited to constipation, irritability, drowsiness, hearing loss, slower body growth, seizures, and behavioral and attention problems resulting in difficulties at school.

Although public funding is always difficult to come by, public-health officials have launched hundreds of programs designed to identify and abate the lead hazard in inner-city housing. Lobbyists have also succeeded in alerting the United States Congress to the problem. In 1992, Congress enacted the Residential Lead-Based Paint Hazard Reduction Act.[28] The act requires landlords to inform tenants of any lead-based paint hazards before allowing tenants to sign leases. In fact, landlords have at their disposal a federally approved disclosure form prepared by the Environmental Protection Agency. If a landlord violates the act, the landlord may be assessed a civil penalty of up to $11,000 per violation and also be required to pay a tenant up to three times the amount of any damages the tenant had finding a new place, moving to it, and setting up house.

How much has the notification requirement accomplished? Many poor tenants do not know of the requirement or want to risk losing an apartment by asking about lead-based paint. My own children are not poor, but I know from watching two of them rent multiple apartments in Chicago and New York City that many landlords are only too willing to leave the notification forms in their back pockets. Some landlords purport, perhaps honestly, to have no knowledge of the federal statute.

People who have lead poisoning or have watched their children suffer from it could of course initiate a personal injury action against their landlords. In litigation related to lead-paint poisoning, the tenant could claim that the landlord's negligence had accidentally caused the lead paint to chip or otherwise deteriorate, and as a result, the tenant or the tenant's family member had sustained a personal injury. That injury, arguably, could merit compensation for inconvenience, pain and suffering, and medical bills. In the case of severe lead-paint poisoning, the latter could be immense.

Unfortunately, personal injury lawsuits of this sort are difficult to win. People alleging they have suffered personal injuries have to file their claims within the statutorily allowed time frames and also show that specific landlords in the chains of ownership were responsible for their injuries. Then, too, many inner-city landlords—especially those of the mom-and-pop variety—do not have what lawyers routinely call "deep pockets." That is, the landlords do not have enough assets to make the large payments personal injury cases involving lead-paint poisoning might dictate.

Starting in the 1990s, local governments in various states argued that paint companies had created a public nuisance in the form of lead-paint poisoning in the inner city. The claimants asked that the companies pay substantial damages and that the monies be used for lead-based paint abatement, an expensive and time-consuming process that involves literally steaming and scraping off the old paint. Courts in California were receptive to the argument and ordered three paint companies to pay $1.1 billion into an abatement fund, but this ruling is an outlier. Courts in a half dozen other states rejected the application of public nuisance notions to the problem of lead-paint poisoning, noting that lead-based paint was a legitimate product when the paint companies sold it and that the paint companies no longer legally owned or controlled the paint when people contracted lead poisoning.[29] Hence, claims that called for corporate accountability and could have affected large swaths of inner city crashed on the shoals of legal principles and the reasoning of the market economy.

In their classic study of law in the lives of the "welfare poor," a subgroup of the urban poor, the researchers found that "the law is all over."[30] But that is not to say that law's relationship to the urban poor's health is necessarily a positive one. Although everyone is aware of the unhealthy ramifications of bars and liquor stores, discount tobacco outlets, and dumps, brownfields, and hazardous waste sites, state and local lawmaking authorities blithely continue to license them. In fact, lawmakers are usually nonplussed that a disproportionate number of these taxpaying businesses and establishments are in the inner city. In their annual budgets, lawmakers also fail to satisfactorily fund the parks and housing that the urban poor would need if they ever hoped to achieve greater collective health. Then, too, even when lawmakers seem poised to address problems related to the urban poor's physical environment and concomitant health problems, they fail to prioritize their legal initiatives. Just as state and local governments seem to have lost interest in their own housing codes they enacted during the 1960s, Congress has backed off such promising initiatives as the Urban Park and Recreation Recovery Program and the Residential Lead-Based Paint Hazard Reduction Act.

Unhealthy Norms and Activities

When public-health scholars assert that "place matters" with regard to a population sector's health, they have in mind not only the physical setting but also the norms and activities in that physical setting. Hence, the urban poor's health problems in part derive from their neighborhoods and housing *and* from their norms and activities in those neighborhoods and housing. Just as law and legal institutions played numerous roles in the urban poor's unhealthy physical environment, law and legal institutions interrelate with the urban poor's unhealthy norms and activities.

As previously mentioned, those unsympathetic to the urban poor often see their unhealthy pursuits as a matter of choice. But just how much "choice" do the urban poor have? Many of the unhealthy activities and undertakings begin when inner-city residents are young, and we normally question the young's ability to choose maturely and intelligently. Then, too, many of the young follow the lead of adult "role models," and some of these supposedly exemplary adults might actually be engaging in the unhealthy activities they started when they were young and immature.

As for the adults in general, certain of their activities and undertakings develop into severe compulsiveness and perhaps even addiction. Addicts are comparable to children in that we question their ability to make decisions thoughtfully and intelligently. Some of the urban poor come to "need" whatever it is that is making them sick, and we should agree that when matters reach this state, something more complicated than "choice" is controlling the decisions people make.

More generally, the pursuits of the urban poor are compromised by the extraordinary number of stressors in their lives, most of which are in part prompted and facilitated by law. Stressors cause anxiety and lead the urban poor to lose sleep, miss appointments, misjudge expectations, and generally live on the edge. The stressors among those living in poverty in fact compound and build on one another. Bad physical and psychological health can result.

Stressful occurrences and developments are ubiquitous and include vandalism, littering, drug sales, and menacing people "hanging out." Residents of the inner city not only see actual violence being perpetrated but also encounter reminders of the violence in the form of unofficial shrines, memorials, and the like. Those moldy piles of stuffed animals that dot the inner city, after all, mark places where somebody was killed. One study explored how even the frequent sight of rats was a stressor among residents of the inner city.[31]

Some of the causes of stress are neither human malefactors nor rodents. The urban poor also have abundant stressful interactions with building managers, landlords, and also government officials such as police, welfare workers, and child welfare investigators. These interactions wear one down, and it appears that inordinate exposure of mothers in disadvantaged neighborhoods to "preconception stressful life events (PSLEs)" contributes to prematurity and low birth weights for babies.[32]

Some of the stressors involve instability and the feelings of uncertainty that go along with it. Matthew Desmond, a Princeton sociologist and winner of a prestigious MacArthur Fellowship, conducted a study of eviction in Milwaukee, Wisconsin. He found that over a two-year period approximately one-eighth of Milwaukee renters went through at least one forced move due to landlord foreclosure, building condemnation, and especially eviction.[33] The evictions fell most heavily on poor women of color. While women from the predominantly African American inner city make up only 9 percent of the city's population, those women made up 30 percent of all evicted tenants. "Among Milwaukee renters, over 1 in 5 black women report having been evicted in their adult lives, compared with 1 in 12 Hispanic and 1 in 15 white women."[34]

Evictions are terribly stressful for individuals who are evicted as well as for their friends, family members, and communities. Eviction destabilizes people who have invested in making their apartments feel like home and getting to know their neighbors. Eviction-related anxiety can lead to depression and, in isolated cases, suicide.[35] Evictions and relocations disrupt daycare arrangements and school enrollment, and, more generally, evictions can wreck whatever social networks the evicted person has developed.[36] An eviction can destabilize an apartment building and even an inner-city block, and the eviction can cause trouble in the new block where the evicted person takes up residence. In general, widespread evictions are bad for neighborhoods and for social capital.[37]

Legal documents, standards, and institutions are of course central in these stressful, destabilizing evictions. The lease is a venerable property-law document that dates back to early modern England if not earlier, and assuming the lease is properly drafted and signed, the lease terms control what happens if tenants are rowdy or fail to pay their rent in a timely manner. The police and the courts stand ready to support the landlord if the tenant is uncooperative. Given landlord-tenant law's forcefulness and the speed with which it can be applied, landlord-tenant law can cast a large shadow, under which de facto informal evictions can take place. In most cities, "off-the-books" evictions most likely outnumber formal ones.[38]

In addition to moves within inner-city communities, a great deal of stressful movement occurs into and out of the communities. Immigrant subcommunities, of course, are constantly welcoming new arrivals, many of whom are poorly educated and unable to speak English. Furthermore, as mentioned in chapter 1, large numbers of young men move frequently from the inner city to prison after being convicted of crimes and then move back into the inner city after having done their time. The movement of these men alters domestic responsibilities and disrupts both marriages and intimate relationships. Parenting grows more difficult, as children are uncertain about authority and chains of command. In some situations, children end up being placed informally with relatives or formally in foster care, and in the worst of situations children head off to juvenile detention facilities or even to the same jails and prisons that their parents themselves occupied.[39]

Excessive alcohol consumption and drug use are the most obvious behaviors and activities contributing to poor health. As I noted earlier, duly licensed and properly zoned alcohol outlets are among the most common businesses in the inner city, and these bars and liquor stores contribute to alcohol abuse virtually as a matter of course. Avid drinkers, after all, are the alcohol outlets' best customers. Poverty ratios are clearly associated with alcohol problems, and both alcoholism and liver problems can and do follow on the heels of heavy drinking.[40]

Drugs are also widely available in the inner city, albeit not through licensed outlets. Addiction can result, and depending on which drug is being used, secondary health problems can also rear their heads. Those who "choose" to inject heroin run the special risk of contracting HIV/AIDS from dirty needles. A study completed in San Francisco demonstrated that neighborhoods that were poorer than surrounding areas also had larger clusters of heroin users and, sadly, higher rates of HIV infection. Furthermore, the data suggest that poverty rather than race was the key among the neighborhoods studied.[41] Researchers in Atlanta, meanwhile, found HIV to be associated with higher levels of poverty and even identified a single geographic cluster that contained 60 percent of all the HIV cases in the entire metropolitan area.[42]

While members of the general public might be well aware that alcoholism and drug use are more prevalent among the poor and working poor, they might be surprised that cigarette smoking is as well. At the turn of the twenty-first century, people living below the poverty line were roughly 50 percent more likely to smoke than those who lived at or above the poverty line.[43] Since then, the overall smoking rates have continued to drop, but people living below the poverty line are now 66 percent more likely to smoke than those at or above the poverty line. One particular indication that smoking has increasingly become a problem concentrated among the poor is that about a third of those Americans insured by Medicaid smoke compared to only 13 percent of those with private insurance.[44]

One revealing aspect of the law's involvement with smoking involves public housing. While the American Lung Association estimates that 17 percent of the adult population now smokes, the estimate for those living in public housing is a striking 40 percent. In hopes of protecting the health of both these smokers and their neighbors and family members, HUD has announced that as of July 31, 2018, cigarettes, cigars, pipes, and hookahs will be banned from public housing's apartments, common areas, offices, and outdoor areas within 25 feet of a given project. Hence, an important legal institution is stepping in to help poor smokers, but at the same time the law is facially discriminating against the poor living in public housing. People with enough money to own their own homes or rent private apartments remain free to smoke themselves into early graves.

The urban poor, and especially poor African Americans, are unfortunately three times as likely to smoke menthol cigarettes. The latter produce a soothing sensation in the throat, and unfortunately, people who smoke menthol cigarettes inhale more deeply and for longer periods of time than do smokers of non-menthol cigarettes.[45] Then, too, "hardcore smoking," defined as more than fifteen cigarettes a day, is also more prevalent among the poor, while attempts to quit smoking are less common and less likely to succeed.[46] Due to this smoking-related behavior, the urban poor have a greater likelihood of asthma, heart disease, stroke, and especially lung cancer due to direct or secondhand inhalation of cigarette smoke.

Massive public-health education campaigns have resulted in reductions in cigarette use *and* in morbidity and mortality attributable to smoking, and some of these efforts seemed especially designed for the urban poor. In 2009, for example, the newly enacted Family Smoking Prevention and Tobacco Control Act required that cigarette packaging include color graphics depicting the negative health consequences of smoking.[47] Poor and poorly educated Americans, the thinking went, were less attentive to the conventional textual warnings on cigarette packaging than middle- and upper-class Americans were, and graphic images might be more effective warnings as deterrents. Relatively large color pictures of diseased lungs or haggard, nicotine-addicted people smoking through holes in their tracheas might literally be eye-catching.

Five tobacco companies, not surprisingly, challenged the graphic warnings requirements, and their challenges were successful. Invoking constitutional guarantees, as did the majority of the courts that considered public nuisance actions against lead-based paint companies, the United States Court of Appeals in Washington, DC, tossed out the graphic warnings in 2012. The United States Congress, the court said, had not stated a "substantial interest" driving the regulations or shown that the graphic warnings advanced the goal of smoking reduction. Hence, according to the court, the Congress had unconstitutionally restricted the tobacco companies' commercial speech rights.[48] Even the conduct of "Big Tobacco," it seems, occurs under the umbrella of protected individual rights and liberties.

Another problematic inner-city behavior involves diet. As I mentioned earlier, the urban poor tend to shop in corner grocery stores in which fresh fruit and vegetables are scarce and/or unappealingly displayed. More fruit and vegetables would be healthy for shoppers and their families, but the foods many buy instead are decidedly less so. They include canned, packaged, and frozen foods with high salt and sugar content, and, to wash things down, a range of sugary soft drinks.

Diets of this sort contribute to obesity, which in turn increases the likelihood of chronic diseases and conditions such as type 2 diabetes, ischemic heart disease, stroke, gall bladder disease, sleep apnea, and arthritis. Much has been written regarding the nation's "obesity epidemic," but, for purposes at hand, underscore that the epidemic has ravaged different sectors of the population inequitably. The prevalence of obesity increases the poorer a population is, and this is especially true for women. A troubling 42 percent of women with income below 130 percent of poverty are obese, and this trend is similar across racial and ethnic groups.[49] As for children, obesity rates increased by 10 percent for American children aged ten to seventeen between 2003 and 2007, but the rate increased 23 percent for low-income children during the same period. Rates of what is called "severe obesity" were, as of 2009, roughly 1.7 times greater for poor children and adolescents than for other children and adolescents.[50]

Financial considerations are contributors to the urban poor's unhealthy obesity. Nutritionists have pointed out that healthier foods cost more than food with loads of fat and sugar. A carton of orange juice, for example, costs four times as much as a comparably sized jug of sugary soda. The former, of course, is much healthier than the latter in the long run, but in the short run the sugary soda fulfills energy needs at a lower cost. The low cost of energy-dense foods and drinks helps explain why the urban poor purchase and consume them. "The key variable, however, is not the macronutrient composition of the diet; rather, what might predict obesity is low diet cost."[51]

The unhealthy food that has created the most concern and led to the most-noticed law reform efforts is the sugary soft drink. According to New York City health commissioner D. Thomas Farley, sugary soft drinks are "the largest source of added sugars in our diets."[52] Forty-six percent of the residents of the Bronx consume at least one sugary soft drink a day, and if any one of those residents simply drank a 16-ounce serving rather than a 20-ounce serving, he or she would save 14,600 calories a year—the equivalent of seventy chocolate candy bars.[53]

Efforts to control the urban poor's consumption of sugary soft drinks in hopes of reducing obesity have included taxes and also limits on the size of these drinks, but these efforts have been challenged in the legislatures and the courts. The beverage industry invested $7.7 million in hopes of defeating a soda tax in San Francisco and still another $1.4 million across the bay in Berkeley, a city of only 117,000. The beverage industry spent over $117 million nationally to stop or roll back soda taxes between 2009 and 2014.[54]

Mayor Michael Bloomberg encountered the power and determination of the fast-food chains and beverage companies when he tried to use local ordinances to control consumption of sugary soft drinks in New York City. Bloomberg proposed in 2013 that restaurants, delis, movie theaters, and sports venues not be allowed to sell sugary soft drinks in containers larger than 16 ounces. The New York City Board of Health enthusiastically endorsed Bloomberg's proposal. However, opponents including the American Beverage Association, the soft drink industry's trade group, argued in court that the 16-ounce restriction arbitrarily interfered with consumer preferences. For obvious self-interested reasons, the soft drink producers thought consumers should have unrestricted opportunities to buy and drink what they wanted.

The New York State Court of Appeals, the state's highest court, vacated the prohibition, saying the Board of Health had exceeded the scope of its regulatory authority. Foes of the "nanny state" counted the decision as a victory, and consumers were once again free to drain their "Big Gulps."[55] One academic even saw the Court of Appeals's decision as an important stop sign for unduly aggressive public health regulators.[56]

In reality, the proposed restrictions might have accomplished very little. Even if Mayor Bloomberg had carried the day, consumers could have purchased large jugs of sugary soft drinks at grocery stores instead of fast-food restaurants, and even at the latter, consumers could simply have purchased two 16-ounce cups of soda instead of a 32-ounce jug. It is difficult to believe that the Bloomberg plan would have altered the status of sugary soft drinks as a popular consumer item, especially among the urban poor. When pressed on the effectiveness of his plan, Bloomberg himself somewhat sheepishly admitted it was only a "speed bump" designed to get consumers to slow down in their buying and, presumably, their drinking of sugary soft drinks.[57]

What's more, Bloomberg's proposals might actually have played into the common attribution of obesity to the personal failures of obese people. These people, Bloomberg and the reformers seemed to be saying, are so weak that they cannot control themselves when it comes to sugary soft drinks. The government is therefore doing them a favor by limiting how many ounces of sugary soft drinks they can purchase and consume.[58]

Law, Wealth, and Urban Poverty

The inner city's shabby and deteriorating physical environment as well as its problematic norms and activities undeniably constitute unhealthy social conditions, and law plays its role in this unfortunate situation. But is it possible to look even further upstream and ask why it is people actually live in this "place," that is, in this type of physical and social environment? On the most fundamental level, the urban poor do not move to a better physical and social place because they lack the assets to do so. They are too poor. Without escaping poverty, the urban poor will not find a better place, and without dramatic changes in their place, the urban poor will not be able to improve their collective health or reduce the health inequity.

Like other Americans, the urban poor can travel two basic avenues to wealth: capital and income from capital, and wages and wage substitutes. Unfortunately for the urban poor, they have almost no capital and therefore no income from capital. At best, a poor African American has a couple of thousand dollars in a low-interest savings or checking account. An impoverished Latino might also own assorted pots and pans, a laptop, a television, and some inexpensive beds and furniture. For both of these individuals, wealth is truly negligible. For the poorest Americans, prominent economist Thomas Piketty has observed, "the very notions of wealth and capital are relatively abstract. . . . The inescapable reality is wealth is so concentrated that a large segment of society is virtually unaware of its existence, so that some people imagine that it belongs to surreal or mysterious entities."[59]

This means that the urban poor must look to the second of the two possibilities for accumulating wealth, namely, wages and wage substitutes. However, the urban poor's undercompensated labor or complete lack of employment greatly deflates hopes of wealth acquisition through wages. Under most current laws, the working poor are not guaranteed much of a wage, and those who are unemployed cannot expect much in the way of state support.

As already pointed out, no bright line exists between the truly impoverished and the working poor. Many of those in poverty temporarily take up low-paying jobs or look on with approval when family members take such jobs. The largest numbers of minimum-wage jobs are in child care, in home health care, and especially in restaurants. One indicator of the difficulty of living on pay from these jobs is that nearly three-quarters of those receiving public support are either employed or members of a family headed by someone who is employed. According to one study, 46 percent of child care workers, 48 percent of home health-care workers, and 52 percent of fast-food workers receive some variety of public assistance.[60] Government support, in some sense, subsidizes low-wage employers; people can work for them and attempt to get the rest of what they need from the state.[61]

Critics frequently point out how small the federally required minimum wage is. It currently stands at $7.25 per hour, and a full-time employee working at that wage would earn $15,080 annually—an amount above the poverty line for an individual but well below the poverty line for a family of four. If one adjusts for inflation, the current minimum wage is actually much lower than the peak minimum wage, which occurred in 1968.[62] In the opinion of many, the federal minimum wage is one of the stingiest of any wealthy country.[63]

In reality, though, the federal minimum wage is only one part of the story, because what people receive as a minimum wage is established by a combination of federal, state, and local laws. In 2018, almost two-thirds of the states had set minimum wages higher than the federal minimum, with Massachusetts and Washington having the highest at $11.00. Chicago, Minneapolis, New York City, Oakland, and other cities also have minimum wages higher than not only the federal minimum wage but also their individual states' higher minimums. San Francisco and Seattle have set their minimum wages at $15.00, more than twice the federal minimum.

What impact would a higher national minimum wage have on the urban poor? Economists heatedly debate the question and point to the many variables other than just a possible increase in the minimum wage. Would it apply to all low-wage jobs or just to, for example, fast-food workers? Does it make a difference what percentage labor costs are of local businesses' overall costs? Most importantly, what difference does the actual size of the proposed minimum wage hike make? After all, past hikes have been much smaller than what some cities have in recent years required.[64]

Overall, raising the minimum wage would obviously have the greatest impact on those currently employed, on the so-called working poor, but there would be ramifications for others as well. According to the Congressional Budget Office, which undertakes nonpartisan analysis for the United States Congress:

> Increasing the minimum wage would have two principal effects on low-wage workers. Most of them would receive higher pay that would increase their family's income, and some of those families would see their income rise above the federal poverty threshold. But some jobs for low-wage workers would probably be eliminated, the income for most workers who became jobless would fall substantially, and the share of low-wage workers who were employed would probably fall slightly.[65]

As for those currently unemployed—the majority of the urban poor—a higher minimum wage would obviously not lift any of them temporarily or permanently out of poverty.

Medicaid, food stamps, and the earned-income tax credit are all important to the urban poor as they struggle to make ends meet, but the type of public support designed to at least partially substitute for wages is Aid to Families with Dependent Children (AFDC) or, more recently, Temporary Assistance for Needy Families (TANF). The latter programs strike Americans as "welfare." According to the welfare scholar and law professor Tonya Brito, "Notwithstanding the broad range of governmental aid programs that exist, at a gut level when people say *welfare* they mean AFDC and its successor program TANF."[66]

Although the amount of venom spewed about supposedly extravagant welfare payments and lazy welfare recipients could fill several large barrels, the reality is that the United States does not have that much of a welfare state. Benefits and entitlements among European social democracies have traditionally been much larger and remain so even with contemporary European budget woes and worries about large numbers of refugees thought to be welfare-seekers.[67]

The reasons for the limited American welfare program involve both financing methods and, more generally, American attitudes regarding welfare and welfare recipients. Dating back to the 1930s, the nation had chosen to finance its welfare system chiefly through an income tax rather than through a national sales tax. The latter would admittedly have been more regressive for the poor, but the income tax presents another set of problems. Americans tend to be leery of and even hostile to an income tax, and elected lawmakers are hesitant to expand and promote it. This makes it difficult to use the income tax for public expenditures, welfare among them.[68]

As for general attitudes, Americans have been leery of welfare for almost a century, and political leaders have pitched to that leeriness. The 1930s-style liberal Franklin D. Roosevelt, who led the nation during the Great Depression and fathered the New Deal, characterized welfare as a narcotic and a destroyer of human spirit. In the 1980s, the conservative Ronald Reagan promoted a welfare reduction program called "Up from Dependency."[69] And in the twenty-first century, Representative Paul Ryan from Wisconsin, while serving as the Republican Speaker of the House, joined the welfare-berating chorus, braying loudly about how welfare is responsible for many aspects of what he takes to be a deterioration of the social fabric. The argument that welfare is more of a problem than a solution "has solidified into a core tenet influencing social policy not only in the United States but also around the world."[70]

Middle- and upper-class Americans usually assume their fellow Americans are autonomous men and women who, if they apply themselves, can realize their full potential. Most Americans assume that individuals are responsible for their own success or failure. This attitude is wildly different from that of many Europeans, who are more likely to emphasize structural explanations of poverty over notions of individual responsibility. Most Americans also take for granted that there are "distinctions between 'deserving poor' (those who have not been able to provide for themselves because of circumstances beyond their control) and the 'undeserving poor' (able-bodied individuals who do not work)."[71] If you give welfare to the "undeserving poor," many Americans think, they will become even lazier, never work that hard, and even persuade the working poor to join in the supposed comfort of a state-supported easy life.

The centerpiece of current American welfare policy dates from the 1990s.

As I reported in chapter 3, Bill Clinton promised during his quest for the presidency in 1992 "to end welfare as we know it."[72] He then kept his promise by guiding the Personal Responsibility and Work Opportunity Reconciliation Act (PRWORA) through Congress. Under the new law, TANF in effect replaced AFDC as the nation's preeminent welfare program, a change sometimes missed by rabid critics of welfare who continue to attack AFDC.

The PRWORA legislation and the substitution of TANF for AFDC dramatically changed the ways the states receive welfare money. For starters, the legislation ended the prior use of matching grants and turned instead to block grants. Current block grants have not adjusted for inflation, and as a result, the block grants have lost more than a third of their buying power over a twenty-year period. More subtly, the block-grant approach provides ways for the states to spend money from the grants on government programs other than cash payments to the poor. "On average, states use only about half of their funds under the TANF program to fund its core objectives: Provide the poor with cash aid or child care, or help connect them to jobs."[73]

Who might actually expect to receive TANF payments? Eligibility standards, income limits, and benefit rules are all different than they used to be, and the most striking changes involve limits on how long recipients might receive welfare and their obligation to work. Hence, a recipient could be cut off when his or her authorized time to receive welfare expired, and/or sanctioned for failing to seek or find employment. The overall effect was to end welfare as an entitlement for mothers with minor children, and to make it into sort of a financial holding pattern for employment seeking, which, if successful, would end dependency. Even against the backdrop of a regime that was already parsimonious, TANF was "a fundamental redirection in government support systems for American families."[74]

Some, of course, claim that the changeover to TANF has been a huge success in that it has reduced the number of people on welfare, and it is true that in an overall sense the welfare rolls have shrunk. But at the same time, only 26 percent of impoverished families with children receive cash payments, and this figure has dropped from 68 percent at the time TANF was instituted. What's more, poor families that continue to receive welfare only receive about one quarter of the amount necessary to lift them out of poverty.[75]

Overall, then, when we travel all the way "upstream" to poverty itself, we see how federal wage and welfare laws contribute to the relative but nevertheless severe poverty that leads the urban poor to reside in an unhealthy physical and social environment. In the contemporary regime, the richest 10 percent of the population owns more than 70 percent of the wealth, and half of that is owned by the richest 1 percent. Poor Americans, by contrast, have virtually no wealth.[76]

While the urban poor suffer from a lack of wealth and being impoverished, they also suffer from the nation's economic inequality. The latter—the way some people have a lot more than some other people—is in itself debilitating. While the United States as a whole is affluent, *New York Times* financial columnist Eduardo Porter is correct in noting that the nation "does an exceptionally dismal job of sharing wealth broadly among Americans."[77] It is hard to believe, but economic inequality in the United States is at its highest level since the 1930s.[78]

As social epidemiologists have pointed out, the greater the degree of economic inequality, the steeper the gradient of health inequity.[79] This appears to be true internationally, among different regions within a country, and even within given metropolitan areas. Hence, the poor in the United States may have lower health status than comparably poor groups in Japan, a country with less income inequality. The wealthy in the United States may not live as long as the wealthy in Sweden, another country with less income inequality. "Stated simply, it is not just the size of the economic pie but how the pie is shared that matters for population health."[80]

Specific findings are complex and somewhat contested, but researchers have found an association between economic inequality and the unhealthy consumption of cigarettes and marijuana.[81] In addition, other studies have found an association between economic inequality and the frequency of alcohol consumption, volume of alcohol consumed, drinking to get drunk, and death from alcohol-attributed illnesses.[82] Researchers even demonstrated that mortality itself is related to a society's degree of economic inequality. In particular, levels of mortality appear higher in societies with pronounced economic inequality.[83]

Is there anything about the nation's economic inequality that is especially harmful to the urban poor's health? One hypothesis is that the poor compare themselves to those who are better off, and the comparison spawns disappointment and even despondency, attitudes that are hardly conducive to good health.[84] Another, more subtle theory is that the urban poor sense that they will never be able to lift themselves off the socioeconomic floor, that they will never be able to get anywhere. This could lead to less investment in health and less determination to lead healthy lives.[85]

Regardless of the pathways and connections between economic inequality and health inequity, the unhealthy ramifications of income inequality are unlikely to decline. If anything, economic inequality is worsening. As a result, the comparatively poor health of the urban poor will grow even worse. The type of extensive reform of wage and welfare laws that would be necessary to reduce urban poverty in itself and economic inequality in general is not even in the discussion stage.

Using Law to Change Unhealthy Social Conditions

From the perspective of the insightful social epidemiologists I mentioned at the beginning of this chapter, the urban poor's social conditions contribute mightily to their unsatisfactory collective health. If new laws could be enacted to change the social conditions, the health of the urban poor might conceivably be improved. If current laws could be altered in substantial ways, the urban poor might have better health outcomes and achieve greater health equity.

The problem is not that bold legal changes are impossible to imagine. The idea of a universal minimum guaranteed income, for example, is occasionally discussed, and it would give all adults a respectable level of income regardless of whether they were employed.[86] African American spokesmen, including but not limited to those in the Black Lives Matter movement, have repeatedly suggested a multifaceted "Marshall Plan" for the inner city.[87] Both of these ideas would have the potential to dramatically change the urban poor's social conditions and collective health.

Unfortunately, these kinds of ideas find little traction in mainstream political debate, much less in Congress. Opponents of the laws say a universal guaranteed income or inner-city "Marshall Plan" would entail governmental overreaching, paternalistic excess, and wasteful expenditures of public monies. Poor Americans, the argument goes, should not rely on handouts but rather pull themselves up by their bootstraps. In this nation, the argument continues, individuals are free to build and shape their success on their own terms, and we do not need the state floating people to the top of the socioeconomic pond.[88]

Furthermore, even more modest laws designed merely to modify the urban poor's social conditions and to thereby improve their collective health a tiny bit are likely to have minimal success or to fail completely. Law on paper, after all, is not the same thing when it plays out on the streets of town. Municipal housing codes, for example, suggest everyone will have safe and hygienic housing, but lax enforcement leaves most of the urban poor renting decrepit apartments from slumlords. Then, too, promising laws go underfunded, and pieces of federal legislation such as the Urban Park and Recreation Recovery Program and the Residential Lead-Based Paint Hazard Reduction Act have basically withered on the vine. Inner-city parks are deteriorating further, and recent tragedies in Flint, Michigan, and elsewhere remind us that lead is in the pipes as well as in the paint. What's more, law itself can stand in the way of sympathetic health-related legal changes. Ordinances and statutes intended to improve health in the inner city can collide with the constitutional promise of liberty, right to privacy, or freedom to own and use one's property as one sees fit. No graphic images will scare the urban poor away from cancerous cigarettes, menthol or otherwise, and merchants can sell sugary soft drinks by the barrel if they are so inclined.

While laws that successfully change the urban poor's social conditions and thereby produce better health outcomes are hard to find, laws contributing to poor health continue to abound. These laws are in fact intimately a part of the urban poor's lives. Those that facilitate and perpetuate poor health contribute in their own way to the containment of the urban poor. Lousy collective health can debilitate a social group and make it challenging indeed for that group to lift itself to a higher socioeconomic plateau. Tending to health problems and even just worrying about health issues make it more difficult to find the energy and wherewithal to deal with other life-management concerns. In addition, the laws, the justifications for them, and even the refusals to change them often condemn the urban poor in the process. If only the poor made better "choices," detractors and skeptics might say, they could avoid alcohol-related diabetes, disabling obesity, lung cancer, and drug addiction.

Overall, the importance of poor health should not be underestimated in an oppressive system. Law, legal proceedings, and legal institutions, meanwhile, generally contribute to the conditions that produce poor collective health. Assuming the urban poor are oppressed, law, legal proceedings, and legal institutions contribute to the urban poor's ongoing oppression. In countless direct and indirect ways, law keeps many of the urban poor in bad health and then blames them for being in that situation.

Conclusion

have used a broad understanding of law in this book concerning the ways law works for, against, and with regard to the urban poor. The preceding chapters have considered law's impact as well as its words—that is, the manner in which law plays out in social life as well as how it appears on the printed page. Then, too, "law" in the work at hand has included not only prescriptions and proscriptions but also legal proceedings as well as government agencies and legal institutions. Overall, my central question has been: How does "law" function in the lives of the urban poor?

The question is not an easy one to answer because the law acts in many ways. In the United States, laws are numerous, bordering on uncountable, and to complicate things further, the laws can overlap and collide. Sometimes the laws even negate and contradict one another. In a social-control vein, the law generally directs individual conduct and various social activities. In an expressive vein, the texts of the law as well as the words of lawmakers and government officials directly and indirectly comment on organizations, sectors of the population, social activities, and public affairs. In a legalistic society such as the United States, neither the complexity of the law nor the range of ways it works should be underestimated.

With all the complexities having been acknowledged, two pronounced tendencies nevertheless emerge in the law's functioning with regard to the urban poor: The law creates and perpetuates types of containment for the urban poor, and the law utters direct and indirect condemnations of the same sector of the population. Put in different terms, the law requires the urban poor to remain in undesirable places and social situations, and the law repeatedly criticizes the urban poor as dysfunctional and unworthy. Containment and condemnation are the most striking functional rhythms in law's relationship to the urban poor.

Criminal Justice, Housing, Family, the Marketplace, and Health

The preceding chapters scrutinized how law works for, against, and with regard to the urban poor in five basic areas—criminal justice, housing, family life, the marketplace, and health. In each of these five areas, containment is evident, and condemnation is audible. Here, in the book's conclusion, I might bring the ways law contains and condemns into higher relief.

Crime and criminal justice are what perhaps sprung first to mind, and crime and criminal justice are in fact pressing concerns among the urban poor. They are the most likely Americans to be victimized by criminal conduct, and the younger men among the urban poor are also the most likely Americans to engage in criminal conduct. However, in chapter 1, I discussed the ways the urban poor are also disproportionately labeled as criminals. While in many cases those labeled as criminals have indeed committed one or more of the criminal offenses that are alleged, the large-scale labeling of the urban poor as criminals has a powerful and lasting impact.

The labeling takes place on our streets and in our courthouses. On the streets, the police take the inner city to be an "offensible space," and they also perceive the urban poor, especially poor young men, as "good collars," that is, arrests that are likely to result in guilty pleas and convictions. Furthermore, many police have a sense of racial superiority and expect more respect than they are prepared to give. When that respect is not forthcoming, arrests are especially likely. Violence perpetrated in conjunction with these arrests or while suspects are in police custody has been so excessive as to prompt Black Lives Matter, a multifaceted national movement demanding not only changes in police conduct but also racial equality and socioeconomic empowerment.

Prosecutors, meanwhile, do not share the language, style, and attitudes of most of those who are arrested, and when they plea-bargain with public defenders representing the indigent, their biases surface. Most prosecutors and public defenders maintain a "soft" adversarial relationship, and in general, procedural fairness is achieved. However, prosecutors are more likely to charge poor defendants with more serious crimes and to encourage them to enter guilty pleas, practices one researcher has criticized as "substantive injustice."[1]

Criminal labeling is especially pronounced when incarceration takes place. The contemporary United States manages to imprison a larger percentage of its citizens than any other nation in the world, and a majority of the imprisoned come from the impoverished inner city. When an inmate has served his or her time, the label "ex-con" is likely to replace that of "felon" or "inmate," and ex-cons relinquish many of their civil rights and encounter an extraordinarily difficult time finding employment. Perhaps not surprisingly, recidivism is common, and over two-thirds of those who have done time end up back in prison.

The labels that result from being arrested, prosecuted, and imprisoned are difficult to shed, and to some extent, once poor men and women are labeled as criminals, the labels stay with them for life. Furthermore, the labeling takes place so frequently and routinely that many unreflectively consider all of the urban poor to be "criminals." That is, the criminal justice system labels individuals as criminals, and, concomitantly, the society criminalizes the urban poor as a social group. A range of processes and attributions usually work together to ostracize a group within the general population, but criminalization obviously plays a major role in marginalizing the urban poor. The law, broadly understood, contributes to making them pariahs in their own country.

In chapter 2, I considered the roles law, legal proceedings, and legal institutions play in the housing and neighborhoods in which the urban poor live. The United States Constitution includes no right to housing of any particular quality or in general, but "The Universal Declaration of Human Rights," among other documents, does include such a right.[2] Housing is a fundamental physical need, and in addition, adequate housing fulfills a personal need for space and privacy. Everyone, human rights advocates insist, should be able to find and then live decently in secure, habitable, and affordable abodes and communities.

Housing in the United States is not as insecure and ramshackle as it is in much of the developing world, but the urban poor's housing is still deplorable compared to national norms. In light of the decline of public housing and the flaws in the voucher and affordable-housing schemes, the urban poor are even more likely than they were twenty-five years ago to live in rundown rental housing in inner-city neighborhoods. Since the 1960s, almost all municipalities have enacted housing codes in hopes of improving this housing, but local officials enforce them selectively and sometimes ignore them completely. By all accounts, the codes are ineffective. According to some, strict and aggressive enforcement of the codes would lead more landlords to abandon inner-city properties and thereby exacerbate the already troubling shortage of inexpensive rental housing.

Why do the urban poor remain in apartments with creepy roaches and diseased rodents? Why do they put up with lead-based paint chips and dust as well as defective wiring and furnaces? Part of the answer is that their options for living elsewhere are limited. Newer outlying suburbs in many metropolitan areas have effectively engaged in exclusionary zoning in order to keep out the urban poor.[3] Suburbs can no longer do this with direct reference to race, but since African Americans are disproportionately overrepresented among the urban poor, efforts to "zone out" the urban poor might surely include racist undercurrents.

How is modern-day exclusionary zoning accomplished? Some zoning boards and local elected officials make no room for apartment complexes or mobile home parks in the plans for their municipalities and villages. More subtly, local officials use minimum lot sizes, large frontage and setback requirements, and limits on the number of bedrooms per housing unit to preclude the development of inexpensive rental housing. Local officials often rationalize this exclusionary zoning as financially prudent or as aesthetically sensitive. Mobile homes depreciate quickly, the argument goes, and large apartment complexes are eyesores. In addition, some suburban zoning boards quite simply admit they want to keep "the city" and "urban life" out of their communities, and unfortunately for the urban poor, they personify both.

Exclusionary zoning not only keeps the urban poor out of the suburbs but also keeps them in the inner-city neighborhoods where they currently reside. Poverty neighborhoods, while rundown and sometimes dangerous, can be useful to the middle and upper classes. The neighborhoods are locales for prostitution and drug sales, and certain suburbanites are known to drive to the inner city for either or both. Poverty neighborhoods, weak in political clout and limited in social capital, are also frequently sites for toxic waste disposal and concentrations of rehabilitation centers and halfway houses. The police can patrol the borders of these neighborhoods, and on a good day, members of the middle and upper classes do not even have to think of the people who live there.

Intimate, loving family life often strikes Americans as a sanctuary of sorts from the stressful realities of social life, and, imbued with an attitude of this sort, the urban poor treasure their families as much as members of the middle and upper classes do. Yet the urban poor also know that their reluctance to marry, their approach to child support, and their child-rearing arrangements are suspect. Members of the middle and upper classes are leery of the urban poor's family life, and the suspicions are evident in the laws, legal proceedings, and legal institutions that attempt to channel them into different approaches to family life.[4]

As I mentioned in chapter 3, sometimes this channeling involving family life is successful, and just as frequently it is not. Sometimes the law, legal proceedings, and legal institutions channel the urban poor toward marriage and toward the faithful paying of child support, but established practices and attitudes often obstruct the channels. Urban poverty, after all, is deeply engrained in social life, and the practices and attitudes associated with poverty are difficult to alter.

The law related to families also purports to be especially concerned with the well-being of children, and American public policy self-righteously supports the healthy development of our society's children. Children, our politicians earnestly remind us, are the key to our society's future. We have to invest in them so that they can grow, almost like living mutual funds. Indeed, states and municipalities have sprawling "child welfare" programs and offices, in which thousands of workers are supposedly engaged in promoting the well-being of American children.

In reality, "child welfare" offices concentrate their efforts on ferreting out child abuse and neglect, and the urban poor dominate among parents investigated for neglecting their children, and also among parents whose parental rights are terminated. Sometimes, charges of neglect and termination of parental rights rest basically on the fact that parents are poor and live their lives like poor people. Sometimes, poverty prevents inner-city residents from effectively thwarting efforts to terminate their parental rights. Throughout "child welfare" investigations and proceedings, many officials and administrators cannot hide their disapproval of how the urban poor parent their children.

Sometimes children in the child welfare system become available for adoption, and law, legal proceedings, and legal institutions are geared to moving those adoptions forward. These adoptions almost always involve poor and working-class children moving to middle- and upper-class homes. Often, the adoptions are truly in the "best interests" of individual children, but the system also rationalizes the adoptions by denigrating the urban poor's parenting. In particular, individualized, possessive motherhood is assumed to be in short supply among the urban poor, and the families of the poor are insufficiently nuclear for middle- and upper-class taste. If children can switch from poor to middle- and upper-class families, these children are thought to be "lucky."

Regardless of the success of the channeling involving marriage and child support, or of the likelihood of adoption, family law for the urban poor has normative dimensions. In purporting to route the urban poor to something more acceptable and in deploring the urban poor for the way they maintain their families, the law implicitly and explicitly condemns the urban poor for the families they try to maintain and for the private, intimate lives they lead.

The familiar notion of a "marketplace" is as much metaphorical as it is actual, but Americans do in fact use money to acquire the goals and services they need and desire. Advertisers and marketers make "soft," nonbinding promises that the goods and services they are hawking will both fulfill the purposes at hand and, more generally, provide purchasers with contentment and happiness.[5] As I described in chapter 4, the urban poor are among those venturing forth from their homes and the sanctuaries of their families into the marketplace. In fact, the urban poor can be especially eager consumers, as they seek the goods and services that can relieve their deprivation and also elevate their social status.

Unfortunately for the urban poor, they routinely turn to small, cramped corner stores in their neighborhoods, where they encounter higher prices than do middle- and upper-class consumers shopping in assorted malls and super-stores. Some have dubbed the price differential a "ghetto tax," and although it is not actually a tax, it is emblematic of the extra financial burdens that the urban poor bear in the marketplace. Furthermore, the urban poor often do not own motor vehicles and cannot rely on declining mass-transit systems. As a result, they find it difficult to get from one store to another and to do anything that might be called "comparative shopping." The so-called ghetto tax is almost impossible to avoid.

When it comes to larger consumer goods, the urban poor can shop at rent-to-own outlets, which promise the urban poor they can come to own flat screens and gas grills if they make large enough rental payments for a long enough period of time. Only a minority of poor consumers succeed in reaching this goal, and if poor consumers added up what it would cost to own a commodity through rent-to-own, they would realize the cost is a great deal higher than it would be in a conventional retail store. If the urban poor lack the cash to launch a rent-to-own transaction, they might instead borrow money at extraordinarily high rates from payday lenders and title pawns. These businesses are as crafty as rent-to-own outlets at exploiting the urban poor.

All three of these businesses employ highly refined and legally enforceable contracts, and the proprietors of rent-to-own stores, payday lending outlets, and title-loan operations realize that these contracts are at the heart of their business models. Well-intentioned judges and legislators have attempted to limit and restrict the operations of these businesses and dictate changes in the standard contracts, but the businesses are usually able to adjust their business operations and to continue thriving. The efforts of the well-intentioned judges and legislators even have the unintended effect of legitimizing blatantly exploitative businesses.

So it goes in the context of consumer capitalism, one might say, but rent-to-own operations, payday lenders, and title pawns not only exploit the urban poor but also perpetuate their poverty. Buoyed by the law, the rent-to-own, payday-lending, and title-pawn businesses hoist the poor onto a debt treadmill. You can burn calories running on a treadmill, but it cannot be ridden out of poverty. The exploitative rent-to-own, payday-lending, and title-pawn businesses help confine the urban poor indefinitely in their undesirable, subordinate socioeconomic situation.

In chapter 5, I turned to the health of the urban poor and underscored that it is worse than that of almost any other sector of the American population. Different interests and groups—some sympathetic to the urban poor and some unsympathetic—have attempted to explain this phenomenon, but social epidemiologists have the most insightful read on things. They tell us that if we want to understand the health of a sector of the population, we have to travel "upstream" to the fundamental social conditions in which that sector of the population lives. In the case of the urban poor, these fundamental social conditions include the poverty in which the poor live and also their undesirable spot on the gradient of wealth distribution. Poverty itself leaves little room to maneuver, and festering about the greater comparative wealth of others is frustrating, alienating, and—ultimately—unhealthy.

Poverty and near-poverty consign the urban poor to the deteriorating neighborhoods of the inner city and of the immediately adjacent older suburbs. In physical terms, these neighborhoods have limited recreational space, abundant liquor outlets, dilapidated housing stock, and a disproportionate percentage of "locally unwanted land uses," that is, dumps and toxic waste sites. Stated simply, the urban poor's neighborhoods are unhealthy places, and if that is not bad enough, the neighborhoods' unhealthy physical features intertwine with the unhealthy attitudes and activities of the people who live in these neighborhoods. These attitudes and activities include comparatively high levels of drug use, alcohol consumption, and cigarette smoking as well as poor eating habits, leading to obesity and a concomitant range of undesirable chronic conditions.

Law, in all its forms and variations, plays a role in the social conditions adversely affecting the health of the urban poor. Zoning and licensing ordinances legally locate the inner city's liquor stores and discount cigarette outlets. Federal statutes and local housing authorities dictate what can or cannot be done in the nation's unhealthy and dwindling public housing, and lengthy and elaborate local housing ordinances supposedly oversee the inexpensive, ramshackle rental housing. More generally, minimum wage laws and stingy welfare options leave the poor with little hope of becoming anything more than the "working poor." The fundamental social conditions of the urban poor lead to the troubling health status for that sector of the population, and law, legal proceedings, and legal institutions are intimately involved in the establishment and continuation of those conditions.

Might "law reform" change any of this? Well-intentioned reformers have succeeded in enacting laws designed to improve the fundamental social conditions and health of the urban poor, but funding for the enforcement of those laws is often lacking. What's more, law itself can hinder and eliminate health-related legal reforms. Legislation intended to help the urban poor can collide with constitutional law's understanding of liberty, privacy, and the freedom to use one's property as one sees fit. Courts and legislatures can quickly put on the brakes, sometimes pontificating in the process about everyone's personal responsibility for deciding how to conduct their lives. Horrors, many think, the "nanny state" is paternalistically overparenting us.

In general, law, legal proceedings, and legal institutions help keep the urban poor in a collectively unhealthy state that has serious ramifications, and then shift the blame for the problem to the urban poor themselves. "Good health," Georgetown University law professor Lawrence Gostin reminds us, "is fundamentally important because it is essential to the happiness, livelihood, political participation, and many of the other elements necessary for a life full of contentment and achievement."[6] To be unhealthy is to be socially and psychologically contained. What's more, lawmakers and average citizens are hardly hesitant to condemn the urban poor for the way they live. The urban poor, the thinking goes and the law reaffirms, could be a lot healthier if they simply made more thoughtful decisions.

I admit that the preceding chapters of this book concerning the law's relationship to criminal justice, housing, family life, marketplace activities, and health among the urban poor read like a multipart indictment. However, the argument is *not* that law, courts, and other legal institutions never do anything to enhance and improve the lives of the urban poor. As I noted in chapter 4, for example, the New Jersey trial and appellate courts were able to resolve the dispute involving the consumer Hilda Perez and Rent-A-Center. The courts concluded that Rent-A-Center was responsible for overcharging Perez in violation of both New Jersey's Retail Installment Act and the state's criminal usury laws. This decision set the stage for even more compensatory claims and rewards. A class of New Jersey consumers who thought they had been wronged in the same way as Perez sued Rent-A-Center, and the nation's largest rent-to-own company agreed to settle a class action lawsuit "out of court" for $109 million.[7] As I mentioned in chapter 5, no less a legislative body than the United States Congress recognized the danger lead-based paint presented in the inner city, especially for young children who eat paint chips and inhale paint dust. The Residential Lead-Based Paint Hazard Reduction Act resulted, and in keeping with that law, landlords are supposed to alert possible tenants to the lead-related dangers in their rental properties.[8]

Were rulings like that in the *Perez* litigation and legislation such as the Residential Lead-Based Paint Hazard Reduction Act common, protectors and champions of the poor would justifiably be pleased. "Look," they could say, "this is how we expect law to work." But unfortunately, law, legal proceedings, and legal institutions work in many ways other than positive, socially enriching ones. Much of what law does is mundane, and sometimes the workings of the law can be quite harmful. When it comes to the urban poor, law often contains and condemns them. The law consigns the urban poor to undesirable places and situations and simultaneously deplores them for the way they supposedly choose to live.

Containment as a legal function can restrict the urban poor to physical locations such as prisons or inner-city neighborhoods, but containment can also involve socioeconomic class and status. As I noted in the introduction to this book, the urban poor are not the "proletariat" of classical Marxist thought, but they do make up a deprived, indebted, and marginalized sector of the population. With good reason, the urban poor might take containment in this section to be permanent. They might understand their situation to be hopeless.

Containment of this sort is not conspiratorial or even consciously crafted by members of the upper classes, but containment is nevertheless extremely deleterious in contemporary society. For the most part, the urban poor do not have rewarding or sustained employment, and the upper classes do not exploit the urban poor in the workplace the way the upper classes of earlier eras exploited farm laborers or industrial workers. The urban poor continue to possess their own "units" of labor, but this labor power ceases to have exploitable value if it is incapable of being deployed.[9] As a result, the urban poor are virtually expendable in the reigning socioeconomic system, and some members of the middle and upper classes might in fact wish they would disappear. That is of course impossible, and in reality the urban poor are growing in number and becoming more and more visible due to increased residential concentration. One alternative is containment, and law can be and is used to develop massive prisons, cordon off zones in cities, and maintain a semipermanent outsider class.

Condemnation, meanwhile, can serve as a crucial rationalization for this containment, and it is audible in both the laws themselves and the descriptions and defenses of those laws by their promoters. Who, after all, wants to admit that a substantial portion of the population is being shunted off to prison, trapped in the inner city, or marginalized as outsiders? It is much more palatable and comforting to condemn the urban poor for their criminal ways, failure to build stable families and raise their children properly, recklessness in the marketplace, and—most generally—imprudence in making lifestyle decisions. Condemnation of this sort makes it easier to dodge any responsibility for the urban poor's plight.

Conventional conceptualizations of law, legal proceedings, and legal institutions rarely include an awareness that they might serve to contain and condemn. Despite the widespread lawyer-baiting and the growing lack of confidence in legal institutions, most Americans remain relatively positive about the law and what they take it to do. If you could somehow get members of the public to think abstractly and to conceptualize what they think law does, they might say it punishes bad people, ends arguments and disagreements, and sorts out who gets what.[10] These pursuits, the populace might proudly add, make the United States the welcome embodiment of a nation living by the "rule of law." If the law's most noteworthy operations with regard to the urban poor's criminal justice, housing, family life, marketplace activities, and health are containment and condemnation, that is terribly difficult to coordinate with a belief in law as a valuable rudder for American life.

Law and Oppression

How might the urban poor be seen as oppressed? What role does law's containing and condemning of the urban poor play in that oppression? As we consider these questions, we should bear in mind that oppression is a fundamentally abhorrent social arrangement. "Oppression," the philosopher Ann Cudd has reminded us, is always wrong.[11] People, institutions, and forces that contribute to oppression are unjust and immoral. If we conclude that the urban poor are oppressed, we have a deplorable condition to contemplate. If we conclude that law plays a major role in the oppression of the urban poor, we will have identified law as an accomplice in unjust and immoral wrongdoing.

The oppression of the urban poor in the United States is not the type of oppression that first springs to mind. In the most familiar variety of oppression, a tyrant, an elite, or a ruling group limits, burdens, and reduces a recognizable group of people. This traditional oppression might take the form of a police state, in which the oppressed live under the thumb of a central armed and authoritarian force. In many cases, despotism and a police state go hand in hand. In the present, oppressive tyrants and police states are surprisingly common and hardly limited to Kim Jong-un in North Korea, Bashar al-Assad in Syria, and Omar al-Bashur in Sudan. The latter has oppressed black Darfurians to such an extent that he has been indicted by the International Criminal Court for genocide.

The proclivity of tyrants and despots for oppression having been noted, oppression in a democratic society is different. Rather than being imposed by a tyrant or by a state-supported police apparatus, oppression in a nation such as the United States derives from a combination of cultural, economic, and political forces, all working to deny, punish, and hold down a given social group. Even something as seemingly benign as humor can contribute—and contribute mightily—to oppression.[12] According to lawyer and political scientist Nicky Gonzalez Yuen, oppression in the United States is neither occasional nor happenstance. "The systematic nature of the oppression, then, is cumulative and the impact is far greater than if the hurts were occasional or isolated occurrences."[13] Because the intertwined oppressive forces do not necessarily call attention to themselves, the oppression in a democratic society can be overlooked or just taken to be the unfortunate way things work out. How many of the people with the troubling "Shit Happens" bumper stickers on their cars are expressing resignation regarding what is actually their oppression?

Given the common and widespread sense of being wronged in the contemporary United States, it is easy to use the term "oppression" too loosely and frequently. Fretful students sometimes say they are oppressed because professors are assigning too much work. Penurious citizens consider the administrative agencies and programs of the federal government to be oppression. But "oppression" does not include all kinds of mistreatment and injustice, and the term "oppression" should not be used for everything we dislike in our society.[14] Oppression requires the systematic limiting, burdening, and reducing of some part of the general population. We usually believe in self-ascription when it comes to membership in social groups; that is, we think individuals have or should have the right to determine and define their group memberships. Oppression, meanwhile, violates the right of voluntary association. Forces outside of individuals' control ascribe membership in the oppressed group. The right to self-ascription, Andrew Pierce maintains, should be a fundamental moral right. Its denial is immoral.[15]

Neither oppressors nor the oppressed are likely to recognize themselves as such. Most of the former, of course, live comfortably and tend to take their advantageous social roles for granted. Few think of themselves primarily with reference to the less fortunate or marginalized. Some oppressors certainly realize that sectors of the population are receiving less than their share of wealth, power, and respect, but rationalizations abound. "For every form of oppression in our society there is a socially sanctioned rationalization for the mistreatment."[16] Then, too, "blaming the victim" is widespread in the context of oppression. Sometimes, this "blaming the victim" is motivated by compassion, but blaming the victims is nevertheless harmful to the victims because it denigrates them while directing attention away from the more fundamental causes of the victims' woes.

The oppressed in a democratic society behave in a range of seemingly irrational ways. According to Paulo Freire, one of the world's most insightful theorists of oppression, oppressed people know they are downtrodden, "but their perception of themselves as oppressed is impaired by their submersion in the reality of oppression."[17] Some become preoccupied with the frequent denials they experience and "develop instinctive automatic ways of perceiving a world that often appears hostile."[18] Their defensive posture becomes virtually permanent. Others become hardened, rigid, and mean, almost daring the injustice to mess with them. Still others identify with their oppressors and find their models of personhood among those who oppress them.[19]

With all the denials and socioeconomic abuse, oppression becomes wearing and disabling. In one classic discussion, Ira Goldberg focuses on the state of being oppressed:

> It is a pattern of hopelessness and helplessness. People only become oppressed when they have been forced (either subtly or with obvious malice) to finally succumb to the insidious process that continually undermines hope and subverts the desire to "become." The process, which is often self-perpetuating and self-reinforcing, leaves in its wake the kinds of human beings who have learned to view themselves and their world as chronically, almost genetically, estranged.[20]

The oppressed often internalize the oppressors' opinion of them and become self-deprecating. "In the end they become convinced of their own unfitness."[21]

The urban poor in the United States surely appear oppressed. They live mostly in dilapidated housing in older inner-city neighborhoods, in which crime and violence are facts of social life. Jobs are hard to find, and supporting a family is a difficult task. When the urban poor go shopping, they find high prices and impossibly high interest rates. In addition, the urban poor are, on average, less healthy than the members of any other sector of the population. As Stanford University law professor Richard Thompson has observed, the urban poor "have almost no contact with mainstream American society or the normal job market."[22] They have few friendships and relationships with people other than the urban poor, and for the most part they keep to themselves.

Indeed, several commentators suggested as early as the 1970s that the urban poor's status resembles that of a caste.[23] In a caste society, one or more social groups have rigidly ascribed status—that is, their lifestyles and positions in society are actually or virtually hereditary. The society assigns traits and characteristics to the members of a caste on the basis of where and to whom they are born. Customarily, the "flawed" members of a caste are expected to occupy a clearly delineated bottom tier of society. Those at the bottom of the American social hierarchy, i.e., the urban poor, are not taken to be inherently impure or physically polluted, as are members of a caste in the traditional caste society. But still, the urban poor are essentially assigned locations and characteristics.

It is little wonder that hopelessness and self-deprecation accompany these material and social conditions. Living in a violent, inadequate, deteriorating, and unhealthy environment, the contemporary urban poor are actually less happy than middle- and upper-class Americans.[24] They stumble along without exercising the previously noted right of self-ascription.[25]

In particular, the urban poor have in recent decades increasingly abandoned the traditional American hope of "moving up" in the world. To be sure, the urban poor might dream of a big win in the lottery or fantasize about wealth and fame as athletes or entertainers, but most have put aside the belief in upward mobility—the idea that through hard work, conscientious saving, and proper conduct one can get ahead. Who could blame them for thinking this way? Studies have shown that American society has much less upward mobility than most think. As Richard Delgado has underscored, "Most children of poor families remain so all their lives, and very few of those who start out in the lowest economic strata wind up at the top."[26]

What is the law's role in the oppression of the urban poor? A threshold point is that oppressed people in a democratic society tend not to vote in large numbers, and this is certainly true of the urban poor. This lack of participation to some extent grows out of the urban poor's alienation and sense of isolation, but sometimes the system prevents the urban poor from voting. As I pointed out in chapter 1, the majority of the convicted felons in American prisons are from inner-city backgrounds, and most states say these individuals are ineligible to vote when they finish their sentences. This means, according to some estimates, that almost 13 percent of the voting-aged urban poor could not cast ballots even if they wanted to do so.[27] In addition, other types of voter suppression efforts, usually in the name of deterring fraud, have a long history in the United States. Although in the past Democrats in the South were the masters of voter suppression, in recent decades Republicans have taken the lead, eagerly endorsing requirements that voters present picture identification cards. The urban poor are among those least likely to have such cards and, as a result, to be turned away at the polls.[28]

The refusal or inability to vote in a democratic society, it bears emphasizing, has serious psychological ramifications beyond actually making a difference at the polls. Disenfranchisement denies the urban poor fundamental opportunity to affirm their citizenship and, by extension, their American identity. Disenfranchisement also chips away the urban poor's already-deficient sense of control over their lives. And, most generally, disenfranchisement undermines the urban poor's dignity. The loss of dignity is especially excruciating "when the mechanisms that violate dignity are discriminatory in origin and institutionalized by law, as in the case with felon disenfranchisement in the United States."[29]

Having stayed away from the polls either voluntarily or involuntarily, oppressed people in a democratic society place fewer supporters, much less champions, in the legislatures. As is typical in societies with socioeconomic stratification, law in the United States tends to flow from the top down, and American law is rarely the handiwork of the urban poor.[30] Middle- and upper-class legislators in the contemporary United States are most likely to be enamored with neoliberal politics and turn to the market for solutions to social problems, in the process supposedly saving money for taxpayers. Working for the most part in a non-conspiratorial fashion, these legislators rarely enact or expand laws aiding the urban poor. Trying to hold down taxes for their constituents, these legislators do not invest to the extent possible in health, education, and welfare programs, which of course are necessary if the urban poor are to find their fair share of health and happiness.[31] Not surprisingly, the urban poor in the end take very little ownership of the laws that play such large roles in their lives.

The urban poor also have little role in administering and enforcing the laws. Their preferences are unlikely to be considered when elected members of the executive branch choose people to head agencies charged with administering the laws and running government programs. Administrative heads and agency personnel also come primarily from the middle and upper classes. In those exceptional cases in which a member of the urban poor is elected to the legislature or named to head a government agency, even one serving the urban poor, these legislators and administrators tend not to receive much respect, especially when their backs are turned.

As this book has insisted, laws and the administration of those laws frequently contain and condemn the urban poor. This containing and condemning of the urban poor virtually establishes who the urban poor are and who they might be. Sadly, it is no exaggeration to say that in the United States law *constitutes* the urban poor, that is, configures and maintains the urban poor as a socioeconomic group. In his study of totalitarian and post-totalitarian societies, Adam Podgorecki concluded that law is "the essential social factor that molds the various faces of oppression,"[32] and this characterization of law seems equally accurate in a purportedly democratic society such as the contemporary United States.

The urban poor, as oppressed people, have little hope of successfully challenging these laws, as the familiar claim of "discrimination" is of little avail. "Discrimination" has become a pronounced and genuine concern in the diverse modern society. However, discrimination is more discrete than oppression and conventionally takes place with regard to a specific location or socioeconomic possibility. One might encounter discrimination, for example, when trying to rent a unit in a housing complex. One might face discrimination with regard to employment or admission to an academic program. Oppression, by contrast, involves multiple limitations and diminutions. It is a complex and compounded restriction on what you can do and say, accomplish and imagine. Oppression keeps a whole sector of the population in its place.

At its core, discrimination in American law is a "methodologically individualist concept."[33] Particular victims may allege in a lawsuit that individual people or individual institutions have discriminated against the petitioners. Even with a so-called class action such as the one pursued by the customers of

Rent-A-Center in New Jersey, American public policy anticipates that individuals with similar claims can come together in a lawsuit against a business or other large institution. But still, no "class" exists in the form of a collective socioeconomic group. The "class action" simply makes it possible for individuals to share the cost of a lawsuit, and if the parties agree on some sort of financial settlement, courts give individuals in the "class" notice and, customarily, the right to opt out. Overall, speaking of the middle and upper classes "discriminating" against the urban poor might be valid, but it is too general and insufficiently individualist to be brought under the legal rubric of "discrimination."

Not surprisingly given their mooring to American individualism, the courts are much more sensitive to claims of discrimination than to claims of oppression. If the discriminatory conduct matches the legal requirements, and a discriminator and/or an agent is properly identified, a judge might in fact find that discrimination has taken place. By contrast, the courts are usually unwilling to recognize a claim pointing to oppression or to general social structure or large and fundamental social groupings. The courts can weaken oppression by finding that discrimination has occurred, but it is possible for oppression to continue even without legal discrimination. While legal discrimination against the native peoples of North America, for example, has been largely eliminated, most would agree they remain oppressed.

In summary, law contributes to the oppression of the urban poor in at least three ways. For starters, law denies the urban poor a major voice in the making of our laws and running of our legal institutions, including even those institutions supposedly created to serve them. Second, law, legal processes, and legal institutions constitute the urban poor as something of a caste-like social group with no right of self-ascription, and this undertaking is more "official" and thereby more forceful than other sources of authority in a democratic society. And third, a petition to the court alleging oppression and demanding its cessation is almost impossible to imagine. The law, to put it bluntly, is potent and unyielding in sustaining the oppressive realities of urban poverty.

To realize that the law is a multifaceted agent of oppression for America's urban poor is disheartening, especially for a believer in the viability of a democratic society and for a legalist working within a democratic society. The population of the United States includes a subordinate sector situated semipermanently below the lowest level of well-being, and law, legal proceedings, and legal institutions contribute to this sorry status quo. Overall, this oppression is harmful and inhumane, not only for the urban poor but also for all of us. American society is not as empowering and enriching as it often claims to be, and American society fails to lift literally millions of its people out of isolation and into the national community. Everyone suffers in the United States when law functions as an agent of oppression and is complicit in the oppression of the urban poor.

Notes

INTRODUCTION

1. David J. Rothman and Sheila M. Rothman, eds., *On Their Own: The Poor in Modern America* (Menlo Park, CA: Addison-Wesley Publishing, 1972), vi.

2. W. J. Rorabaugh, *The Alcoholic Republic: An American Tradition* (New York: Oxford University Press, 1979), 28–29.

3. David S. Reynolds, *Waking Giant: America in the Age of Jackson* (New York: HarperCollins, 2008), 176.

4. Ibid., 34.

5. Paul Boyer, *Urban Masses and Moral Order in America, 1820–1920* (Cambridge, MA: Harvard University Press, 1978), 3.

6. Between 1790 and 1830, Philadelphia tripled in size, and New York grew sixfold from a mere 33,000 to 215,000. Ibid., 4.

7. Seth Rockman, *Welfare Reform in the Early Republic* (Boston: Bedford/St. Martin's, 2003), 20; David J. Rothman, *The Discovery of the Asylum: Social Order and Disorder in the New Republic* (Boston: Little, Brown and Co., 1971), 180.

8. Stephen Pimpare, *A People's History of Poverty in America* (New York: New Press, 2008), 43–44.

9. Boyer, *Urban Masses*, 13.
10. Only tailors earned more. Reynolds, *Waking Giant*, 202.
11. Quoted in Boyer, *Urban Masses*, 19.
12. Jodie Collins, "Why Was Masturbation Such a Medical Concern in the 19th Century?," https://jodebloggs.wordpress.com.
13. Marie Boyd, "Zoning for Apartments: A Study of the Role of Law in the Control of Apartment Houses in New Haven, Connecticut," *Pace Law Review* 33 (2013): 604.
14. Roy Lubove, *The Progressives and the Slums: Tenement House Reform in New York City, 1890–1917* (Pittsburgh: University of Pittsburgh Press, 1962), 233.
15. Ibid., 230.
16. Stephen J. Polaha, "Housing Codes and the Prevention of Urban Blight," *Villanova Law Review* 17 (1972): 492.
17. Robin K. Berson, *Jane Addams: A Biography* (Westport, CT: Greenwood Press, 2004), 23.
18. The best study of Addams is Louise W. Knight, *Citizen Jane Addams and the Struggle for Democracy* (Chicago: University of Chicago Press, 2005).
19. Robert Hunter, *Poverty* (New York: Macmillan Co., 1905), 3.
20. Stephanie Christensen, "The Great Migration (1915–1960)," *Black Past*, https://www.blackpast.org.
21. Nicholas Lemann, *The Promised Land: The Great Black Migration and How It Changed America* (New York: Alfred A. Knopf, 1991), 6.
22. A poll from 1964, for example, revealed that almost 70 percent of the respondents thought some or most of those receiving welfare were doing so dishonestly. Rothman and Rothman, *On Their Own*, xxii.
23. Michael Harrington, *The Other America: Poverty in the United States* (New York: Macmillan, 1962).
24. Maurice Isserman, "Warrior on Poverty," *New York Times Book Review*, June 21, 2009, 20.
25. Lyndon Baines Johnson, "First State of the Union Address," January 8, 1964, American Rhetoric Speechbank (online).
26. Edgar S. Cahn and Jean C. Cahn, "The War on Poverty: A Civilian Perspective," *Yale Law Journal* 73 (1964): 1317.
27. Annalise Orleck and Lisa Gayle Harerjian, eds., *War on Poverty: A New Grassroots History, 1864–1980* (Athens: University of Georgia Press, 2011) contains fifteen

articles on representative local "War on Poverty" programs.

28. Polaha, "Housing Codes," 494.

29. Annie Lowrey, "50 Years Later, War on Poverty Is a Mixed Bag," *New York Times*, January 5, 2014, A1.

30. Many commentators bemoan the failure of the "War on Poverty" to live up to its promise. M. B. Katz, *The Undeserving Poor: From the War on Poverty to the War on Welfare* (New York: Pantheon Books, 1989); and Frank Stricker, *Why America Lost the War on Poverty—and How to Win It* (Chapel Hill: University of North Carolina Press, 2007).

31. Karl Marx, "The Eighteenth Brumaire of Louis Bonaparte," in *Karl Marx and Friedrich Engels: Basic Writings on Politics and Philosophy*, ed. Lewis S. Feuer (New York: Anchor Books, 1959), 320, 343–44.

32. Karl Marx, "Manifesto of the Communist Party," in Feuer, *Karl Marx and Friedrich Engels*, 18.

33. The Swedish economist Gunnar Myrdal had referred to the "under-class" as early as 1963, hyphenating the term in the process. Gunnar Myrdal, *Challenge to Affluence* (New York: Pantheon Books, 1983), 34. However, Myrdal's work seems not to have prompted the later widespread use of the term "underclass."

34. "The American Underclass: Destitute and Dirty in the Land of Plenty," *Time*, August 27, 1977, 17–27.

35. Herbert Gans, *The War against the Poor: The Underclass and Antipoverty Policy* (New York: Basic Books, 1995), 37.

36. These exquisite works include *Power, Racism and Privilege: Race Relations in Theoretical and Sociohistorical Perspective* (New York: Macmillan, 1973); *The Declining Significance of Race: Blacks and Changing Institutions* (Chicago: University of Chicago Press, 1978); *The Truly Disadvantaged: The Inner City, the Underclass, and Public Policy* (Chicago: University of Chicago Press, 1984); and *When Work Disappears: The World of the New Urban Poor* (New York: Knopf, 1996).

37. Wilson, *Declining Significance of Race*, 156.

38. Barbara Ehrenreich, "It Is Expensive to Be Poor," *The Atlantic*, January 13, 2014.

39. Myron Magnet, "America's Underclass: What to Do?," *Fortune*, May 11, 1987, 13.

40. Christopher Jencks, *Rethinking Social Policy: Race, Poverty, and the Underclass* (Cambridge, MA: Harvard University Press, 1992), 201–2.

41. For a discussion of Wilson's disavowal of the term "underclass," see Bill E. Larson,

"Meditations on Integration," in *The Underclass Question*, ed. Bill E. Larson (Philadelphia: Temple University Press, 1992), 57.

42. Wilson's *More Than Just Race: Being Black and Poor in the Inner City* (New York: W.W. Norton & Co., 2009) argues forcefully that racism and deindustrialization are more important than ghetto culture in explaining the state of the urban poor. In his opinion, an aggressive public policy that is committed to creating meaningful economic opportunity is the only way to break the cycle.

43. While 22 percent of African Americans live in poverty, 19.4 percent of Hispanics of any race and 10.1 percent of Asians live in poverty. Non-Hispanic whites have the lowest poverty rate at 8.8 percent. "U.S. Poverty Statistics," Federal Safety Net (online).

44. Tanzina Vega, "Report Finds Hispanics Faring Better Than Blacks," *New York Times*, April 13, 2014, A19.

45. Miriam Jordan, "When Syria Came to Fresno: A Strain on Welcoming Arms," *New York Times*, July 21, 2017, A10.

46. Vega, "Report Finds Hispanics Faring Better Than Blacks," A19.

47. Alan Ehrenhalt, "Trading Places: The Demographic Inversion of the American City," *New Republic*, August 13, 2008; and Christopher B. Leinberger, "The Next Slum?," *Atlantic Monthly*, March 2008, 70.

48. Earl R. Hutchison Jr., "Black Suburbanization: A History of Social Change in a Working Class Suburb" (PhD diss., University of Chicago, 1984).

49. Darnell Little and Dan Mihalopoulos, "Black Chicagoans Fuel Growth in South Suburbs," *New York Times*, July 3, 2011, 21A.

50. Elizabeth Kneebone, "The Growth and Spread of Concentrated Poverty," July 31, 2014, Brookings Institution (online).

51. Tracey Ross, "Addressing Urban Poverty in America Must Remain a Priority," June 5, 2013, Center for American Progress (online).

52. Rachel D. Godsil, "The Gentrification Trigger: Autonomy, Mobility, and Affirmatively Furthering Fair Housing," *Brooklyn Law Review* 78 (2013): 325.

53. Book-length studies of "gentrification" include Loretta Lees, Tom Slater, and Elvin K. Wyly, *Gentrification* (New York: Routledge, 2008); and Kathryn B. Nelson, *Gentrification and Distressed Cities* (Madison: University of Wisconsin Press, 1988). A useful collection of essays is J. John Palen and Bruce London, eds., *Gentrification, Displacement, and Neighborhood Revitalization* (Albany: SUNY Press, 1984).

54. Emily Badger, "The Suburbanization of Poverty," May 20, 2013, CityLab (online).

55. Helle Porsdam, *Legally Speaking: Contemporary American Culture and the Law* (Amherst: University of Massachusetts Press, 1999), 1.

56. Austin Sarat and Susan Silbey, "Critical Traditions in Law and Society Research," *Law & Society Review* 2 (1987): 173.

57. Steven E. Barkan, *Law and Society: An Introduction* (Upper Saddle River, NJ: Pearson Prentice Hall, 2009), 5–6; Donald Black, *The Behavior of Law* (New York: Academic Press, 1976), 106.

58. James Boyd White, *Heracles' Bow: Essays on Rhetoric and the Poetics of the Law* (Madison: University of Wisconsin Press, 1985), 28.

59. Eli K. Best, "Atypical Actors and Tort Law's Expressive Function," *Marquette Law Review* 96 (2012): 474. For a review, albeit a highly critical one, of articles discussing law's expressive function in the areas of punishment, constitutions, and regulation, see Matthew A. Adler, "Expressive Theories of Law: A Skeptical Overview," *University of Pennsylvania Law Review* 148 (2000): 1413–62.

60. Elizabeth S. Anderson and Richard H. Pildes, "Expressive Theories of Law: A Skeptical Overview," *University of Pennsylvania Law Review* 148 (2000): 1525.

61. Lawrence Lessig, "Social Meaning and Social Norms," *University of Pennsylvania Law Review* 144 (1996): 2188.

62. Alex Geisinger, "A Belief Change Theory of Expressive Law," *Iowa Law Review* 88 (2002): 40.

CHAPTER 1. LABELING THE URBAN POOR AS CRIMINALS

1. Edwin M. Schur, *Labeling Deviant Behavior: Its Sociological Implications* (New York: Harper and Row, 1971), 4.

2. Howard Becker, *Outsiders: Studies in the Sociology of Deviance* (London: Free Press, 1963), 14.

3. Robert J. Sampson and William Julius Wilson, "Toward a Theory of Race, Class, and Urban Inequality," in *Crime and Inequality*, ed. John Hagan and Ruth D. Peterson (Palo Alto, CA: Stanford University Press, 1995), 38.

4. John Hagan and Ruth Peterson, "Criminal Inequality in America: Patterns and Consequences," in Hagan and Peterson, *Crime and Inequality*, 20.

5. Richard Delgado, "Law Enforcement in Subordinated Communities: Innovation and

Response," *Michigan Law Review* 106 (2008): 1197.

6. Hagan and Peterson, "Criminal Inequality," 20.

7. In a discussion of "visual cues," Robert Sampson reminds us that the cues do not in and of themselves create the impression of crime and disorder. "Intersubjectively shared historical assessments" provide a meaningful definition of a given area, and this established definition invites extrapolations from the bulletproof shields and metallic graffiti. Robert J. Sampson, *Great American City: Chicago and the Enduring Neighborhood Effect* (Chicago: University of Chicago Press, 2012), 146–48.

8. William J. Chambliss, "Policing the Ghetto Underclass: The Politics of Law Enforcement," *Social Problems* 41 (1994): 191.

9. Joseph Goldstein, "Judge Rejects New York's Stop-and-Frisk Policy," *New York Times*, May 2, 2013, A1; Joseph Goldstein, "Police Department's Focus on Race Is at Core of Ruling against Stop-and-Frisk," *New York Times*, August 15, 2013, A18.

10. Floyd v. City of New York, 959 F.Supp.2d 540, 561 (S.D.N.Y. 2013).

11. Benjamin Weiser, "Parting Words as Judge Steps Down, in Defense of Stop-and-Frisk Ruling," *New York Times*, May 2, 2016, A14.

12. Benjamin Weiser and Joseph Goldstein, "New York to End Frisking Lawsuit with Settlement," *New York Times*, January 31, 2014, A20.

13. Ibid.

14. Chambliss, "Policing," 191, 192.

15. Hagan and Peterson, "Criminal Inequality," 25.

16. Becker, *Outsiders*, 158.

17. Douglas A. Smith and Christy A. Visher, "Street-Level Justice: Situational Determinants of Police Arrest Decisions," *Social Problems* 29 (1981): 72.

18. David Cole, *No Equal Justice: Race and Class in the American Criminal Justice System* (New York: New Press, 1999), 16–55.

19. "Because a consent search requires no objective individualized suspicion, it is more likely to be directed at poor black men than wealthy white women"; Cole, *No Equal Justice*, 31.

20. David A. Harris, "Factors for Reasonable Suspicion: When Black and Poor Means Stopped and Frisked," *Indiana Law Journal* 69 (1994): 660.

21. Ibid., 680.

22. Chambliss, "Policing," 179.

23. Ibid.

24. Jonathan Simon, *Poor Discipline: Parole and the Social Control of the Underclass, 1890–1990* (Chicago: University of Chicago Press, 1993), 252.

25. Delgado, "Law Enforcement," 1194.

26. N.W.A., "Fuck the Police," in *Straight Outta Compton* (Priority, 1998), compact disc.

27. Ice-T, "Cop Killer," in *Body Count* (Warner Brothers, 1992), compact disc.

28. Delgado, "Law Enforcement," 1194.

29. David Ray Papke, "The Black Panther Party's Narratives of Resistance," *Vermont Law Review* 18 (1994): 645–80.

30. Nissa Rhee, "In Black Lives Matter's Shift to Economic Issues, Echoes of Black Panthers," *Christian Science Monitor*, May 24, 2016 https://www.csmonitor.com/USA/Society/2016/0524/In-Black-Lives-Matter-s-shift-to-economic-issues-echoes-of-Black-Panthers; Janell Ross, "What a Black Lives Matter Economic Agenda Looks Like," *Washington Post*, August 29, 2016.

31. Brakkton Booker, "Federal Ferguson Review Finds More Than 100 Lessons for Police," September 2, 2015, NPR (online).

32. David C. Gorlin, "Evaluating Punishment in Purgatory: The Need to Separate Pretrial Detainees' Condition-of-Confinement Claims from Inadequate Eighth Amendment Analysis," *Michigan Law Review* 108 (2009): 417.

33. Erica Haber, "Demystifying a Legal Twilight Zone: Resolving the Circuit Court Split on When Seizure Ends and Pretrial Detention Begins," *New York Law School Journal of Human Rights* 19 (2003): 939; Eamonn O'Hagan, "Judicial Illumination of the Constitutional 'Twilight Zone,'" *Boston College Law Review* 44 (2003): 1357; Tiffany Ritchie, "A Legal Twilight Zone: From the Fourth to the Fourteenth Amendment, What Constitutional Protection Is Afforded a Pretrial Detainee," *Southern Illinois University Law Journal* 27 (2003): 613.

34. John Irwin, *The Jail: Managing the Underclass in American Society* (Berkeley: University of California Press, 1985), 57.

35. David Ray Papke, *Framing the Criminal: Crime, Cultural Work, and the Loss of Critical Perspective, 1830–1900* (Hamden, CT: Archon Books, 1987), 136.

36. Irwin, *The Jail*, 58.

37. Timothy Williams, "Jails Have Become Warehouses for the Poor, Ill and Addicted, a Report Says," *New York Times*, February 11, 2015, A19.

38. Catherine T. Struve, "The Conditions of Pretrial Detention," *University of Pennsylvania Law Review* 161 (2013): 1055.

39. Ibid.

40. Chad M. Oldfather, "Heuristics, Biases, and Criminal Defendants," *Marquette Law Review* 91 (2007): 258.

41. Douglas L. Colbert et al., "Do Attorneys Really Matter? The Empirical and Legal Case for the Right to Counsel at Bail," *Cardozo Law Review* 23 (2002): 1724.

42. Struve, "Conditions of Pretrial Detention," 1059.

43. Human Rights Watch, *The Price of Freedom: Bail and Pretrial Detention of Low Income Nonfelony Defendants in New York City* (New York: Human Rights Watch, 2010), 24.

44. Stephanos Bibas, "Plea Bargaining outside the Shadow of Trial," *Harvard Law Review* 117 (2004): 2540.

45. For two authors who studied local criminal courts in Boston in the 1970s, the pervasive bargaining seemed the dominant aspect of the entire enterprise. Suzann R. Buckle and Leonard Buckle, *Bargaining for Justice: Case Disposition and Reform in the Criminal Courts* (New York: Praeger Publishers, 1977).

46. Missouri v. Frye, 132 S. Ct. 1399, 1407, quoting Robert E. Scott and William J. Stuntz, "Plea Bargaining as Contract," *Yale Law Journal* 101 (1992): 1912.

47. Ibid., Missouri v. Frye.

48. Malcolm M. Feeley, "Perspectives on Plea Bargaining," *Law and Society Review* 13 (1979): 200.

49. Julian A. Cook, "Plea Bargaining, Sentence Modifications, and the Real World," *Wake Forest Law Review* 48 (2013): 81.

50. Michel Foucault, *Discipline and Punish: The Birth of the Prison* (New York: Vintage Books, 1979), 276.

51. William F. McDonald, "From Plea Negotiation to Coercive Justice: Notes in the Respecification of a Concept," *Law and Society Review* 13 (1979): 385–92.

52. Bruce A. Green, "Why Should Prosecutors Seek Justice?," *Fordham Urban Law Journal* 26 (1999): 609; Andrew E. Taslitz, "Eyewitness Identification, Democratic Deliberation, and the Politics of Science," *Cardozo Public Law, Policy, and Ethics Journal* 4 (2006): 304.

53. Jack Katz, "Legality and Equality: Plea Bargaining in the Prosecution of White-Collar and Common Crimes," *Law and Society Review* 13 (1979): 443.

54. Taslitz, "Eyewitness Identification," 296.

55. Ibid.

56. Martin Guggenheim, "Divided Loyalties: Musings on Some Ethical Dilemmas for

the Institutional Criminal Defense Attorney," *New York University Review of Law and Social Change* 14 (1986): 14–15.

57. A. W. Alschuler, "Personal Failure, Institutional Failure, and the Sixth Amendment," *New York University Review of Law and Social Change* 14 (1986): 150–52.

58. For a fine study of how defense counsel and prosecutors interact with one another, see Douglas W. Maynard, *Inside Plea Bargaining: The Language of Negotiation* (New York: Plenum Press, 1984).

59. Bibas, "Plea Bargaining," 2469.

60. Debra S. Emmelman, *Justice for the Poor: A Study of Criminal Defense Work* (Burlington, VT: Ashgate, 2003), 124.

61. Ibid., 121.

62. I summarized some of these conventions in David Ray Papke, "The American Courtroom Trial: Pop Culture, Courthouse Realities, and the Dream World of Justice," *South Texas Law Review* 40 (1999): 919–32.

63. Since "plea bargaining" encompasses so many approaches and concerns, it is difficult to calculate with any precision the percentage of cases plea-bargained and the percentage going to trial, but surely trial is the exception rather than the rule. A 2002 study estimated that only 2 percent of felony convictions in state courts were the result of trials. U.S. Department of Justice, *Sourcebook of Criminal Justice Statistics* (Washington, DC: U.S. Government Printing Office, 2004), table 546.2002. Furthermore, the reliance on guilty pleas in criminal cases has increased dramatically in recent decades. Marc Galanter, "The Hundred-Year Decline in Trials and the Thirty Years War," *Stanford Law Review* 57 (2005): 1255.

64. Missouri v. Frye, 1407.

65. Hagan and Peterson, "Criminal Inequality," 28–29.

66. Imani Perry, "Acts of Aggression," *New York Times Book Review*, May 29, 2016, 15.

67. Sampson, *Great American City*, 102.

68. Matt Apuzo, "Holder Endorses Proposal to Reduce Drug Sentences," *New York Times*, March 14, 2014, A15.

69. David Cole, "Punitive Damage," *New York Times*, May 18, 2014, 24.

70. Simon, *Poor Discipline*, 255, 259.

71. Chambliss, "Policing," 184–87; Joachim J. Savelsberg, "Knowledge, Domination, and Criminal Punishment," *American Journal of Sociology* 99 (1994): 938; Eduardo Porter, "In the U.S., Punishment Comes before the Crimes," *New York Times*, April 30, 2014, B9.

72. Katherine Beckett, *Making Crime Pay* (New York: New York University Press, 1997), 23–25.

73. Cole, *No Equal Justice*, 139.

74. Anthony Chase, *Movies on Trial: The Legal System on the Silver Screen* (New York: New Press, 2002), 68–75.

75. The number of Americans imprisoned is five times as high on a per capita basis as that in any Western European country, *and* American prison sentences are also much longer on average than those in most parts of the world. Sarah Sun Beale, "The Many Faces of Overcriminalization," *American University Law Review* 54 (2005): 750.

76. Perry, "Acts of Aggression," 15.

77. Ibid.

78. Paul Shepard, "Focusing on Prevention and Neuroscience, President Ends Reagan's War on Drugs," April 24, 2013, NewsOne (online).

79. Julian Hattem, "Obama Seeks New Approach to the War on Drugs," *The Hill*, April 24, 2013, http://thehill.com/blogs/regwatch/administration/295889-obama-seeks-new-approach-to-the-war-on-drugs.

80. Don Winslow, "President Trump's War on Drugs Is Catastrophic," *Time*, June 20, 2017.

81. Madison Pauly, "A Brief History of America's Private Prison Industry," *Mother Jones*, July-August 2016.

82. Ibid.

83. Joshua Holland, "Higher Profits Explain Why There Are More People of Color in Private Prisons," *Moyers & Company*, February 7, 2014, http://www.billmoyers.com.

84. According to one journalist, inmates in federal private prisons are more likely to be placed in lockdown, and individual inmates are more frequently subjected to solitary confinement. Complaints about meals and medical treatment are also more common. Oliver Laughland, "Private Federal Prisons More Dangerous, Damaging DOJ Investigation Reveals," *The Guardian*, August 12, 2016.

85. Valerie Strauss, "Mass Incarceration of African Americans Affects the Achievement Gap," *Washington Post*, March 15, 2017.

86. Antonio Moore, "The Black Male Incarceration Problem Is Real and It's Catastrophic," *Huffington Post*, February 17, 2015.

87. Naomi Murakawa, *The First Civil Right: How Liberals Built Prison America* (New York: Oxford University Press, 2014), 1.

88. Loïc Wacquant, "Class, Race, and Hyperincarceration in Revanchist America," *Daedalus* 139, no. 3 (2010): 74–90.

89. Bernadette Raybury and Daniel Kopf, "Prisons of Poverty: Uncovering the Pre-Incarceration Incomes of the Imprisoned," National Council on Crime and Delinquency, July 21, 2015, https://nccdglobal.org.

90. Sendhil Mullainathan, "A Top-Heavy Focus on Income Inequality," *New York Times*, March 9, 2014, 4.

91. Cynthia Golembeski and Robert Fullilove, "Criminal (In)Justice in the City and Its Associated Health Consequences," *American Journal of Public Health* 95 (2005): 1703.

92. Harold Pollack, "The Most Embarrassing Graph in American Drug Policy," Wonkblog, *Washington Post*, May 29, 2013.

93. Josh Katz and Abby Goodnough, "Opioid Deaths Rising Swiftly among Blacks," *New York Times*, December 22, 2017, A1.

94. Olga Khazan, "The Link between Opioids and Unemployment," *The Atlantic*, April 18, 2017; H. Henry Spiller et al., "Epidemiological Trends in Abuse and Misuse of Prescription Opioids," *Journal of Addictive Diseases* 28 (2009): 130–36.

95. Lisa D. Moore and Amy Elkavish, "Who's Using and Who's Doing Drugs: Incarceration, the War on Drugs, and Public Health," *American Journal of Public Health* 98 (2008): 782.

96. Noam Chomsky, "Drug Policy as Social Control," in *Prison Nation: The Warehousing of America's Poor*, ed. Tara Herviel and Paul Wright (New York: Routledge, 2003), 57, 59.

97. As Jonathan Simon puts it, "The massive expansion of criminal custody over the last decade in the United States must be seen in relationship to changes in the political economy including the restructuring of the labor force away from industrial employment, the emergence of an urban underclass living in zones of hardened poverty and made up primarily of minorities, and the heightened accountability of political power—what we call due process—that has emerged since the Second World War." Simon, *Poor Discipline*, 5.

98. Golembeski and Fullilove, "Criminal (In)Justice," 1704.

99. Ibid.

100. Nicholas Freudenberg, "Jails, Prisons, and the Health of Urban Populations: A Review of the Impact of the Correctional System in Community Health," *Journal of Urban Health* 78 (2001): 223.

101. Golembeski and Fullilove, "Criminal (In)Justice," 1704.

102. Lorelei Laird, "Doing Time Extended," *ABA Journal*, June 2013, 55.

103. Freudenberg, "Jails, Prisons, and the Health of Urban Populations," 222.

104. Golembeski and Fullilove, "Criminal (In)Justice," 1705.

105. Freudenberg, "Jails, Prisons, and the Health of Urban Populations," 215.

106. Eric Lichtblau, "Trump May Reverse Obama Policy of Freeing Inmates," *New York Times*, January 16, 2017, A12.

107. Eric Tucker, "Prison Time May Be Cut for Drugs," *Milwaukee Journal Sentinel*, July 9, 2014, 3A.

108. Jeremy W. Peters, "G.O.P. Moving to Ease Stance on Sentencing," *New York Times*, March 14, 2014, A1.

109. Winslow, "President Trump's War on Drugs."

110. In the present, drug offenders comprise half the federal prison population in the United States. Shepard, "Focusing on Prevention and Neuroscience."

111. Timothy Williams, "A '90s Legacy That Is Filling Prisons Today," *New York Times*, July 5, 2016, A1.

112. Cole, "Punitive Damage," 24.

113. Ibid.

114. Loïc Wacquant, "Deadly Symbiosis: When Ghetto and Prison Meet," in *Mass Imprisonment: Social Cause and Consequences*, ed. David Garland (London: Sage Publications, 2001).

115. David Garland discusses what he calls the "crime complex of late modernity." Garland, *Mass Imprisonment*, 163.

116. Jonathan Simon, *Governing through Crime: How the War on Crime Transformed American Democracy and Created a Culture of Fear* (New York: Oxford University Press, 2007), 78.

CHAPTER 2. NO PLACE TO CALL HOME

1. Gail Radford, "The Federal Government and Housing during the Great Depression," in *From Tenements to the Taylor Homes: In Search of Urban Housing Policy in the Twentieth Century*, ed. John F. Baumer, Roger Biles, and Kristin M. Szylvian (University Park: Pennsylvania State University Press, 2000), 104–8.

2. Wagner-Steagall Act, 42 U.S.C. 1437 et seq.

3. Nathaniel S. Keith, *Politics and the Housing Crisis since 1930* (New York: Universe

Books, 1973), 37.

4. Harry S. Truman, "Statement by the President Upon Signing the Housing Act of 1949," July 15, 1949, The American Presidency Project (online), http://www.presidency.ucsb.edu/ws/?pid=13246.

5. Ginia Bellafante, "In Marcus Garvey Village, a Housing Solution Gone Awry," *New York Times*, June 1, 2013.

6. J. A. Stoloff, "A Brief History of Public Housing" (Washington, DC: U.S. Department of Housing and Urban Development, 2004), 1.

7. Ibid., 6.

8. Lawrence M. Friedman, *Government and Slum Housing: A Century of Frustration* (Chicago: Rand McNally & Co., 1968), 21.

9. Peter Dreier, "The New Politics of Housing," *Journal of the American Planning Association* 63, no. 1 (Winter 1997): 7.

10. National Economic and Social Rights Initiative, "Realizing Human Rights in Public Housing," http://www.nesri.org/programs/realizing-human-rights-in-public-housing.

11. Gary Rivlin, "The Cold Hard Lessons of Mobile Home U.," *New York Times Magazine*, March 13, 2014, 38.

12. Dreier, "New Politics of Housing," 7.

13. Ben Austen, "The Last Tower: The Decline and Fall of Public Housing," *Harper's Magazine*, May 2012, 42.

14. C. J. Hughes, "Ahead of the Pack: Is Land inside Public Housing Complexes the Next Big Thing?," *New York Times*, June 28, 2015, Business 8.

15. "Housing Choice Voucher Fact Sheets," Center on Budget and Policy Priorities, https://www.cbpp.org/housing-choice-voucher-fact-sheets.

16. Ann K. Pikus, "Wanted: Affordable Housing in Wisconsin," *Wisconsin Law Review* 2007 (2007): 209.

17. Robert C. Ellickson, "The False Promise of the Mixed-Income Housing Project," *UCLA Law Review* 57 (2010): 994.

18. John Arena, *Driven from New Orleans: How Nonprofits Betray Public Housing and Promote Privatization* (Minneapolis: University of Minnesota Press, 2012), 219, 225.

19. Brentin Mock, "Chicago Developers Are Pushing Back against Affordable Housing Rules," September 1, 2015, CityLab (online).

20. Janet Babin, "New York Skyscraper's Separate 'Poor Door' Called a Disgrace," July 30, 2014, NPR (online).

21. Zachary Kussin and Rob Smith, "City Beef: From 'Pricing Out' to 'Poor Doors,'" *New York Post*, December 25, 2014, 33.

22. Dreier, "New Politics of Housing," 9.

23. Robert M. Buckley and Alex F. Schwartz, "Housing Policy in the U.S.," International Working Affairs Paper (New York: The New School, 2010), 30.

24. Kriston Capps, "Every Single County in America Is Facing an Affordable Housing Crisis," June 18, 2015, CityLab (online).

25. Stephen J. Polaha, "Housing Codes and the Prevention of Urban Blight: Administrative and Enforcement Problems and Proposals," *Villanova Law Review* 17 (1972): 501.

26. "Conservation of Dwellings: The Prevention of Blight," *Indiana Law Journal* 29 (1953): 109–11.

27. H. Laurence Ross, "Housing Code Enforcement and Urban Decline," *Journal of Affordable Housing and Community Development Law* 6 (1996): 40.

28. Joint Center for Housing Studies of Harvard University, *The State of the Nation's Housing* (Cambridge, MA: President and Fellows of Harvard College, 2003), 27.

29. Polaha, "Housing Codes," 494.

30. Samuel Bassett Abbott, "Housing Policy, Housing Codes and Tenant Remedies," *Boston University Law Review* 56 (1976): 44.

31. Ross, "Housing Code Enforcement," 41.

32. Shaila Dewan, "Evictions Soar in Hot Market; Renters Suffer," *New York Times*, August 28, 2014.

33. Joint Center for Housing Studies of Harvard University, *The State of the Nation's Housing*, 28.

34. Erik Eckholm, "A Sight All Too Familiar in Poor Neighborhoods," *New York Times*, February 18, 2010.

35. Elizabeth Gudrais, "Disrupted Lives," *Harvard Magazine*, January–February 2014, 38.

36. Dewan, "Evictions Soar."

37. Ross, "Housing Code Enforcement," 29–46.

38. Ibid., 29.

39. Lawrence M. Friedman, *American Law in the 20th Century* (New Haven, CT: Yale University Press, 2002), 409.

40. Abbott, "Housing Policy, Housing Codes and Tenant Remedies," 91. One scholar in the 1960s accurately characterized housing as a type of "social overhead." Leland

Burns, "Housing as Social Overhead Capital," in *Essays in Urban Land Economics*, ed. James Gillies (Los Angeles: University of California Real Estate Research Program, 1966), 3–30.

41. Displeased by what he has observed, Peter Dreier, the E.P. Clap Distinguished Professor of Politics at Occidental College in Los Angeles, put it bluntly: "Other major industrial nations do not permit the level of sheer destitution and decay found in our cities." Dreier, "New Politics of Housing," 6.

42. National Economic and Social Rights Initiative, "What Is the Human Right to Housing?," https://www.nesri.org.

43. Bill Bishop, *The Big Sort: Why the Clustering of Like-Minded America Is Tearing Us Apart* (New York: Houghton Mifflin, 2008), 14, 302.

44. J. Gordon Hylton et al., *Property Law and the Public Interest* (Charlottesville, VA: Lexis, 2003), 130.

45. Miller v. Board of Public Works, 234 P. 381, 387 (Cal. 1925).

46. Ibid.

47. Marie Boyd, "Zoning for Apartments: A Study of the Role of Law in the Control of Apartment Houses in New Haven, Connecticut, 1912–1932," *Pace Law Review* 33 (2013): 600–601.

48. Ibid., 601.

49. Village of Euclid v. Ambler Realty Co., 272 U.S. 365, 394 (1926).

50. The voluminous literature on changes in suburbanization includes Robert Fishman, *Bourgeois Utopias: The Rise and Fall of Suburbia* (New York: Basic Books, 1998); Joel Garreau, *Edge City: Life on the New Frontier* (New York: Doubleday, 1991); Kenneth T. Jackson, *Crabgrass Frontier: The Suburbanization of the United States* (New York: Oxford University Press, 1985); and Peter O. Muller, *Contemporary Suburban America* (Englewood Cliffs, NJ: Prentice-Hall, 1981).

51. Joseph Rodriguez, *City against Suburb: The Culture Wars in an American Metropolis* (Westport, CT: Praeger, 1999), 10.

52. David L. Kirp, "Here Comes the Neighborhood," *New York Times*, "Sunday Review," October 20, 2013, 3.

53. Steve Macek, *Urban Nightmares: The Media, the Right, and the Moral Panic over the City* (Minneapolis: University of Minnesota Press, 2006), 71.

54. James S. Duncan and Nancy G. Duncan, *Landscapes of Privilege: The Politics of the Aesthetic in an American Suburb* (New York: Routledge, 2004), 10.

55. Ibid., 3.

56. Gerald E. Frug, *City Making: Building Communities without Building Walls* (Princeton, NJ: Princeton University Press, 1999), 77.

57. Macek, *Urban Nightmares*, xvii.

58. Buchanan v. Warley, 245 U.S. 60, 82 (1917).

59. Quoted in Richard D. Kahlenberg, "The Walls We Won't Tear Down," *New York Times*, August 6, 2017.

60. Patricia E. Salkin, *American Law of Zoning*, 5th ed. (St. Paul, MN: Thomson-West, 2008); Peter W. Salsich Jr. and Timothy J. Tryniecki, *Land Use Regulation*, 2nd ed. (New York: Shepard's/McGraw-Hill, 2003).

61. Ybarra v. The City of the Town of Los Altos Hills, 503 F.2d 250, 254 (9th Cir. 1974).

62. Town of Edgartown, 680 N.E.2d 37, 41–42 (Mass. 1977).

63. Duncan and Duncan, *Landscapes of Privilege*, 87.

64. David A. Thornburg, *Galloping Bungalows: The Rise and Demise of the American House Trailer* (Hamden, CT: Archon Books, 1991), 174.

65. Rivlin, "The Cold, Hard Lessons of Mobile Home U.," 37, 45.

66. Allan D. Wallis, *Wheel Estate: The Rise and Decline of Mobile Homes* (Baltimore: Johns Hopkins University Press, 1997), 199.

67. Ibid., 173.

68. Quoted in Adam Cohen, "Will She Have Her Day in Court?," *Time*, January 25, 2010, 32.

69. Lawrence H. Davis et al., eds., *Shepard's Mobile Homes and Mobile Home Parks* (Colorado Springs: Shepard's Citations, 1975), 274–76.

70. Appeal of Groff, 274 A.2d 574 (Pa. 1971).

71. In the Matter of Village Board of Trustees of the Village of Malone v. Zoning Board of Appeals of the Village of Malone, 164 A.D.2d 24 (N.Y. App. Div. 1990).

72. Rivlin, "Cold, Hard Lessons of Mobile Home U.," 37.

73. John Fraser Hart, Michelle J. Rhodes, and John T. Morgan, *The Unknown World of the Mobile Home* (Baltimore: Johns Hopkins University Press, 2002), 22–23.

74. Wallis, *Wheel Estate*, 179.

75. Constance Perin, *Everything in Its Place: Social Order and Land Use in America* (Princeton, NJ: Princeton University Press, 1977), 4.

76. Southern Burlington County NAACP v. Township of Mount Laurel, 336 A.2d 713, 723 (New Jersey 1975).

77. Ibid., 732.

78. Southern Burlington County NAACP v. Township of Mount Laurel, 456 A.2d 390, 410 (New Jersey 1983).
79. Ibid., 415.
80. Ibid., 419.
81. Harold E. Spaeth, "Strict Scrutiny," in *The Oxford Companion to the Supreme Court of the United States*, ed. Kermit L. Hall et al. (New York: Oxford University Press, 2005), 845.
82. Bullock v. Carter, 404 U.S. 1354 (1972); Griffin v. Illinois, 351 U.S. 12 (1956); Douglas v. California, 372 U.S. 353 (1963); Williams v. Illinois, 399 US. 235 (1970).
83. Lindsey v. Normet, 405 U.S. 56, 74 (1972).
84. Ibid.
85. U.S. Constitution, Amendment IX, Section 1.
86. James v. Valtierra, 402 U.S. 137, 141 (1971).
87. Ibid.
88. Ibid., 142.
89. Ibid., 145.
90. David H. Moskowitz, *Exclusionary Zoning Litigation* (Cambridge, MA: Ballinger, 1977), 502.
91. Hutchison, "Black Suburbanization."
92. Robert J. Sampson, *Great American City: Chicago and the Enduring Neighborhood Effect* (Chicago: University of Chicago Press, 2012), 57.
93. For an intriguing commentary on New Jersey's *Mount Laurel* decision by its author, see Frederick W. Hall, "A Review of the Mount Laurel Decision," in *After Mount Laurel: The New Suburban Zoning*, ed. Jerome G. Rose and Robert E. Rothman (New Brunswick, NJ: Center for Urban Policy Research, 1977), 39–45.
94. Brian R. Lerman, "Mandatory Inclusionary Zoning: The Answer to the Affordable Housing Problem," *Boston College Environmental Affairs Law Review* 33 (2006): 383; Douglas R. Porter, *Covenants and Zoning for Research/Business Parks* (Washington, DC: Urban Land Institute, 2004).
95. Motoko Rich, "Percentage of Poor Students in Public Schools Rises," *New York Times*, January 16, 2015, A13.
96. Douglas S. Massey et al., *Climbing Mount Laurel: The Struggle for Affordable Housing and Social Mobility in an American Suburb* (Princeton, NJ: Princeton University Press, 2013).

97. Kirp, "Here Comes the Neighborhood," 3.

98. Herbert J. Gans, *The War Against the Poor: The Underclass and Antipoverty Policy* (New York: Basic Books, 1995), 99.

99. Jonathan Simon, *Poor Discipline: Parole and the Social Control of the Underclass, 1890–1990* (Chicago: University of Chicago Press, 1993), 260.

CHAPTER 3. CHANNELING FAMILY LIFE

1. Carl E. Schneider, "The Channelling Function in Family Law," *Hofstra Law Review* 20 (1992): 532. Some have wondered if, in light of the rapidly changing realities of family life, channeling through law remains possible, and one commentator has even announced that the channeling function in family law is currently "on life support." June Carbone, "Out of the Channel and into the Swamp: How Family Law Fails in a New Era of Class Division," *Hofstra Law Review* 39 (2011): 864.

2. Articles that explore the ways dominant attitudes about family life might be expressed through law include Katherine T. Bartlett, "Re-Expressing Parenthood," *Yale Law Journal* 98 (1988): 293; and Carol Weisbrod, "On the Expressive Functions of Family Law," *UC Davis Law Review* 22 (1989): 991.

3. Kathryn Edin and Joanna M. Reed, "Why Don't They Just Get Married? Barriers to Marriage among the Disadvantaged," *Future of Children* 15 (Fall 2005): 117–18.

4. Amy L. Wax, "Engines of Inequality: Class, Race, and Family Structure," *Family Law Quarterly* 41 (2007): 570–71.

5. Kate Zernike, "Why Are There So Many Single Americans?," *New York Times*, January 21, 2007, D1.

6. Andrew L. Yarrow, "Falling Marriage Rates Reveal Economic Fault Lines," *New York Times*, February 8, 2015, ST-15.

7. Gary S. Becker, *A Treatise on the Family* (Cambridge, MA: Harvard University Press, 1981), 14–37. For a challenge to Becker's thesis, see generally Valerie Kincade Oppenheimer, "Women's Rising Employment and the Future of the Family in Industrial Societies," *Population and Development Review* 20 (1994): 293.

8. "Economic Situation Summary," Bureau of Labor Statistics, http://www.bls.gov/news.release/empsit.nr0.htm.

9. William Julius Wilson, *The Truly Disadvantaged: The Inner City, the Underclass, and Public Policy* (Chicago: University of Chicago Press, 1987), 94–95.

10. Ibid., 91.

11. Barbara Ehrenreich, "TANF, or 'Torture and Abuse of Needy Families,'" *Seattle Journal for Social Justice* 1 (2002): 423.

12. Rachel Cohen, "Two Steps Forward, One Step Back: Evaluating the Healthy Marriage Initiative in Light of American Welfare History," *Georgetown Journal on Poverty Law & Policy* 17 (2010): 145.

13. Christina M. Gibson-Davis, Kathryn Edin, and Sara McLanahan, "High Hopes but Even Higher Expectations: The Retreat from Marriage among Low-Income Couples," *Journal of Marriage and the Family* 67 (2005): 1301–4.

14. Ibid., 1307–8.

15. Quentin Fottrell, "10 Things Married Couples Won't Tell You," *Milwaukee Journal Sentinel*, November 2, 2014, 5D.

16. Gibson-Davis, Edin, and McLanahan, "High Hopes but Even Higher Expectations," 1308.

17. Ehrenreich, "TANF, or 'Torture and Abuse of Needy Families,'" 423.

18. Cohen, "Two Steps Forward, One Step Back," 145.

19. Vice President Dan Quayle, "Address to the Commonwealth Club of California," May 19, 1992, http://www.vicepresidentdanquayle.com.

20. Ibid.

21. Tom Harper, "Who Hijacked Our Country," September 2, 2008, http://whohijackedourcountry.blogspot.com.

22. Personal Responsibility and Work Opportunity Reconciliation Act of 1996, 42 U.S.C. §601(101) (1996).

23. Robert Pear and Daniel D. Kirkpatrick, "Bush Plans $1.5 Billion Drive for Promotion of Marriage," *New York Times*, January 14, 2004, A1.

24. Monica Davey, "Promoting Marriage Becomes Major Phase of Welfare Reform," *Indianapolis Star*, December 2, 2001, A1.

25. Deficit Reduction Act, 42 U.S.C. §603(a)(2)(D) (2006).

26. "The Healthy Marriage Initiative," U.S. Department of Health and Human Services, Office of Family Assistance, https://www.acf.hhs.gov/ofa/resource/the-healthy-marriage-initiative-hmi.

27. Pear and Kirkpatrick, "Bush Plans $1.5 Billion Drive," A1.

28. "The Oklahoma Marriage Initiative," Oklahoma Marriage Initiative, http://www.okmarriage.org.

29. Teresa Kominos, "What Do Marriage and Welfare Reform Really Have in Common? A Look into TANF Programs," *St. John's Journal of Legal Comment* 21 (2006): 928–29.

30. "Healthy Marriage Initiative.".

31. Eugene D. Genovese, *Roll, Jordan, Roll: The World the Slaves Made* (New York: Pantheon Books, 1974), 475.

32. *Jump the Broom*, African American Healthy Marriage Initiative, http://www.aahmi.net/docs/jumpthebroom.pdf.

33. Robin Dion, "Healthy Marriage Programs: What Works?," *Future of Children* 15 (Fall 2005): 146.

34. Ibid.

35. Pear and Kirkpatrick, "Bush Plans $1.5 Billion Drive," A1.

36. Lynn Marie Kohm and Rachel K. Toberty, "A Fifty-State Survey of the Cost of Family Fragmentation," *Regent University Law Review* 25 (2012): 38–76.

37. 42 U.S.C. 603(a)(2)(D), Section 402(a)(2)(D).

38. Julia M. Fisher, "Marriage Promotion Policies and the Working Poor: A Match Made in Heaven?," *Boston College Third World Law Journal* 25 (2005): 487.

39. Council on Contemporary Families, "Promoting Marriage among Single Mothers," Brief Reports for January 6, 2014, http://www.contemporaryfamilies.org/marriage-ineffective-in-war-on-poverty-report.

40. Annie Lowrey, "For Richer, For Poorer," *New York Times Sunday Magazine*, February 9, 2014, 17.

41. Timothy Grail, "Custodial Mothers and Fathers and Their Child Support: 2011," U.S. Census Bureau Current Population Report, October 2013, 9.

42. Jeff Guo, "How Our Child Support System Can Push the Poor Deeper into Poverty," *Washington Post*, January 26, 2014.

43. Frances Robles and Shaila Dewan, "Skip Child Support. Go to Jail. Lose Job. Repeat." *New York Times*, April 20, 2015, A1.

44. Kathleen Mullan Harris, "Family Structure, Poverty, and Family Well-Being," *Employee Rights and Employment Policy Journal* 10 (2006), 57.

45. Catherine Wimberly, "Deadbeat Dads, Welfare Moms, and Uncle Sam: How the Child Support Recovery Act Punishes Single-Mother Families," *Stanford Law Review* 53 (2000): 735.

46. Tonya L. Brito, "The Welfarization of Family Law," *University of Kansas Law Review* 48 (2000): 261–62.

47. Sandra Evans, "Putting a Face on Deadbeat Dads," *Washington Post*, May 29, 1991, D1.

48. Paul Taylor, "Delinquent Dads: When Child Support Lags, 'Deadbeats' May Go to Jail," *Washington Post*, December 16, 1990, A1.

49. Sarah E. Button, "Bounties on Deadbeat Dads," *Money*, March 1984, 202.

50. David L. Chambers, *Making Fathers Pay: The Enforcement of Child Support* (Chicago: University of Chicago Press, 1979), 118–19.

51. Quoted in Dennis Chapman, "Top Court Refuses Case of State Dad," *Milwaukee Journal Sentinel*, October 8, 2002, A1.

52. Quoted in "No-Kids Appeal to Be Heard," *Beloit Daily News*, April 30, 2001, 1.

53. A symposium regarding the decision appears at *Western New England Law Review* 26 (2004): 1, and the symposium includes my own "State v. Oakley, Deadbeat Dads, and American Poverty," 9–26.

54. State v. Oakley, 629 N.W. 2d 200, 204 (Wis. 2001).

55. Ibid., 216.

56. Joseph L. Lieberman, *Child Support in America: Practical Advice for Negotiating—and Collecting—a Fair Settlement* (New Haven, CT: Yale University Press, 1986), x.

57. Ibid., 122.

58. Ibid, v.

59. Child Support Enforcement Amendments of 1984, 42 U.S.C. §651–669 (2006).

60. Child Support Recovery Act of 1992, 18 U.S.C. §228 (2006).

61. Catherine Wimberly, "Deadbeat Dads, Welfare Moms, and Uncle Sam," 739.

62. Ibid., 743.

63. Deadbeat Parents Punishment Act of 1998, 18 U.S.C. §228 (2006).

64. Presidential candidate William Clinton used this line during his 1992 campaign and also included it in his first State of the Union Address. Richard Delgado, "The Myth of Upward Mobility," *University of Pittsburgh Law Review* 68 (2007): 908. Clinton's call for the poor to get off welfare and get to work drew robust bipartisan support. Stephen D. Sugarman, "Financial Support of Children and the End of Welfare as We Know It," *Virginia Law Review* 81 (1995): 2548.

65. Personal Responsibility and Work Opportunity Reconciliation Act of 1996, 42 U.S.C. 601 (1996).

66. "Remarks on Signing the Personal Responsibility and Work Opportunity Reconciliation Act of 1996 and an Exchange with Reporters, August 22, 1996," http://www.presidency.ucsb.edu/ws/?pid=53218.

67. Brito, "The Welfarization of Family Law," 256–62.

68. Paul K. Legler, "The Coming Revolution in Child Support Policy: Implications of the 1996 Welfare Act," *Family Law Quarterly* 30 (1996): 538.

69. Ibid.

70. Robles and Dewan, "Skip Child Support," A1.

71. "Obama Urges Black Men to Be Better Fathers," *Milwaukee Journal Sentinel*, June 16, 2008, 4A.

72. Quoted in Eduardo Porter, "Time to Try Compassion, Not Censure, for Families," *New York Times*, March 15, 2014, B1.

73. Annette R. Appell, "'Bad' Mothers and Spanish-Speaking Caregivers," *Nevada Law Journal* 7 (2007): 760.

74. Tanya Asim Cooper, "Racial Bias in American Foster Care: The National Debate," *Marquette Law Review* 97 (2013): 223.

75. Patricia E. Erickson, "Federal Child Abuse and Child Neglect Policy in the United States since 1974," *Criminal Justice Review* 25 (2000): 89.

76. Appell, "'Bad' Mothers and Spanish-Speaking Caregivers," 760.

77. Lucy Wieland and Jenny L. Nelson, "Aging Out of Foster Care: How Extended Foster Care for Youth Eighteen to Twenty-One Has Fostered Independence," *William Mitchell Law Review* 40 (2014): 1117.

78. Jean C. Lawrence, "ASFA in the Age of Mass Incarceration: Go to Prison—Lose Your Child?," *William Mitchell Law Review* 40 (2014): 993.

79. Dorothy E. Roberts, "Poverty, Race, and New Directions in Child Welfare Policy," *Washington University Journal of Law and Policy* 1 (1999): 64.

80. Andrea J. Sedlar and Diane D. Broadhurst, *Third National Incidence Study of Child Abuse and Neglect* (Washington, DC: U.S. Department of Health and Human Services, 1996), 10.

81. Kashana Cauley, "How America Destroys Black Families," *New York Times*, January 3, 2018, A13.

82. Ibid.

83. Cooper, "Racial Bias in American Foster Care," 228.

84. Candra Bullock, "Low-Income Parents Victimized by Child Protective Services," *Journal of Gender, Social Policy & the Law* 11 (2003): 1048.

85. Cooper, "Racial Bias in American Foster Care," 240.

86. Ibid.

87. Anita Ortiz Maddali, "The Immigrant 'Other': Racialized Identity and the Devaluation of Immigrant Family Relations," *Indiana Law Journal* 89 (2014): 666–73.

88. Appell, "'Bad' Mothers and Spanish-Speaking Caregivers," 759.

89. Elizabeth J. Samuels, "Surrender and Subordination: Birth Mothers and Adoption Law Reform," *Michigan Journal of Gender & Law* 20 (2013): 36.

90. Maureen A. Sweeney, who as a college student placed a child for adoption, at first understood her decision in terms of her child's welfare but then realized self-interest played a role. "After time and reflection," she writes, "I believe within that genuine desire for my son was also a desire for myself. I knew that if I kept him I would probably marry his father (who had in the weeks before the birth become the one pushing for marriage), and my instincts were clamoring that this would be a disastrous move for me." Maureen A. Sweeney, "Between Sorrow and Happy Endings: A New Paradigm of Adoption," *Yale Journal of Law & Feminism* 2 (1998): 332.

91. Kathy S. Stolley, "Statistics on Adoption in the United States," in *Family Law in Action: A Reader*, ed. Margaret F. Brinig et al. (Cincinnati: Anderson Publishing Co., 1999), 106.

92. Viviana Zelizer, *Pricing the Priceless Child: The Changing Social Value of Children* (New York: Basic Books, 1985), 169, 193.

93. David Ray Papke, "Transracial Adoption in the United States: The Reflection and Reinforcement of Racial Hierarchy," *Journal of Law and Family Studies* 15 (2013): 74.

94. Elizabeth Bartholet, "Where Do Black Children Belong? The Politics of Race Matching in Adoption," *University of Pennsylvania Law Review* 139 (1991): 1178.

95. James S. Bowen, "Cultural Convergences and Divergences: The Nexus between Putative Afro-American Family Values and the Best Interests of the Child," *Journal of Family Law* 26 (1987): 487; Cynthia G. Hawkins-Leon and Carla Bradley, "Race and Transracial Adoptions: The Answer Is Neither Black or White Nor Right or Wrong," *Catholic University Law Review* 51 (2002): 1227; Asher D. Isaacs, "Interracial Adoption: Permanent Placement and Racial Identity—An Adoptee's Perspective," *National Black Law Journal* 14 (1995): 126; David Ray Papke, "Transracial Adoption in the United States: The Reflection and Reinforcement of Racial Hierarchy," *Journal of Law & Family Studies* 15 (2013): 57; Marlon N. Yarbrough, "Trans-Racial Adoption: The Genesis of Minority Cultural Existence," *Southern University Law Review* 15 (1988): 353.

96. David Ray Papke, "Pondering Past Purposes: A Critical History of American Adoption

Law," *West Virginia Law Review* 102 (1999): 470–74.

97. Diane S. Kaplan, "The Baby Richard Amendments and the Law of Unintended Consequences," *Children's Legal Rights Journal* 22 (2002): 2; Donna L. Moore, "Implementing a National Putative Father Registry by Utilizing Existing Federal/ State Collaborative Databases," *John Marshall Law Review* 36 (2003): 1033.

98. In a much-discussed Connecticut case, a biological father argued that it could not possibly be in the "best interests" of his son to terminate the father's parental rights and send the son to foster care when no adoptive parents had stepped forward. Among other things, the father noted, this would sever the boy's positive relationships with other members of his biological family. Courts at the trial and appellate levels disagreed, and they allowed the foster care placement to go forward. See In re Davanta V., 280 Conn. 947 (2006).

99. Elisabeth M. Landes and Richard A. Posner, "The Economics of the Baby Shortage," *Journal of Legal Studies* 7 (1978): 324.

100. Tamar Frankel and Francis H. Miller, "The Inapplicability of Market Theory to Adoptions," *Boston University Law Review* 67 (1987): 99; J. Robert S. Prichard, "A Market for Babies?," *University of Toronto Law Review* 34 (1984): 341; Robin West, "Submission, Choice, and Ethics: A Rejoinder to Judge Posner," *Harvard Law Review* 99 (1986): 1449.

101. Richard A. Posner, "The Regulation of the Market in Adoptions," *Boston University Law Review* 67 (1987): 59.

102. Gilbert A. Holmes, "The Extended Family System in the Black Community: A Child-Centered Model for Adoption Policy," *Temple Law Review* 68 (1995): 1653.

103. Melanie Nicholson, "Without Their Children: Rethinking Motherhood among Transnational Migrant Women," *Social Text* 24, no. 3 (2006): 13, 15–16.

104. Ibid.

105. Nancy Chodorow, *The Reproduction of Mothering: Psychoanalysis and the Sociology of Gender* (Berkeley: University of California Press, 1978), 76.

106. Elmer P. Martin and Joanne Mitchell Martin, *The Black Extended Family* (Chicago: University of Chicago Press, 1978); David M. Schneider and Raymond T. Smith, *Class Differences in American Kinship* (Ann Arbor: University of Michigan Press, 1978).

107. Rayna Rapp, "Family and Class in Contemporary America: Notes toward an Understanding of Ideology," *Science & Society*, 42 (1978): 292.

108. Cynthia G. Hawkins-Leon, "The Indian Child Welfare Act and the African American

Tribe: Facing the Adoption Crisis," *Brandeis Journal of Family Law* 36 (1997): 211.

109. Appell, "'Bad' Mothers and Spanish-Speaking Caregivers," 778.

110. Twila L. Perry, "Transracial and International Adoption: Mothers, Hierarchy, Race, and Feminist Legal Theory," *Yale Journal of Law & Feminism* 10 (1998): 121.

111. Andrew Adam Newman, "Wendy's Turns Up Volume on Adoption Drive," *New York Times*, March 14, 2014, B8.

112. Beth Wilson, "What Is 'Poverty Porn,' and Are We Guilty of Indulging in It?," *Trespass* magazine, February 4, 2010, http://ww.trespassmag.com.

113. Perry, "Transracial and International Adoption," 123–24.

CHAPTER 4. MARKETPLACE EXPLOITATION

1. Elizabeth Sweet, "Symbolic Capital Consumption and Health Inequality," *American Journal of Public Health* 101 (2011): 260.

2. Robert G. Dunn, "Identity, Commodification, and Consumer Culture," in *Identity and Social Change*, ed. Joseph E. Davis (New Brunswick, NJ: Transaction, 2000), 113.

3. David Caplovitz, *The Poor Pay More: Consumer Practices of Low-Income Families* (New York: Free Press, 1967); Gregory D. Squires, *Why the Poor Pay More* (Westport, CT: Praeger Publishers, 2004).

4. Erik Eckholm, "Study Documents 'Ghetto Tax' Being Paid by the Urban Poor," *New York Times*, July 19, 2006, A16; Matthew Fellowes, "The High Price of Being Poor," *Los Angeles Times*, July 23, 2006, A14; Bruce Katz, "Concentrated Poverty in New Orleans and Other Cities," *Chronicle of Higher Education*, August 4, 2006, 6–7.

5. Debabrata Talukdar, "Cost of Being Poor: Retail Price Differences across Inner-City and Suburban Neighborhoods," *Journal of Consumer Research* 25 (2008): 457.

6. Ibid., 467, 470.

7. Bruce Speight and Greg Hart, "Rent-to-Own Rip-off: Why Wisconsin Shouldn't Exempt the Predatory Rent-to-Own Industry from Consumer Protection Laws" (Madison, WI: WISPIRG Report, 2013), 2.

8. Bruce M. Lacko, Signe-Mary McKernan, and Mary Hastak, *Survey of Rent-to-Own Customers*, Federal Trade Commission Bureau of Economics Staff Report (Washington, DC: United States Government Printing Office, 2000), 3.

9. Michael Ralph, "Commodity," *Social Text* 27 (2009): 78.

10. David Ray Papke, "Pondering Past Purposes: A Critical History of American Adoption

Law," *West Virginia Law Review* 102 (1999): 468–70.

11. Daniel Horowitz, *The Morality of Spending: Attitudes toward the Consumer Society, 1875–1940* (Baltimore: Johns Hopkins University Press, 1985), 135.

12. Stephen Garey, "Brands R Us: How Advertising Works," Center for Media Literacy, n.d., http://www.medialit.org/reading-room/brands-r-us-how-advertising-works.

13. Christopher Lasch, *The Culture of Narcissism: American Life in an Age of Diminishing Expectations* (New York: W.W. Norton & Co., 1978), 72.

14. Lacko, McKernan, and Hastak, *Survey of Rent-to-Own Customers*, 32.

15. James P. Nehf, "Effective Regulation of Rent-to-Own Contracts," *Ohio State Law Journal* 52 (1991): 752.

16. Kathleen E. Keest, Jeffrey I. Langer, and Michael F. Day, "Interest Rate Regulation Developments: High-Cost Mortgages, Rent-to-Own Transactions, and Unconscionability," *Business Lawyer* 50 (1995): 1086.

17. Speight and Hart, "Rent-to-Own Rip-off," 1–2.

18. Jim Hawkins, "Renting the Good Life," *William and Mary Law Review* 49 (2008): 2055.

19. Lacko, McKernan, and Hastak, *Survey of Rent-to-Own Customers*, 47.

20. Hawkins, "Renting the Good Life," 2055.

21. "Rent-A-Center Is a Ripoff That Preys on the Poor," *New York Daily News*, November 25, 2009.

22. Kim Christensen, "Payday Loans Mushroom," *Pittsburgh Tribune Review*, January 11, 2009.

23. Josh Boak, "'Payday' Loan Rules Sought," *Milwaukee Journal Sentinel*, March 27, 2015, 1D.

24. Karen E. Francis, "Rollover, Rollover: A Behavioral Law and Economics Analysis of the Payday Loan Industry," *Texas Law Review* 88 (2010): 618–19.

25. Meera Louis, "Consumer Credit in U.S. Increases by Most in 10 Years," *Bloomberg News*, January 9, 2012.

26. Michelle Jamrisko, "Consumer Credit in U.S. Rises by $17.1 Billion, Fed Says," *Bloomberg News*, July 9, 2012, https://www.bloomberg.com/news/articles/2012-07-09/consumer-credit-in-u-s-jumped-by-17-1-billion-in-may-fed-says.

27. Jessica Silver-Greenberg, "Banks Are a Key in the Machinery of Payday Loans," *New York Times*, February 24, 2013, A1.

28. Creola Johnson, "Payday Loans: Shrewd Business or Predatory Lending?," *Minnesota*

Law Review 87 (2000): 9.

29. Diane Hellwig, "Exposing the Loansharks in Sheep's Clothing: Why Regulating the Consumer Credit Market Makes Sense," *Notre Dame Law Review* 80 (2015): 1567–611.

30. Mark H. Haller and John V. Alviti, "Loansharking in American Cities: Historical Analysis of a Marginal Enterprise," *American Journal of Legal History* 21 (1977): 125–56.

31. Ibid., 11.

32. Jessica Silver-Greenberg, "Consumer Protection Agency Seeks Limits on Payday Lenders," *New York Times*, February 9, 2015, A1.

33. Ibid., B2.

34. Nathalie Martin, "Regulating Payday Loans: Why This Should Make the CFPB's Short List," *Harvard Business Law Review Online* 2 (2011): 46 (online).

35. Francis, "Rollover, Rollover," 627–31.

36. Shane Mendenhall, "Payday Loans: The Effects of Payday Lending on Society and the Need for More State and Federal Regulation," *Oklahoma City Law Review* 32 (2007): 314–15.

37. Paige Marta Skiba, "Regulation of Payday Loans Misguided?," *Washington and Lee Law Review* 69 (2012): 1023.

38. Lynn Drysdale and Kathleen E. Keest, "The Two-Tiered Consumer Financial Services Marketplace: The Fringe Banking System and Its Challenges to Current Thinking about the Role of Usury Laws in Today's Society," *South Carolina Law Review* 51 (2000): 605.

39. Ibid., 600.

40. Lacko, McKernan, and Hastak, *Survey of Rent-to-Own Customers*, 3.

41. Ibid.

42. Patrick Moulding, "Fair or Unfair? The Importance of Mass Transit for America's Poor," *Georgetown Journal on Poverty Law & Policy* 12 (2005): 155.

43. Joseph B. Cahill, "License to Owe: Title-Loan Firms Can Offer Car Owners a Solution That Often Backfires," *Wall Street Journal*, March 3, 1999.

44. Susan Payne Carter and Paige Martin Skiba, "Pawnshops, Behavioral Economics, and Self-Regulation," *Review of Banking and Financial Law* 32 (2012): 200–201.

45. Ibid., 202–3.

46. Jarret C. Oeltjen, "Florida Pawnbroking: An Industry in Transition," *Florida State University Law Review* 22 (1996): 995–96.

47. Carter and Skiba, "Pawnshops, Behavioral Economics, and Self-Regulation," 193.

48. Stephanie Clifford and Jessica Silver-Greenberg, "Platinum Card and Text Alert, via Pawnshop," *New York Times*, August 28, 2013, 14.

49. Kathleen C. Engel and Patricia A. McCoy, "A Tale of Three Markets: The Law and Economics of Predatory Lending," *Texas Law Review* 80 (2002): 1261–62.

50. Center for Responsible Lending, *Car Title Lending: Driving Borrowers to Financial Ruin*, 4–7, April 14, 2005, http://www.responsiblelending.org.

51. Ibid., 4–5.

52. Nathalie Martin and Ozymandias Adams, "Grand Theft Auto Loans," *Missouri Law Review* 71 (2012): 85–86.

53. Todd J. Zywicki, "Consumer Use and Government Regulation of Title Pledge Lending," *Loyola Consumer Law Review* 22 (2010): 435.

54. Jim Hawkins, "Credit on Wheels: The Law and Business of Auto-Title Lending," *Washington and Lee Law Review* 69 (2012): 590.

55. Zywicki, "Consumer Use and Government Regulation of Title Pledge Lending," 427.

56. Hawkins, "Credit on Wheels," 590.

57. Martin and Adams, "Grand Theft Auto Loans," 85.

58. Center for Responsible Lending, *Car Title Lending*, 6.

59. Perez v. Rent-A-Center, 892 A.2d 1255, 1260 (N.J. 2006).

60. Ibid.

61. Drysdale and Keest, "The Two-Tiered Consumer Financial Services Marketplace," 641–42.

62. Hamilton v. York, 987 F. Supp. 953 (E.D. Ky. 1997); White v. Check Holder, Inc., 996 S.W. 2d 496 (Ky. 1999).

63. Pendleton v. American Title Brokers, 754 F. Supp. 860 (S.D. Ala. 1991); Lynn v. Financial Solutions Corp., 173 B.R. 894 (Bankr. M.D. Tenn. 1994); State ex rel. McGraw v. Pawn America, 518 S.E. 2d 859 (W. Va. 1998).

64. Susan Lorde Martin and Nancy White Hutchins, "Consumers Advocates vs. The Rent-to-Own Industry: Reaching a Reasonable Accommodation," *American Business Law Journal* 34 (1997): 396–408.

65. Patrick Marley, "Payday Lenders Escape Limits," *Milwaukee Journal Sentinel*, December 10, 2012, 11A.

66. Martin and Adams, "Grand Theft Auto Loans," 55.

67. Nathalie Martin and Ernesto Longa, "High-Interest Loans and Class: Do Payday and

Title Loans Really Serve the Middle Class," *Loyola Consumer Law Review* 24 (2012): 525. For a discussion of predatory lending involving military personnel, see Jessica Silver-Greenberg and Peter Eavis, "Service Members Left Vulnerable to Payday Loans," *New York Times*, November 22, 2013, A1.

68. Hawkins, "Credit on Wheels," 586–88.

69. "Progress on Payday Lending," *New York Times*, March 3, 2015, SR8.

70. "New Rules to Ban Payday Lending 'Debt Traps,'" The Two-Way: NPR (online).

71. Alan Rappeport, "Defenders See Rules Easing under Trump," *New York Times*, February 5, 2018, A1.

72. Zywicki, "Consumer Use and Government Regulation of Title Pledge Lending," 429.

73. Ibid., 431.

74. Marley, "Payday Lenders Escape Limits," 1A.

75. Michael Booth, "Suit over Rent-to-Own Agreements Settles for $109 Million in New Jersey," *New Jersey Law Journal*, May 3, 2007, A1.

76. Boak, "'Payday' Loan Rules Sought," 3D.

77. Francis, "Rollover, Rollover," 618; Martin and Longa, "High-Interest Loans and Class," 526.

78. James Livingston, *Against Thrift: Why Consumer Culture Is Good for the Economy, the Environment, and Your Soul* (New York: Basic Books, 2011), 195–96.

79. Satz says those with no choice have "weak agency." Debra Satz, *Why Some Things Should Not Be for Sale: The Moral Limits of Markets* (New York: Oxford University Press, 2010), 9.

80. Ibid.

81. Zoë Elizabeth Lees, "Payday Peonage: Thirteenth Amendment Implications in Payday Lending," *Scholar: St. Mary's Law Review on Race and Justice* 15 (2012): 63.

CHAPTER 5. HEALTH INEQUITY

1. Scott Burris, "From Health Care to the Social Determinants of Health," *University of Pennsylvania Law Review* 159 (2011): 1652.

2. Lisa F. Berkman and Ichiro Kawachi, eds., *Social Epidemiology* (Oxford: Oxford University Press, 2000).

3. Scott Burris, "Law in a Social Determinants Strategy: A Public Health Law Research Perspective," *Public Health Reports* 126 (2011): 22.

4. Norman Daniels, Bruce P. Kennedy, and Ichiro Kawachi, "Why Justice Is Good for Our Health: The Social Determinants of Health Inequalities," *Daedalus* 128, no. 4 (1999): 216, 237.

5. Scott Burris, Ichiro Kawachi, and Austin Sarat, "Health, Law, and Human Rights: Background and Key Concepts Integrating Law and Social Epidemiology," *Journal of Law, Medicine & Ethics* 30 (2002): 511.

6. Rolf Pendall et al., *A Lost Decade: Neighborhood Poverty and the Urban Crisis of the 2000s* (Washington, DC: Joint Center for Political and Economic Studies, 2011), 26; Darrell J. Gaskin et al., "Disparities in Diabetes: The Nexus of Race, Poverty, and Place," *American Journal of Public Health* 104 (2014): 2151.

7. Paul M. Sherer, *The Benefits of Parks: Why America Needs More Parks and Open Space* (Washington, DC: Trust for Public Land, 2006), 8.

8. Ibid., 5.

9. "Urban Park and Recreation Recovery Program," National Park Service, https://www.nps.gov/uparr.

10. Sherer, *The Benefits of Parks*, 13–14.

11. Eugenia C. South et al., "Neighborhood Blight, Stress, and Health: A Walking Trial of Urban Greening and Ambulatory Heart Rate," *American Journal of Public Health* 105 (2015): 911.

12. Robert Lipton et al., "The Geography of Violence, Alcohol Outlets, and Drug Arrests in Boston," *American Journal of Public Health* 103 (2013): 657–64.

13. Shannon N. Zenk et al., "Relative and Absolute Availability of Healthier Food and Beverage Alternatives across Communities in the United States," *American Journal of Public Health* 104 (2014): 2170.

14. One study found that only 18 percent of the small grocery stores in a minority neighborhood carried healthy foods compared with 58 percent in a white area. C. R. Horowitz et al., "Barriers to Buying Healthy Foods for People with Diabetes," *American Journal of Public Health* 94 (2004): 1549–54.

15. Neil Wrigley et al., "Assessing the Impact of Improved Retail Access on Diet in a Food Desert," *Urban Studies* 39 (2002): 2061–82.

16. "Food Deserts," U.S. Department of Agriculture Agricultural Marketing Service, http://apps.ams.usda.gov.

17. Gaskin et al., "Disparities in Diabetes," 2151.

18. Ibid.

19. Robert Bullard, "Residential Segregation and Urban Quality of Life," in *Environmental Justice: Issues, Policies, and Solutions*, ed. Bunyan Bryant (Washington, DC: Island Press, 1995), 77.

20. Alex Geisinger, "The Benefits of Development and Environmental Justice," *Columbia Journal of Environmental Law* 37 (2012): 205; Feng Liu, "Dynamics and Causation of Environmental Equity, Locally Unwanted Land Uses, and Neighborhood Changes," *Environmental Management* 21 (2015): 643–56.

21. Dennis C. Cory and Tauhidur Rahman, *Environmental Justice and Federalism* (Northampton, MA: Edward Elgar Publishing, 2012), 2.

22. J. A. Stoloff, "A Brief History of Public Housing" (Washington, DC: U.S. Department of Housing and Urban Development, 2004), 6.

23. National Heart and Lung Institute, *Public Health in Public Housing* (Washington, DC: U.S. Department of Health and Human Services, 2005), vi.

24. Erin Ruel et al., "Is Public Housing the Cause of Poor Health or a Safety Net for the Unhealthy Poor?," *Journal of Urban Health* 87 (2010): 827.

25. Patricia J. Martens et al., "The Effect of Neighborhood Socioeconomic Status on Education and Health Outcomes for Children Living in Social Housing," *American Journal of Public Health* 104 (2014): 2103.

26. Lisa M. Cleveland et al., "Lead Hazards for Pregnant Women and Children: Part I; Immigrants and the Poor Shoulder Most of the Burden of Lead Exposure in This Country," *American Journal of Nursing* 108 (2008): 40–49.

27. Brady Dennis, "In Some Zip Codes 1 in 7 Children Suffer from Dangerously High Blood Lead Levels," *Washington Post*, June 15, 2016.

28. Residential Lead-Based Paint Hazard Reduction Act, 42 U.S.C. 4851.

29. Amanda Bronstad, "Lead Paint Litigation Is Beginning to Fade," *National Law Journal*, August 21, 2007, 17; Robert Tyson and Morgan Van Buren, "Lead Paint Litigation and the Future of Public Nuisance Law," n.d., Tyson & Mendes, http://www.tysonmendes.com/blog-lead-paint.

30. Austin Sarat, "'The Law Is All Over': Power, Resistance, and the Legal Consciousness of the Welfare Poor," *Yale Journal of Law and the Humanities* 2 (1990): 343.

31. Danielle German and Carl A. Latkin, "Exposure to Urban Rats as a Community Stressor among Low-Income Urban Residents," *Journal of Community Psychology* 44 (2016): 249, 251.

32. Whitney P. Witt et al., "Neighborhood Disadvantage, Preconception Stressful Life

Events, and Infant Birth Weight," *American Journal of Public Health* 105 (2015): 1044, 1048.

33. Matthew Desmond, *Evicted: Poverty and Profit in the American City* (New York: Crown Books, 2016), 296.

34. Ibid., 330.

35. Ibid., 298.

36. Elizabeth Gudrais, "Disrupted Lives," *Harvard Magazine*, January–February 2014, 38.

37. Desmond, *Evicted*, 97, 298.

38. Ibid., 99.

39. Stephanos Bibas, "Plea Bargaining outside the Shadow of Trial," *Harvard Law Review* 117 (2004): 2540.

40. Katherine J. Karriker-Jaffee, Sarah C. M. Roberts, and Jason Bond, "Income Inequality, Alcohol Use, and Alcohol-Related Problems," *American Journal of Public Health* 103 (2013): 649.

41. Alexis N. Martinez et al., "Spatial Analysis of HIV Positive Injection Drug Users in San Francisco, 1987 to 2005," *International Journal of Environmental Research and Public Health* 11 (2014): 3937.

42. Brooke A. Hixson et al., "Spatial Clustering of HIV Prevalence in Atlanta, Georgia and Population Characteristics Associated with Case Concentrations," *Journal of Urban Health* 88 (2011): 129–41.

43. Gary A. Giovino, "Epidemiology of Tobacco Use in the United States," *Oncogene* 21 (2002): 7333; Oral Cancer Foundation, "Demographics," https://oralcancerfoundation.org.

44. Sabrina Tavernise, "Socioeconomic Divide in Smoking Rates," *New York Times*, November 13, 2015, A23.

45. Center for Disease Control and Prevention, "Fact Sheet—Adult Smoking in the United States," http://www.cdc.gov/tobacco/data_statistics/fact_sheets/.

46. Rosemary Hiscock et al., "Socioeconomic Status and Smoking: A Review," *Annals of the New York Academy of Sciences* 1248 (2012): 111–17.

47. Public Law No. 111–3, 123 Stat. 1776 (codified as amended in scattered sections of 21 U.S.C. (2112).

48. R.J. Reynolds Company, et al., v. Food and Drug Administration, et al., 696 F.3d 1205 (D.C. Cir. 2012).

49. Cynthia L. Ogden et al., "Obesity and Socioeconomic Status in Adults: United States,

2005–2008," *NCHS Data Brief* 50 (December 2010): 1–2.

50. Food Research and Action Center, "Relationships between Poverty and Obesity," http://frac.org/obesity-health/relationship-poverty-obesity.

51. Adam Drewnowski, "Obesity, Diets, and Social Inequalities," *Nutrition Reviews* 67 (2009): S37.

52. "NYC Passes Ban on Supersized Sugary Drinks," *TODAY*, October 13, 2016, http://www.today.com/health/nyc-passes-ban-supersized-sugar-drinks-995552.

53. Ibid.

54. Adam Nagourney, "Berkeley Officials Outspent but Optimistic in Battle over Soda Tax," *New York Times*, October 8, 2014, A16.

55. New York Statewide Coalition of Hispanic Chambers of Commerce v. New York City Department of Health and Mental Hygiene, 23 N.Y.3d 945 (2014); Michael M. Grynbaum, "New York's Ban on Big Sodas Is Rejected by Final Court," *New York Times*, June 27, 2014, A24.

56. David Adam Friedman, "Public Health Regulation and the Limits of Paternalism," *Connecticut Law Review* 46 (2014): 1694.

57. Ibid., 1739.

58. The tendency to hold obese people personally responsible for their obesity dovetails to some extent with class and racial biases. Poor people of color who happen to be obese are in this sense double and/or triple-marginalized. Lindsay F. Wiley, "Shame, Blame, and the Emerging Law of Obesity Control," *UC Davis Law Review* 121 (2013): 165.

59. Thomas Piketty, *Capital in the Twenty-First Century* (Cambridge, MA: Belknap Press, 2014), 259.

60. Patricia Cohen, "Counting Up Hidden Costs of Low Pay," *New York Times*, April 13, 2015, D1.

61. Ibid.

62. Pew Research Center, "5 Facts about the Minimum Wage," July 23, 2015, http:www.pewrsr.ch/18mdJTD.

63. Christopher Ingraham, "The U.S. Has One of the Stingiest Minimum Wage Policies of Any Wealthy Nation," *Washington Post*, December 29, 2017.

64. Noam Scheiber, "Raising the Floor for Wages Moves Economy into Unknown," *New York Times*, July 27, 2015, A1.

65. Congressional Budget Office, "The Effects of a Minimum-Wage Increase on

Employment and Family Income," February 18, 2014, http:www.cbo.gov/publication/44995.

66. Tonya L. Brito, "The Welfarization of Family Law," *University of Kansas Law Review* 48 (2000): 233.

67. Eduardo Porter, "Income Inequality Is Costing the Nation on Social Issues," *New York Times*, April 29, 2015.

68. Monica Prasad, *The Land of Too Much: American Abundance and the Paradox of Poverty* (Cambridge, MA: Harvard University Press, 2012), 249.

69. Eduardo Porter, "Discredited Notions Still Guide Policy on Aid to the Poor," *New York Times*, October 2, 2015, B1.

70. Ibid.

71. Brito, "The Welfarization of Family Law," 235.

72. Bill Clinton, "Acceptance Speech to the Democratic National Convention, July 16, 1992," www.4president.org/speeches/billclinton1992acceptance.htm.

73. Eduardo Porter, "A Party's Strategy to Ignore Poverty," *New York Times*, October 28, 2015, B1.

74. Paul K. Legler, "The Coming Revolution in Child Support Policy: Implications of the 1996 Welfare Act," *Family Law Quarterly* 30 (1996): 519.

75. Porter, "A Party's Strategy to Ignore Poverty," B1.

76. Steven Erlanger, "Taking on Adam Smith (and Karl Marx)," *New York Times*, April 20, 2014, Business 1.

77. Eduardo Porter, "What Debate on Inequality Is Missing," *New York Times*, May 5, 2015, B1.

78. Michael Kraus, Shai Davidai, and A. David Nussbaum, "American Dream? Or Mirage," *New York Times*, May 3, 2015, SR9.

79. Daniels et al., "Why Justice Is Good for Our Health," 215.

80. Ibid., 221.

81. Sandro Galea et al., "Neighborhood Income and Income Distribution and the Use of Cigarettes, Alcohol, and Marijuana," *American Journal of Preventive Medicine* 32 (2007): S195–S202.

82. Frank J. Elgar et al., "Income Inequality and Alcohol Use: A Multilevel Analysis of Drinking and Drunkenness in Adolescents in 34 Countries," *European Journal of Public Health* 15 (2003): 245–50.

83. John Lynch et al., "Income Inequality and Mortality: Importance to Health of

Individual Income, Psychological Environment, or Material Conditions," *British Medical Journal* 320 (2000): 1200–1204.

84. Karriker-Jaffe et al., "Income Inequality, Alcohol Use, and Alcohol-Related Problems," 649.

85. Atheendar S. Venkataramani et al., "Economic Opportunity, Health Behaviors, and Mortality in the United States," *American Journal of Public Health* 106 (2016): 478, 483.

86. Eduardo Porter, "Plan to End Poverty Is Wide of the Target," *New York Times*, June 1, 2016, B1.

87. Ron Daniels, "A Domestic Marshall Plan to Transform America's 'Dark Ghettos,'" *Black Scholar* 37 (2007): 10–13.

88. The tendency to cast these types of public health law and regulations as "paternalistic" seems to have become more common after the publication of Richard Thaler and Cass Sunstein's *Nudge: Improving Decisions about Health, Wealth, and Happiness* (New Haven, CT: Yale University Press, 2008). One law review devoted an entire issue to public health paternalism and its various types and categories: *Connecticut Law Review* 46 (2014): 1687–936.

CONCLUSION

1. Debra Emmelman, *Justice for the Poor: A Study of Criminal Defense Work* (Burlington, VT: Ashgate, 2003), 121.

2. United Nations, "The Universal Declaration of Human Rights" (1948), Article 25:1.

3. David Ray Papke, "Keeping the Underclass in Its Place: Zoning, the Urban Poor, and Residential Segregation," *Urban Lawyer* 41 (2009): 787.

4. Carl E. Schneider, "The Channelling Function in Family Law," *Hofstra Law Review* 20 (1992): 532.

5. Robert G. Dunn, "Identity, Commodification, and Consumer Culture," in *Identity and Social Change*, ed. Joseph E. Davis (New Brunswick, NJ: Transaction, 2000), 113.

6. Lawrence O. Gostin, *Public Health Law: Power, Duty, Restraint* (Berkeley: University of California Press, 2000), xvii.

7. David Ray Papke, "Perpetuating Poverty: Exploitative Businesses, the Urban Poor, and the Failure of Reform," *The Scholar* 16 (2014): 251.

8. 42 U.S.C. 4851.

9. Erik Olin Wright, "Class Analysis," in *Social Class and Stratification*, ed. Rhonda E. Levine (Lanham, MD: Rowman & Littlefield, 1998), 143, 154.

10. A social scientist might choose to say that law should allocate responsibility for wrongdoing, settle disputes, and distribute the good and desirable things in life. Richard Lempert and Joseph Sanders, *An Invitation to Law and the Social Sciences* (Philadelphia: University of Pennsylvania Press, 1986), 4–8.

11. Ann E. Cudd, *Analyzing Oppression* (New York: Oxford University Press, 2006), 23.

12. J. Harvey, "Humor as Social Act," *Journal of Value Inquiry* 29, no. 1 (1995): 19–30.

13. Nicky Gonzalez Yuen, "Oppression and Democracy," in *The Politics of Liberation*, ed. Nicky Gonzalez Yuen, 3rd ed. (Dubuque, IA: Kendall/Hunt Publishing, 2000), 13.

14. Andrew Pierce warns against allowing the term "oppression" to become an "empty signifier"—that is, a term that stands for so much that it stands for nothing. Andrew J. Pierce, *Collective Identity, Oppression, and the Right to Self-Ascription* (Lanham, MD: Lexington Books, 2012), 29.

15. Ibid., 3–4.

16. Yuen, "Oppression and Democracy," 13.

17. Paulo Freire, *Pedagogy of the Oppressed* (New York: Seabury Press, 1970), 30.

18. Yuen, "Oppression and Democracy," 13.

19. Freire, *Pedagogy of the Oppressed*, 31.

20. Ira Goldberg, *Oppression and Social Intervention: Essays on the Human Condition and the Problems of Change* (Chicago: Nelson-Hall, 1978), 2–3.

21. Freire, *Pedagogy of the Oppressed*, 49.

22. Richard Thompson Ford, "Why the Poor Stay Poor," *New York Times Book Review*, March 8, 2009, 8.

23. Carol Andreas, *Sex and Caste in America* (Englewood Cliffs, NJ: Prentice-Hall, 1971); Lucile Duberman, *Social Inequality: Class and Caste in America* (Philadelphia: Lippincott, 1976).

24. Arthur C. Brooks, "Love People, Not Pleasure," *New York Times*, July 27, 2014, SR 1.

25. Pierce, *Collective Identity, Oppression, and the Right to Self-Ascription*, 3.

26. Richard Delgado, "The Myth of Upward Mobility," *University of Pittsburgh Law Review* 68 (2007): 879.

27. Jonathan Purtle, "Felon Disenfranchisement in the United States: A Health Equity Perspective," *American Journal of Public Health* 103 (2013): 632.

28. Tova Andrea Wang, *The Politics of Voter Suppression: Defending and Expanding*

Americans' Right to Vote (Ithaca, NY: Cornell University Press, 2012).

29. Purtle, "Felon Disenfranchisement," 636.

30. David J. Rothman and Sheila M. Rothman, eds., *On Their Own: The Poor in Modern America* (Menlo Park, CA: Addison-Wesley Publishing, 1972), vi.

31. Norman Daniels, Bruce P. Kennedy, and Ichiro Kawachi, "Why Justice Is Good for Our Health: The Social Determinants of Health Inequalities," *Daedalus* 128, no. 4 (Fall 1999): 224.

32. Adam Podgorecki, *Social Oppression* (London: Greenwood Press, 1993), 60.

33. Iris Marion Young, "Five Faces of Oppression," in *Rethinking Power*, ed. Thomas Wartenberg (New York: SUNY Press, 1992), 174.

Bibliography

Abbott, Samuel Bassett. "Housing Policy, Housing Codes and Tenant Remedies." *Boston University Law Review* 56 (1976): 2–90.

Adler, Matthew A. "Expressive Theories of Law: A Skeptical Overview." *University of Pennsylvania Law Review* 148 (2000): 1413–62.

Alschuler, A. W. "Personal Failure, Institutional Failure, and the Sixth Amendment." *New York University Review of Law and Social Change* 14 (1986): 149–56.

Anderson, Elizabeth S., and Richard H. Pildes. "Expressive Theories of Law: A Skeptical Overview." *University of Pennsylvania Law Review* 148 (2000): 1504–75.

Andreas, Carol. *Sex and Caste in America.* Englewood Cliffs, NJ: Prentice-Hall, 1971.

Appell, Annette R. "'Bad' Mothers and Spanish-Speaking Caregivers." *Nevada Law Journal* 7 (2007): 759–79.

Apuzo, Matt. "Holder Endorses Proposal to Reduce Drug Sentences." *New York Times,* March 14, 2014.

Arena, John. *Driven from New Orleans: How Nonprofits Betray Public Housing and Promote Privatization.* Minneapolis: University of Minnesota Press, 2012.

Austen, Ben. "The Last Tower: The Decline and Fall of Public Housing." *Harper's Magazine,* May 2012.

Badger, Emily. "The Suburbanization of Poverty." May 20, 2013. CityLab (online).

Barkan, Steven E. *Law and Society: An Introduction.* Upper Saddle River, NJ: Pearson Prentice Hall, 2009.

Bartholet, Elizabeth. "Where Do Black Children Belong? The Politics of Race Matching in Adoption." *University of Pennsylvania Law Review* 139 (1991): 1163–257.

Bartlett, Katherine T. "Re-Expressing Parenthood." *Yale Law Journal* 98 (1988): 293–340.

Baumer, John F., Roger Biles, and Kristin M. Szylvian, eds. *From Tenements to the Taylor Homes: In Search of Urban Housing Policy in the Twentieth Century.* University Park: Pennsylvania State University Press, 2000.

Beale, Sarah Sun. "The Many Faces of Overcriminalization." *American University Law Review* 54 (2005): 747–80.

Becker, Gary S. *A Treatise on the Family.* Cambridge, MA: Harvard University Press, 1981.

Becker, Howard. *Outsiders: Studies in the Sociology of Deviance.* London: Free Press, 1963.

Beckett, Katherine. *Making Crime Pay.* New York: New York University Press, 1997.

Bellafante, Ginia. "A Housing Solution Gone Awry." *New York Times,* June 2, 2013.

Berkman, Lisa F., and Ichiro Kawachi, eds. *Social Epidemiology.* Oxford: Oxford University Press, 2000.

Berson, Robin K. *Jane Addams: A Biography.* Westport, CT: Greenwood Press, 2004.

Best, Eli K. "Atypical Actors and Tort Law's Expressive Function." *Marquette Law Review* 96 (2012): 463–514.

Bibas, Stephanos. "Plea Bargaining Outside the Shadow of Trial." *Harvard Law Review* 117 (2004): 2464–547.

Bishop, Bill. *The Big Sort: Why the Clustering of Like-Minded America Is Tearing Us Apart.* New York: Houghton Mifflin, 2008.

Black, Donald. *The Behavior of Law.* New York: Academic Press, 1976.

Boak, Josh. "'Payday' Loan Rules Sought." *Milwaukee Journal Sentinel,* March 27, 2015.

Booker, Brakkton. "Federal Ferguson Review Finds More Than 100 Lessons for Police." September 3, 2015. NPR (online).

Booth, Michael. "Suit over Rent-to-Own Agreements Settles for $109 Million in New Jersey." *New Jersey Law Journal,* May 3, 2007.

Bowen, James S. "Cultural Convergences and Divergences: The Nexus between Putative Afro-American Family Values and the Best Interests of the Child." *Journal of Family Law* 26 (1987): 487–544.

Boyd, Marie. "Zoning for Apartments: A Study of the Role of Law in the Control of

Apartment Houses in New Haven, Connecticut, 1912–1932." *Pace Law Review* 33 (2013): 600–684.

Boyer, Paul. *Urban Masses and Moral Order in America, 1820–1920*. Cambridge, MA: Harvard University Press, 1978.

Brito, Tonya L. "The Welfarization of Family Law." *University of Kansas Law Review* 48 (2000): 229–84.

Bronstad, Amanda. "Lead Paint Litigation Is Beginning to Fade." *National Law Journal*, August 21, 2007.

Brooks, Arthur C. "Love People, Not Pleasure." *New York Times*, July 27, 2014.

Buckle, Suzann R., and Leonard Buckle. *Bargaining for Justice: Case Disposition and Reform in the Criminal Courts*. New York: Praeger Publishers, 1977.

Buckley, Robert M., and Alex F. Schwartz. "Housing Policy in the U.S." International Working Affairs Paper. New York: The New School, 2010.

Bullard, Robert. "Residential Segregation and Urban Quality of Life." In *Environmental Justice: Issues, Policies, and Solutions*, edited by Bunyan Bryant, 76–85. Washington, DC: Island Press, 1995.

Bullock, Candra. "Low-Income Parents Victimized by Child Protective Services." *Journal of Gender, Social Policy & the Law* 11 (2003): 1–31.

Burris, Scott. "From Health Care to the Social Determinants of Health." *University of Pennsylvania Law Review* 159 (2011): 1649–67.

———. "Law in a Social Determinants Strategy: A Public Health Law Research Perspective." *Public Health Reports* 126 (2011): 22–27.

Burris, Scott, Ichiro Kawachi, and Austin Sarat. "Health, Law, and Human Rights: Background and Key Concepts Integrating Law and Social Epidemiology." *Journal of Law, Medicine & Ethics* 30 (2002): 510–21.

Button, Sara E. "Bounties on Deadbeat Dads." *Money*, March 1984.

Cahill, Joseph B. "License to Owe: Title-Loan Firms Can Offer Owners a Solution That Often Backfires." *Wall Street Journal*, March 3, 1999.

Cahn, Edgar S., and Jean C. Cahn. "The War on Poverty: A Civilian Perspective." *Yale Law Journal* 73 (1964): 1317–52.

Caplovitz, David. *The Poor Pay More: Consumer Practices of Low-Income Families*. New York: Free Press, 1967.

Carbone, June. "Out of the Channel and into the Swamp: How Family Law Fails in a New Era of Class Division." *Hofstra Law Review* 39 (2011): 859–95.

Carter, Susan Payne, and Paige Martin Skiba. "Pawnshops, Behavioral Economics, and Self-Regulation." *Review of Banking and Financial Law* 32 (2012): 193–220.

Cauley, Kashana. "How America Destroys Black Families." *New York Times*, January 3, 2018.

Chambers, David L. *Making Fathers Pay: The Enforcement of Child Support* (Chicago: University of Chicago Press, 1979).

Chambliss, William J. "Policing the Ghetto Underclass: The Politics of Law Enforcement." *Social Problems* 41 (1994): 177–94.

Chase, Anthony. *Movies on Trial: The Legal System on the Silver Screen*. New York: New Press, 2002.

Chodorow, Nancy. *The Reproduction of Mothering: Psychoanalysis and the Sociology of Gender.* Berkeley: University of California Press, 1978.

Christensen, Kim. "Payday Loans Mushroom." *Pittsburgh Tribune Review*, January 11, 2009.

Christensen, Stephanie. "The Great Migration (1915–1960)." N.d. Black Past, https://www.blackpast.org.

Cleveland, Lisa M., Monica L. Minter, Kathleen A. Cobb, Anthony A. Scott, and Victor F. German. "Lead Hazards for Pregnant Women and Children: Part I; Immigrants and the Poor Shoulder Most of the Burden of Lead Exposure in This Country." *American Journal of Nursing* 108 (2008): 40–49.

Clifford, Stephanie, and Jessica Silver-Greenberg. "Platinum Card and Text Alert, via Pawnshop." *New York Times*, August 28, 2013.

Clinton, Bill. "Acceptance Speech to the Democratic National Convention, July 16, 1992." www.4president.org/speeches/billclinton1992acceptance.htm.

Cohen, Patricia. "Counting Up Hidden Costs of Low Pay." *New York Times*, April 13, 2015.

Cohen, Rachel. "Two Steps Forward, One Step Back: Evaluating the Healthy Marriage Initiative in Light of American Welfare History." *Georgetown Journal on Poverty Law & Policy* 17 (2010): 145–61.

Colbert, Douglas E., Ray Paternoster, and Shawn Bushway. "Do Attorneys Really Matter? The Empirical and Legal Case for the Right to Counsel at Bail." *Cardozo Law Review* 23 (2002): 1719–93.

Cole, David. *No Equal Justice: Race and Class in the American Criminal Justice System.* New York: New Press, 1999.

———. "Punitive Damage." *New York Times*, May 18, 2014.

Collins, Jodie. "Why Was Masturbation Such a Medical Concern in the 19th Century?"

https://jodebloggs.wordpress.com.

"Conservation of Dwellings: The Prevention of Blight." *Indiana Law Journal* 29 (1953): 109–25.

Cook, Julian A. "Plea Bargaining, Sentence Modifications, and the Real World." *Wake Forest Law Review* 48 (2013): 65–95.

Cooper, Tanya Asim. "Racial Bias in American Foster Care: The National Debate." *Marquette Law Review* 97 (2013): 215–77.

Cory, Dennis C., and Tauhidur Rahman. *Environmental Justice and Federalism.* Northampton, MA: Edward Elgar Publishing, 2012.

Cudd, Ann E. *Analyzing Oppression.* New York: Oxford University Press, 2006.

Daniels, Norman, Bruce P. Kennedy, and Ichiro Kawachi. "Why Justice Is Good for Our Health: The Social Determinants of Health Inequalities." *Daedalus* 128, no. 4 (1999): 215–51.

Daniels, Ron. "A Domestic Marshall Plan to Transform America's 'Dark Ghettos.'" *Black Scholar* 37 (2007): 10–13.

Davey, Monica. "Promoting Marriage Becomes Major Phase of Welfare Reform." *Indianapolis Star*, December 2, 2001.

Davis, Lawrence H., et al., eds. *Shepard's Mobile Homes and Mobile Home Parks.* Colorado Springs, CO: Shepard's Citations, 1975.

Delgado, Richard. "Law Enforcement in Subordinated Communities: Innovation and Response." *Michigan Law Review* 106 (2008): 1193–212.

———. "The Myth of Upward Mobility." *University of Pittsburgh Law Review* 68 (2007): 879–913.

Dennis, Brady. "In Some Zip Codes 1 in 7 Children Suffer from Dangerously High Blood Lead Levels." *Washington Post*, June 15, 2016.

DeSilver, Drew. "5 Facts about the Minimum Wage." Pew Research Center (online).

Desmond, Matthew. *Evicted: Poverty and Profit in the American City.* New York: Crown Books, 2016.

Dewan, Shaila. "Evictions Soar in Hot Market; Renters Suffer." *New York Times*, August 28, 2014.

Dion, Robin. "Healthy Marriage Programs: What Works?" *Future of Children* 15 (2005): 139–56.

Dreier, Peter. "The New Politics of Housing." *Journal of the American Planning Association* 63 (Winter 1997): 5–27.

Drewnowski, Adam. "Obesity, Diets, and Social Inequalities." *Nutrition Reviews* 67 (2009): S36–S39.

Drysdale, Lynn, and Kathleen E. Keest. "The Two-Tiered Consumer Financial Services Marketplace: The Fringe Banking System and Its Challenges to Current Thinking about the Role of Usury Laws in Today's Society." *South Carolina Law Review* 51 (2000): 589–669.

Duberman, Lucile. *Social Inequality: Class and Caste in America.* Philadelphia: Lippincott, 1976.

Duncan, James S., and Nancy G. Duncan. *Landscapes of Privilege: The Politics of the Aesthetic in an American Suburb.* New York: Routledge, 2004.

Dunn, Robert G. "Identity, Commodification, and Consumer Culture." In *Identity and Social Change*, edited by Joseph E. Davis, 11–37. New Brunswick, NJ: Transaction, 2000.

Eavis, Peter. "Service Members Left Vulnerable to Payday Loans." *New York Times*, November 22, 2013.

Eckholm, Erik. "A Sight All Too Familiar in Poor Neighborhoods." *New York Times*, February 18, 2010.

———. "Study Documents 'Ghetto Tax' Being Paid by the Urban Poor." *New York Times*, July 19, 2006.

Edin, Kathryn, and Joanna M. Reed. "Why Don't They Just Get Married? Barriers to Marriage among the Disadvantaged." *Future of Children* 15 (Fall 2005): 117–37.

Ehrenhalt, Alan. "Trading Places: The Demographic Inversion of the American City." *New Republic*, August 13, 2008.

Ehrenreich, Barbara. "It Is Expensive to Be Poor." *The Atlantic*, January 13, 2014.

———. "TANF, or 'Torture and Abuse of Needy Families.'" *Seattle Journal for Social Justice* 1 (2002): 419–26.

Elgar, Frank J., Chris Roberts, Nina Parry-Langdon, and William Boyce. "Income Inequality and Alcohol Use: A Multilevel Analysis of Drinking and Drunkenness in Adolescents in 34 Countries." *European Journal of Public Health* 15 (2003): 245–50.

Ellickson, Robert C. "The False Promise of the Mixed-Income Housing Project." *UCLA Law Review* 57 (2010): 983–1021.

Emmelman, Debra S. *Justice for the Poor: A Study of Criminal Defense Work.* Burlington, VT: Ashgate, 2003.

Engel, Kathleen C., and Patricia A. McCoy. "A Tale of Three Markets: The Law and

Economics of Predatory Lending." *Texas Law Review* 80 (2002): 1255–381.

Erickson, Patricia E. "Federal Child Abuse and Child Neglect Policy in the United States since 1974." *Criminal Justice Review* 25 (2000): 77–92.

Erlanger, Steven. "Taking on Adam Smith (and Karl Marx)." *New York Times*, April 20, 2014.

Evans, Sandra. "Putting a Face on Deadbeat Dads." *Washington Post*, May 29, 1991.

Feeley, Malcolm M. "Perspectives on Plea Bargaining." *Law & Society Review* 13 (1979): 199–209.

Fellowes, Matthew. "The High Price of Being Poor." *Los Angeles Times*, July 23, 2006.

Feuer, Lewis S., ed. *Karl Marx and Friedrich Engels: Basic Writings on Politics and Philosophy*. New York: Anchor Books, 1959.

Fisher, Julia M. "Marriage Promotion Policies and the Working Poor: A Match Made in Heaven?" *Boston College Third World Law Journal* 25 (2005): 475–97.

Fishman, Robert. *Bourgeois Utopias: The Rise and Fall of Suburbia*. New York: Basic Books, 1998.

Ford, Richard Thompson. "Why the Poor Stay Poor." *New York Times Book Review*, March 8, 2009.

Fottrell, Quentin. "10 Things Married Couples Won't Tell You." *Milwaukee Journal Sentinel*, November 2, 2014.

Foucault, Michel. *Discipline and Punish: The Birth of the Prison*. New York: Vintage Books, 1979.

Francis, Karen E. "Rollover, Rollover: A Behavioral Law and Economics Analysis of the Payday Loan Industry." *Texas Law Review* 88 (2010): 611–38.

Frankel, Tamar, and Francis H. Miller. "The Inapplicability of Market Theory to Adoptions." *Boston University Law Review* 67 (1987): 99–103.

Freire, Paulo. *Pedagogy of the Oppressed*. New York: Seabury Press, 1970.

Freudenberg, Nicholas. "Jails, Prisons, and the Health of Urban Populations: A Review of the Impact of the Correctional System in Community Health." *Journal of Urban Health* 78 (2001): 214–35.

Friedman, David Adam. "Public Health Regulation and the Limits of Paternalism." *Connecticut Law Review* 46 (2014): 1687–770.

Friedman, Lawrence. *American Law in the 20th Century*. New Haven, CT: Yale University Press, 2002.

———. *Government and Slum Housing: A Century of Frustration*. Chicago: Rand McNally

& Co., 1968.

Frug, Gerald E. *City Making: Building Communities without Building Walls.* Princeton, NJ: Princeton University Press, 1999.

Galanter, Marc. "The Hundred-Year Decline in Trials and the Thirty Years War." *Stanford Law Review* 57 (2005): 1255–74.

Galea, Sandro, Jennifer Ahern, Melissa Tracy, and David Vlahov. "Neighborhood Income and Income Distribution and the Use of Cigarettes, Alcohol, and Marijuana." *American Journal of Preventive Medicine* 32 (2007): S195–S202.

Gans, Herbert. *The War against the Poor: The Underclass and Antipoverty Policy.* New York: Basic Books, 1995.

Garey, Stephen. "Brands R Us: How Advertising Works." February 17, 2018. Center for Media Literacy (online).

Garland, David, ed. *Mass Imprisonment: Social Causes and Consequences.* London: Sage Publications, 2001.

Garreau, Joel. *Edge City: Life on the New Frontier.* New York: Doubleday, 1991.

Gaskin, Darrell J., et al. "Disparities in Diabetes: The Nexus of Race, Poverty, and Place." *American Journal of Public Health* 104 (2014): 2147–55.

Geisinger, Alex. "A Belief Change Theory of Expressive Law." *Iowa Law Review* 88 (2002): 35–73.

———. "The Benefits of Development and Environmental Justice." *Columbia Journal of Environmental Law* 37 (2012): 177–214.

Genovese, Eugene D. *Roll, Jordan, Roll: The World the Slaves Made.* New York: Pantheon Books, 1974.

German, Danielle, and Carl A. Latkin. "Exposure to Urban Rats as a Community Stressor among Low-Income Urban Residents." *Journal of Community Psychology* 44 (2016): 249–62.

Gibson-Davis, Christina M., Kathryn Edin, and Sara McLanahan. "High Hopes but Even Higher Expectations: The Retreat from Marriage among Low-Income Couples." *Journal of Marriage and the Family* 67 (2005): 1301–12.

Gillies, James, ed. *Essays in Urban Land Economics.* Los Angeles: University of California Real Estate Research Program, 1966.

Giovino, Gary A. "Epidemiology of Tobacco Use in the United States." *Oncogene* 21 (2002): 7326–40.

Godsil, Rachel D. "The Gentrification Trigger: Autonomy, Mobility, and Affirmatively

Furthering Fair Housing." *Brooklyn Law Review* 78 (2013): 319–38.

Goldberg, Ira. *Oppression and Social Intervention: Essays on the Human Condition and the Problems of Change.* Chicago: Nelson-Hall, 1978.

Goldstein, Joseph. "Judge Rejects New York's Stop-and-Frisk Policy." *New York Times*, August 13, 2013.

———. "Police Department's Focus on Race Is at Core of Ruling against Stop-and-Frisk." *New York Times*, May 2, 2013.

Golembeski, Cynthia, and Robert Fullilove. "Criminal (In)Justice in the City and Its Associated Health Consequences." *American Journal of Public Health* 95 (2005): 1701–6.

Gorlin, David C. "Evaluating Punishment in Purgatory: The Need to Separate Pretrial Detainees' Condition-of-Confinement Claims from Inadequate Eighth Amendment Analysis." *Michigan Law Review* 108 (2009): 417–44.

Gostin, Lawrence O. *Public Health Law: Power, Duty, Restraint.* Berkeley: University of California Press, 2000.

Grail, Timothy. "Custodial Mothers and Fathers and Their Child Support: 2011." U.S. Census Bureau Current Population Report, October 2013. https://www.census.gov/prod/2013pubs/p60-246.pdf.

Green, Bruce A. "Why Should Prosecutors Seek Justice?" *Fordham Urban Law Journal* 26 (1999): 607–43.

Grynbaum, Michael M. "New York's Ban on Big Sodas Is Rejected by Final Court." *New York Times*, June 27, 2014.

Gudrais, Elizabeth. "Disrupted Lives." *Harvard Magazine*, January–February 2014.

Guggenheim, Martin. "Divided Loyalties: Musings on Some Ethical Dilemmas for the Institutional Criminal Defense Attorney." *New York University Review of Law and Social Change* 14 (1986): 13–22.

Guo, Jeff. "How Our Child Support System Can Push the Poor Deeper into Poverty." *Washington Post*, January 26, 2014.

Haber, Erica. "Demystifying a Legal Twilight Zone: Resolving the Circuit Court Split on When Seizure Ends and Pretrial Detention Begins." *New York Law School Journal of Human Rights* 19 (2003): 939–80.

Hagan, John, and Ruth D. Peterson. *Crime and Inequality.* Palo Alto, CA: Stanford University Press, 1995.

Haller, Mark H., and John V. Alviti. "Loansharking in American Cities: Historical Analysis of a Marginal Enterprise." *American Journal of Legal History* 21 (1977): 125–56.

Harrington, Michael. *The Other America: Poverty in the United States.* New York: Macmillan, 1962.

Harris, David A. "Factors for Reasonable Suspicion: When Black and Poor Means Stopped and Frisked." *Indiana Law Review* 69 (1994): 659–88.

Harris, Kathleen Mullan. "Family Structure, Poverty, and Family Well-Being." *Employee Rights and Employment Policy Journal* 10 (2006): 45–80.

Hart, John Fraser, Michelle J. Rhodes, and John T. Morgan. *The Unknown World of the Mobile Home.* Baltimore: Johns Hopkins University Press, 2002.

Harvey, J. "Humor as Social Act." *Journal of Value Inquiry* 29, no. 1 (1995): 19–30.

Hattem, Julian. "Obama Seeks New Approach to the War on Drugs." *The Hill*, April 24, 2013. http://thehill.com/blogs/regwatch/administration/295889-obama-seeks-new-approach-to-the-war-on-drugs.

Hawkins, Jim. "Credit on Wheels: The Law and Business of Auto-Title Lending." *Washington and Lee Law Review* 69 (2012): 535–606.

———. "Renting the Good Life." *William and Mary Law Review* 49 (2008): 2041–117.

Hawkins-Leon, Cynthia G. "The Indian Child Welfare Act and the African American Tribe: Facing the Adoption Crisis." *Brandeis Journal of Family Law* 36 (1997): 201–18.

Hawkins-Leon, Cynthia G., and Carla Bradley. "Race and Transracial Adoptions: The Answer Is Neither Black or White Nor Right or Wrong." *Catholic University Law Review* 51 (2002): 1227–86.

Hellwig, Diane. "Exposing the Loansharks in Sheep's Clothing: Why Regulating the Consumer Credit Market Makes Sense." *Notre Dame Law Review* 80 (2015): 1567–611.

Herviel, Tara, and Paul Wright. *Prison Nation: The Warehousing of America's Poor.* New York: Routledge, 2003.

Hiscock, Rosemary, et al. "Socioeconomic Status and Smoking: A Review." *Annals of the New York Academy of Sciences* 1248 (2012): 111–17.

Hixson, Brooke A., Saad B. Omer, Carlos del Rio, and Paula M. Frew. "Spatial Clustering of HIV Prevalence in Atlanta, Georgia and Population Characteristics Associated with Case Concentrations." *Journal of Urban Health* 88 (2011): 129–41.

Holland, Joshua. "Higher Profits Explain Why There Are More People of Color in Private Prisons." *Moyers & Company*, February 7, 2014. http://www.billmoyers.com.

Holmes, Gilbert A. "The Extended Family System in the Black Community: A Child-Centered Model for Adoption Policy." *Temple Law Review* 68 (1995): 1649–87.

Horowitz, C. R., K. A. Colson, P. L. Hebert, and K. Lancaster. "Barriers to Buying Healthy Foods for People with Diabetes." *American Journal of Public Health* 94 (2004): 1549–54.

Horowitz, Daniel. *The Morality of Spending: Attitudes toward the Consumer Society, 1875–1940*. Baltimore: Johns Hopkins University Press, 1985.

Hughes, C. J. "Ahead of the Pack: Is Land inside Public Housing Complexes the Next Big Thing?" *New York Times*, June 28, 2015.

Human Rights Watch. *The Price of Freedom: Bail and Pretrial Detention of Low Income Nonfelony Defendants in New York City*. New York: Human Rights Watch, 2010.

Hunter, Robert. *Poverty*. New York: Macmillan Co., 1905.

Hutchison, Earl R., Jr. "Black Suburbanization: A History of Social Change in a Working Class Suburb." PhD diss., University of Chicago, 1984.

Hylton, J. Gordon, et al. *Property Law and the Public Interest*. Charlottesville, VA: Lexis, 2003.

Ingraham, Christopher. "The U.S. Has One of the Stingiest Minimum Wage Policies of Any Wealthy Nation." *Washington Post*, December 29, 2017.

Irwin, John. *The Jail: Managing the Underclass in American Society*. Berkeley: University of California Press, 1985.

Isaacs, Asher D. "Interracial Adoption: Permanent Placement and Racial Identity—An Adoptee's Perspective." *National Black Law Journal* 14 (1995): 126–56.

Isserman, Maurice. "Warrior on Poverty." *New York Times Book Review*, June 21, 2009.

Jackson, Kenneth T. *Crabgrass Frontier: The Suburbanization of the United States*. New York: Oxford University Press, 1985.

Jamrisko, Michelle. "Consumer Credit in U.S. Rises by $17.1 Billion, Fed Says." *Bloomberg News*, July 9, 2012.

Jencks, Christopher. *Rethinking Social Policy: Race, Poverty, and the Underclass*. Cambridge, MA: Harvard University Press, 1992.

Johnson, Creola. "Payday Loans: Shrewd Business or Predatory Lending?" *Minnesota Law Review* 87 (2000): 1–52.

Johnson, Lyndon Baines. "First State of the Union Address, January 8, 1964." http://www.americanrhetoric.com/speechbank.htm.

Joint Center for Housing Studies of Harvard University. *The State of the Nation's Housing*. Cambridge, MA: President and Fellows of Harvard College, 2003.

Jordan, Miriam. "When Syria Came to Fresno." *New York Times*, July 21, 2017.

Kaplan, Diane S. "The Baby Richard Amendments and the Law of Unintended Consequences." *Children's Legal Rights Journal* 22 (2002): 2–16.

Karriker-Jaffe, Katherine J., Sarah C. M. Roberts, and Jason Bond. "Income Inequality, Alcohol Use, and Alcohol-Related Problems." *American Journal of Public Health* 103 (2013): 649–56.

Katz, Bruce. "Concentrated Poverty in New Orleans and Other Cities." *Chronicle of Higher Education*, August 4, 2006.

Katz, Jack. "Legality and Equality: Plea Bargaining in the Prosecution of White-Collar and Common Crimes." *Law & Society Review* 13 (1979): 431–59.

Katz, Josh, and Abby Goodnough. "Opioid Deaths Rising Swiftly among Blacks." *New York Times*, December 23, 2017.

Katz, M. B. *The Undeserving Poor: From the War on Poverty to the War on Welfare.* New York: Pantheon Books, 1989.

Kazan, Olga. "The Link between Opioids and Unemployment." *The Atlantic*, April 2017.

Keest, Kathleen E., Jeffrey I. Langer, and Michael F. Day. "Interest Rate Regulation Developments: High-Cost Mortgages, Rent-to-Own Transactions, and Unconscionability." *Business Lawyer* 50 (1995): 1081–91.

Keith, Nathaniel S. *Politics and the Housing Crisis since 1930.* New York: Universe Books, 1973.

Kirp, David L. "Here Comes the Neighborhood." *New York Times*, October 20, 2013.

Kneebone, Elizabeth. "The Growth and Spread of Concentrated Poverty." July 31, 2014. Brookings Institution (online).

Knight, Louise W. *Citizen Jane Addams and the Struggle for Democracy.* Chicago: University of Chicago Press, 2005.

Kohm, Lynn Marie, and Rachel K. Toberty. "A Fifty-State Survey of the Cost of Family Fragmentation." *Regent University Law Review* 25 (2012): 25–89.

Kominos, Teresa. "What Do Marriage and Welfare Reform Really Have in Common? A Look into TANF Programs." *St. John's Journal of Legal Comment* 21 (2006): 915–49.

Kraus, Michael, Shai Davidai, and A. David Nussbaum. "American Dream? Or Mirage?" *New York Times*, May 3, 2015.

Kussin, Zachary, and Rob Smith. "City Beef: From 'Pricing Out' to 'Poor Doors,'" *New York Post*, December 25, 2014.

Lacko, Bruce M., Signe-Mary McKernan, and Mary Hastak. *Survey of Rent-to-Own Customers.* Federal Trade Commission Bureau of Economics Staff Report.

Washington, DC: United States Government Printing Office, 2000.

Laird, Lorelei. "Doing Time Extended." *ABA Journal*, June 2013.

Landes, Elisabeth M., and Richard A. Posner. "The Economics of the Baby Shortage." *Journal of Legal Studies* 7 (1978): 323–48.

Larson, Bill E., ed. *The Underclass Question*. Philadelphia: Temple University Press, 1992.

Lasch, Christopher. *The Culture of Narcissism: American Life in an Age of Diminishing Expectations*. New York: W.W. Norton & Co., 1978.

Laughland, Oliver. "Private Federal Prisons More Dangerous, Damaging DOJ Investigation Reveals." *The Guardian*, August 12, 2016.

Lawrence, Jean C. "AFSA in the Age of Mass Incarceration: Go to Prison—Lose Your Child?" *William Mitchell Law Review* 40 (2014): 990–1007.

Lees, Loretta, Tom Slater, and Elvin K. Wyly. *Gentrification*. New York: Routledge, 2008.

Lees, Zoë Elizabeth. "Payday Peonage: Thirteenth Amendment Implications in Payday Lending." *The Scholar: St. Mary's Law Review on Race and Justice* 15 (2012): 63–100.

Legler, Paul K. "The Coming Revolution in Child Support Policy: Implications of the 1996 Welfare Act." *Family Law Quarterly* 30 (1996): 519–63.

Leinberger, Christopher B. "The Next Slum?" *Atlantic Monthly*, March 2008.

Lemann, Nicholas. *The Promised Land: The Great Black Migration and How It Changed America*. New York: Alfred A. Knopf, 1991.

Lempert, Richard, and Joseph Sanders. *An Invitation to Law and the Social Sciences*. Philadelphia: University of Pennsylvania Press, 1986.

Lerman, Brian R. "Mandatory Inclusionary Zoning: The Answer to the Affordable Housing Problem." *Boston College Environmental Affairs Law Review* 33 (2006): 383–416.

Lessig, Lawrence. "Social Meaning and Social Norms." *University of Pennsylvania Law Review* 144 (1996): 2181–90.

Lichtblau, Eric. "Trump May Reverse Obama Policy of Freeing Inmates." *New York Times*, January 17, 2016.

Lieberman, Joseph L. *Child Support in America: Practical Advice for Negotiating—and Collecting—a Fair Settlement*. New Haven, CT: Yale University Press, 1986.

Lipton, Robert L., et al. "The Geography of Violence, Alcohol Outlets, and Drug Arrests in Boston." *American Journal of Public Health* 103 (2013): 657–64.

Little, Darnell, and Dan Mihalopoulos. "Black Chicagoans Fuel Growth in South Suburbs." *New York Times*, July 3, 2011.

Liu, Feng. "Dynamics and Causation of Environmental Equity, Locally Unwanted Land

Uses, and Neighborhood Changes." *Environmental Management* 21 (2015): 643–56.

Livingston, James. *Against Thrift: Why Consumer Culture Is Good for the Economy, the Environment, and Your Soul.* New York: Basic Books, 2011.

Lowrey, Annie. "50 Years Later, War on Poverty Is a Mixed Bag." *New York Times,* January 5, 2014.

———. "For Richer, for Poorer." *New York Times Sunday Magazine,* February 9, 2014.

Lubove, Roy. *The Progressives and the Slums: Tenement House Reform in New York City, 1890–1917.* Pittsburgh: University of Pittsburgh Press, 1962.

Lynch, John, George Davey-Smith, George A. Kaplan, and James S. House. "Income Inequality and Mortality: Importance to Health of Individual Income, Psychological Environment, or Material Conditions." *British Medical Journal* 320 (2000): 1200–1204.

Macek, Steve. *Urban Nightmares: The Media, the Right, and the Moral Panic over the City.* Minneapolis: University of Minnesota Press, 2006.

Maddali, Anita Ortiz. "The Immigrant 'Other': Racialized Identity and the Devaluation of Immigrant Family Relations." *Indiana Law Journal* 89 (2014): 644–702.

Magnet, Myron. "America's Underclass: What to Do? *Fortune,* May 11, 1987.

Marley, Patrick. "Payday Lenders Escape Limits." *Milwaukee Journal Sentinel,* December 10, 2012.

Martens, Patricia J., et al. "The Effect of Neighborhood Socioeconomic Status on Education and Health Outcomes for Children Living in Social Housing." *American Journal of Public Health* 104 (2014): 2103–13.

Martin, Elmer P., and Joanne Mitchell Martin. *The Black Extended Family.* Chicago: University of Chicago Press, 1978.

Martin, Nathalie. "Regulating Payday Loans: Why This Should Make the CFPB's Short List." *Harvard Business Law Review Online* 2 (2011): 44–51.

Martin, Nathalie, and Ozymandias Adams. "Grand Theft Auto Loans." *Missouri Law Review* 71 (2012): 41–94.

Martin, Nathalie, and Ernesto Longa, "High-Interest Loans and Class: Do Payday and Title Loans Really Serve the Middle Class." *Loyola Consumer Law Review* 24 (2012): 524–61.

Martin, Susan Lorde, and Nancy White Hutchins. "Consumer Advocates vs. the Rent-to-Own Industry: Reaching a Reasonable Accommodation." *American Business Law Journal* 34 (1997): 396–408.

Martinez, Alexis N., et al. "Spatial Analysis of HIV Positive Injection Drug Users in San Francisco, 1987 to 2005." *International Journal of Environmental Research and Public*

Health 11 (2014): 3937–55.

Massey, Douglas S., et al. *Climbing Mount Laurel: The Struggle for Affordable Housing and Social Mobility in an American Suburb.* Princeton, NJ: Princeton University Press, 2013.

Maynard, Douglas W. *Inside Plea Bargaining: The Language of Negotiation.* New York: Plenum Press, 1984.

McDonald, William F. "From Plea Negotiation to Coercive Justice: Notes in the Respecification of a Concept." *Law and Society Review* 13 (1979): 385–92.

Meera, Louis. "Consumer Credit in U.S. Increases by Most in 10 Years." *Bloomberg News,* January 9, 2012.

Mendenhall, Shane. "Payday Loans: The Effects of Payday Lending on Society and the Need for More State and Federal Regulation." *Oklahoma City Law Review* 32 (2007): 299–332.

Moore, Antonio. "The Black Male Incarceration Problem Is Real and It's Catastrophic." *Huffington Post,* February 17, 2015.

Moore, Donna. "Implementing a National Putative Father Registry by Utilizing Existing Federal/State Collaborative Databases." *John Marshall Law Review* 36 (2003): 1033–52.

Moore, Lisa D., and Amy Elkavish. "Who's Using and Who's Doing Drugs: Incarceration, the War on Drugs, and the Public Health." *American Journal of Public Health* 98 (2008): 782–86.

Moskowitz, David H. *Exclusionary Zoning Litigation.* Cambridge, MA: Ballinger, 1977.

Moulding, Patrick. "Fair or Unfair? The Importance of Mass Transit for America's Poor." *Georgetown Journal on Poverty Law & Policy* 12 (2005): 155–80.

Mullainathan, Sendhil. "A Top-Heavy Focus on Income Inequality." *New York Times,* March 9, 2014.

Muller, Peter O. *Contemporary Suburban America.* Englewood Cliffs, NJ: Prentice-Hall, 1981.

Murakawa, Naomi. *The First Civil Right: How Liberals Built Prison America.* New York: Oxford University Press, 2014.

Myrdal, Gunnar. *Challenge to Affluence.* New York: Pantheon Books, 1983.

Nagourney, Adam. "Berkeley Officials Outspent but Optimistic in Battle over Soda Tax." *New York Times,* October 8, 2014.

National Heart and Lung Institute. *Public Health in Public Housing.* Washington, DC: U.S. Department of Health and Human Services, 2005.

Nehf, James P. "Effective Regulation of Rent-to-Own Contracts." *Ohio State Law Journal* 52

(1991): 751–845.

Nelson, Kathryn B. *Gentrification and Distressed Cities.* Madison: University of Wisconsin Press, 1988.

Newman, Andrew Adam. "Wendy's Turns Up Volume on Adoption Drive." *New York Times,* March 14, 2014.

Nicholson, Melanie. "Without Their Children: Rethinking Motherhood among Transnational Migrant Women." *Social Text* 24, no. 3 (2006): 13–33.

Ogden, Cynthia L., Molly M. Lamb, Margaret D. Carroll, and Katherine M. Flegal. "Obesity and Socioeconomic Status in Adults: United States, 2005–2008." *NCHS Data Brief* 50 (December 2010).

O'Hagan, Eamonn. "Judicial Illumination of the Constitutional 'Twilight Zone.'" *Boston College Law Review* 44 (2003): 1357–95.

Oldfather, Chad M. "Heuristics, Biases, and Criminal Defendants." *Marquette Law Review* 91 (2007): 249–62.

Oppenheimer, Valerie Kincade. "Women's Rising Employment and the Future of the Family in Industrial Societies." *Population and Development Review* 20 (1994): 293–342.

Orleck, Annalise, and Lisa Gayle Hazirjian, eds. *The War on Poverty: A New Grassroots History, 1864–1980.* Athens: University of Georgia Press, 2011.

Palen, J. John, and Bruce London, eds. *Gentrification, Displacement, and Neighborhood Revitalization.* Albany, NY: SUNY Press, 1984.

Papke, David Ray. "The American Courtroom Trial: Pop Culture, Courthouse Realities, and the Dream World of Justice." *South Texas Law Review* 40 (1999): 919–32.

———. "The Black Panther Party's Narratives of Resistance." *Vermont Law Review* 18 (1994): 645–80.

———. *Framing the Criminal: Crime, Cultural Work, and the Loss of Critical Perspective, 1830–1900.* Hamden, CT: Archon Books, 1987.

———. "Keeping the Underclass in Its Place: Zoning, the Urban Poor, and Residential Segregation." *Urban Lawyer* 41 (2009): 787–806.

———. "Perpetuating Poverty: Exploitative Businesses, the Urban Poor, and the Failure of Reform." *The Scholar: St. Mary's Law Review on Race & Social Justice* 16 (2014): 223–53.

———. "Pondering Past Purposes: A Critical History of American Adoption Law." *West Virginia Law Review* 102 (1999): 459–74.

————. "State v. Oakley, Deadbeat Dads, and American Poverty." *Western New England Law Review* 26 (2004): 9–26.

————. "Transracial Adoption in the United States: The Reflection and Reinforcement of Racial Hierarchy." *Journal of Law and Family Studies* 15 (2013): 57–80.

Pauly, Madison. "A Brief History of America's Private Prison Industry." *Mother Jones*, July-August 2016.

Pear, Robert, and Daniel D. Kirkpatrick. "Bush Plans $1.5 Billion Drive for Promotion of Marriage." *New York Times*, January 14, 2004.

Pendall, Rolf, Elizabeth Davies, Lesley Freiman, and Rob Pitingolo. *A Lost Decade: Neighborhood Poverty and the Urban Crisis of the 2000s.* Washington, DC: Joint Center for Political and Economic Studies, 2011.

Perin, Constance. *Everything in Its Place: Social Order and Land Use in America.* Princeton, NJ: Princeton University Press, 1977.

Perry, Imani. "Acts of Aggression." *New York Times Book Review*, May 29, 2016.

Perry, Twila L. "Transracial and International Adoption: Mothers, Hierarchy, Race, and Feminist Legal Theory." *Yale Journal of Law & Feminism* 10 (1998): 101–64.

Peters, Jeremy W. "G.O.P. Moving to Ease Stance on Sentencing." *New York Times*, March 14, 2014.

Pierce, Andrew J. *Collective Identity, Oppression, and the Right to Self-Ascription.* Lanham, MD: Lexington Books, 2012.

Piketty, Thomas. *Capital in the Twenty-First Century.* Cambridge, MA: Belknap Press, 2014.

Pikus, Ann K. "Wanted: Affordable Housing in Wisconsin." *Wisconsin Law Review* (2007): 202–32.

Pimpare, Stephen. *A People's History of Poverty in America.* New York: New Press, 2008.

Pittenger, Mark. *Class Unknown: Undercover Investigations of American Work and Poverty from the Progressive Era to the Present.* New York: New York University Press, 2012.

Podgorecki, Adam. *Social Oppression.* London: Greenwood Press, 1993.

Polaha, Stephen J. "Housing Codes and the Prevention of Urban Blight: Administrative and Enforcement Problems and Proposals." *Villanova Law Review* 17 (1972): 490–523.

Pollack, Harold. "The Most Embarrassing Graph in American Drug Policy." *Washington Post*, May 29, 2013.

Porsdam, Helle. *Legally Speaking: Contemporary American Culture and the Law.* Amherst: University of Massachusetts Press, 1999.

Porter, Douglas R. *Covenants and Zoning for Research/Business Parks.* Washington, DC:

Urban Land Institute, 2004.

Porter, Eduardo. "Discredited Notions Still Guide Policy on Aid to the Poor." *New York Times*, October 2, 2015.

———. "In the U.S., Punishment Comes before the Crimes." *New York Times*, April 30, 2014.

———. "Income Inequality Is Costing the Nation on Social Issues." *New York Times*, April 29, 2015.

———. "A Party's Strategy to Ignore Poverty." *New York Times*, October 28, 2015.

———. "Plan to End Poverty Is Wide of the Target." *New York Times*, June 1, 2016.

———. "Time to Try Compassion, Not Censure, for Families." *New York Times*, March 15, 2014.

———. "What Debate on Inequality Is Missing." *New York Times*, May 5, 2015.

Posner, Richard A. "The Regulation of the Market in Adoptions." *Boston University Law Review* 67 (1987): 59–72.

Prasad, Monica. *The Land of Too Much: American Abundance and the Paradox of Poverty.* Cambridge, MA: Harvard University Press, 2012.

Prichard, J. Robert S. "A Market for Babies?" *University of Toronto Law Review* 34 (1984): 341–57.

Purtle, Jonathan. "Felon Disenfranchisement in the United States: A Health Equity Perspective." *American Journal of Public Health* 103 (2013): 632–37.

Oeltjen, Jarret C. "Florida Pawnbroking: An Industry in Transition." *Florida State University Law Review* 22 (1996): 995–1042.

Ralph, Michael. "Commodity." *Social Text* 27, no. 3 (2009): 78–84.

Rapp, Rayna. "Family and Class in Contemporary America: Notes toward an Understanding of Ideology." *Science and Society* 42 (1978): 278–300.

Rappeport, Alan. "Defenders See Rules Easing under Trump." *New York Times*, February 5, 2018.

Raybury, Bernadette, and Daniel Kopf. "Prisons of Poverty: Uncovering the Pre-Incarceration Incomes of the Imprisoned." July 21, 2015. www.nccdglobal.org.

"Rent-A-Center Is a Rip-Off That Preys on the Poor." *New York Daily News*, November 25, 2009.

Reynolds, David S. *Waking Giant: America in the Age of Jackson.* New York: HarperCollins, 2008.

Rhee, Nissa. "In Black Lives Matter's Shift to Economic Issues, Echoes of Black Panthers."

Christian Science Monitor, May 24, 2016.

Rich, Motoko. "Number of Poor Students in Public Schools Rises." *New York Times*, January 17, 2015.

Ritchie, Tiffany. "A Legal Twilight Zone: From the Fourth to the Fourteenth Amendment." *Southern Illinois University Law Journal* 27 (2003): 169–94.

Rivlin, Gary. "The Cold, Hard Lessons of Mobile Home U." *New York Times Magazine*, March 13, 2014.

Roberts, Dorothy E. "Poverty, Race, and New Directions in Child Welfare Policy." *Washington University Journal of Law and Policy* 1 (1999): 63–77.

Robles, Frances, and Shaila Dewan. "Skip Child Support. Go to Jail. Lose Job. Repeat." *New York Times*, April 20, 2015.

Rockman, Seth. *Welfare Reform in the Early Republic*. Boston: Bedford/St. Martin's, 2003.

Rodriguez, Joseph. *City against Suburb: The Culture Wars in an American Metropolis*. Westport, CT: Praeger, 1999.

Rorabaugh, W. J. *The Alcoholic Republic: An American Tradition*. New York: Oxford University Press, 1979.

Rose, Jerome G., and Robert E. Rothman, eds. *After Mount Laurel: The New Suburban Zoning*. New Brunswick, NJ: Center for Urban Policy Research, 1977.

Ross, H. Laurence. "Housing Code Enforcement and Urban Decline." *Journal of Affordable Housing and Community Development Law* 6 (1996): 29–46.

Ross, Janell. What a Black Lives Matter Economic Agenda Looks Like." *Washington Post*, August 29, 2016.

Ross, Tracey. "Addressing Urban Poverty in America Must Remain a Priority." June 15, 2013. Center for American Progress (online).

Rothman, David J. *The Discovery of the Asylum: Social Order and Disorder in the New Republic*. Boston: Little, Brown and Co., 1971.

Rothman, David J., and Sheila M. Rothman, eds. *On Their Own: The Poor in Modern America*. Menlo Park, CA: Addison-Wesley Publishing, 1972.

Ruel, Erin, D. Oakley, G. E. Wilson, and R. Maddox. "Is Public Housing the Cause of Poor Health or a Safety Net for the Unhealthy Poor?" *Journal of Urban Health* 87 (2010): 827–38.

Salkin, Patricia E. *American Law of Zoning*. 5th ed. St. Paul, MN: Thomson-West, 2008.

Salsich, Peter W., Jr., and Timothy J. Tryniecki. *Land Use Regulation*. 2nd ed. New York: Shepard's/McGraw-Hill, 2003.

Sampson, Robert J. *Great American City: Chicago and the Enduring Neighborhood Effect.* Chicago: University of Chicago Press, 2012.

Samuels, Elizabeth J. "Surrender and Subordination: Birth Mothers and Adoption Law Reform." *Michigan Journal of Gender & Law* 20 (2013): 33–81.

Sarat, Austin, et al. "'The Law Is All Over': Power, Resistance, and the Legal Consciousness of the Welfare Poor." *Yale Journal of Law and the Humanities* 2 (1990): 343–79.

Sarat, Austin, and Susan Silbey. "Critical Traditions in Law and Society Research." *Law & Society Review* 2 (1987): 166–74.

Satz, Debra. *Why Some Things Should Not Be for Sale: The Moral Limits of Markets.* New York: Oxford University Press, 2010.

Savelsberg, Joachim J. "Knowledge, Domination, and Criminal Punishment." *American Journal of Sociology* 99 (1994): 911–43.

Scheiber, Noam. "Raising the Floor for Wages Moves Economy into Unknown." *New York Times,* July 27, 2015.

Schneider, Carl E. "The Channelling Function in Family Law." *Hofstra Law Review* 20 (1992): 495–532.

Schneider, David M., and Raymond T. Smith. *Class Differences in American Kinship.* Ann Arbor: University of Michigan Press, 1978.

Schur, Edwin M. *Labeling Deviant Behavior: Its Sociological Implications.* New York: Harper and Row, 1971.

Scott, Robert E., and William J. Stuntz. "Plea Bargaining as Contract." *Yale Law Journal* 101 (1992): 1909–68.

Sedlar, Andrea J., and Diane D. Broadhurst. *Third National Incidence Study of Child Abuse and Neglect.* Washington, DC: U.S. Department of Health and Human Services, 1996.

Shepard, Paul. "Focusing on Prevention and Neuroscience, President Ends Reagan's War on Drugs." April 24, 2013. NewsOne (online).

Sherer, Paul M. *The Benefits of Parks: Why America Needs More Parks and Open Space.* Washington, DC: Trust for Public Land, 2006.

Silver-Greenberg, Jessica. "Banks Are a Key in the Machinery of Payday Loans." *New York Times,* February 24, 2013.

———. "Consumer Protection Agency Seeks Limits on Payday Lenders." *New York Times,* February 9, 2015.

Silver-Greenberg, Jessica, and Peter Eavis. "Service Members Left Vulnerable to Payday Loans." *New York Times,* November 22, 2013.

Simon, Jonathan. *Governing through Crime: How the War on Crime Transformed American Democracy and Created a Culture of Fear.* New York: Oxford University Press, 2007.

———. *Poor Discipline: Parole and the Social Control of the Underclass, 1890–1990.* Chicago: University of Chicago Press, 1993.

Skiba, Paige Marta. "Regulation of Payday Loans Misguided?" *Washington and Lee Law Review* 69 (2012): 1023–49.

Smith, Douglas A., and Christy A. Visher. "Street-Level Justice: Situational Determinants of Police Arrest Decisions." *Social Problems* 29 (1981): 167–77.

South, Eugenia, Michelle C. Kondo, Rose A. Cheney, and Charles C. Branas. "Neighborhood Blight, Stress, and Health: A Walking Trial of Urban Greening and Ambulatory Heart Rate." *American Journal of Public Health* 105 (2015): 909–13.

Spaeth, Harold E. "Strict Scrutiny." In *The Oxford Companion to the Supreme Court of the United States,* edited by Kermit L. Hall et al. New York: Oxford University Press, 2005.

Speight, Bruce, and Greg Hart. "Rent-to-Own Rip-off: Why Wisconsin Shouldn't Exempt the Predatory Rent-to-Own Industry from Consumer Protection Laws." Madison, WI: WISPIRG, 2013.

Spiller, H. Henry, et al. "Epidemiological Trends in Abuse and Misuse of Prescription Opioids." *Journal of Addictive Diseases* 28 (2009): 130–36.

Squires, Gregory D. *Why the Poor Pay More.* Westport, CT: Praeger Publishers, 2004.

Stolley, Kathy S. "Statistics on Adoption in the United States." In *Family Law in Action: A Reader,* edited by Margaret F. Brinig et al. Cincinnati: Anderson Publishing Co., 1999.

Stoloff, J. A. "A Brief History of Public Housing." Washington, DC: U.S. Department of Housing and Urban Development, 2004.

Strauss, Valerie. "Mass Incarceration of African Americans Affects the Racial Achievement Gap." *Washington Post,* March 15, 2017.

Stricker, Frank. *Why America Lost the War on Poverty—and How to Win It.* Chapel Hill: University of North Carolina Press, 2007.

Struve, Catherine T. "The Conditions of Pretrial Detention." *University of Pennsylvania Law Review* 161 (2013): 1009–79.

Sugarman, Stephen D. "Financial Support of Children and the End of Welfare as We Know It." *Virginia Law Review* 81 (1995): 2523–73.

Sweeney, Maureen A. "Between Sorrow and Happy Endings: A New Paradigm of Adoption." *Yale Journal of Law and Feminism* 2 (1998): 329–69.

Sweet, Elizabeth. "Symbolic Capital, Consumption and Health Inequality." *American*

Journal of Public Health 101 (2011): 260–64.

Talukdar, Debabrata. "Cost of Being Poor: Retail Price Differences across Inner-City and Suburban Neighborhoods." *Journal of Consumer Research* 25 (2008): 457–71.

Taslitz, Andrew E. "Eyewitness Identification, Democratic Deliberation, and the Politics of Science." *Cardozo Public Law, Policy, and Ethics Journal* 4 (2006): 271–327.

Tavernise, Sabrina. "Socioeconomic Divide in Smoking Rates." *New York Times*, November 13, 2015.

Taylor, Paul. "Delinquent Dads: When Child Support Lags, 'Deadbeats' May Go to Jail." *Washington Post*, December 16, 1990.

Thaler, Richard, and Cass Sunstein. *Nudge: Improving Decisions about Health, Wealth, and Happiness.* New Haven, CT: Yale University Press, 2008.

Thornburg, David A. *Galloping Bungalows: The Rise and Demise of the American House Trailer.* Hamden, CT: Archon Books, 1991.

Tucker, Eric. "Prison Time May Be Cut for Drugs." *Milwaukee Journal Sentinel*, July 9, 2014.

U.S. Department of Justice. *Sourcebook of Criminal Justice Statistics.* Washington, DC: U.S. Government Printing Office, 2004.

Vega, Tanzina. "Report Finds Hispanics Faring Better Than Blacks." *New York Times*, April 13, 2014.

Venkataramani, Atheendar S., Paula Chatterjee, Ichiro Kawachi, and Alexander C. Tsai. "Economic Opportunity, Health Behaviors, and Mortality in the United States." *American Journal of Public Health* 106 (2016): 478–84.

Wacquant, Loïc. "Class, Race, and Hyperincarceration in Revanchist America." *Daedalus* 139, no. 3 (2010): 74–90.

Wallis, Allan D. *Wheel Estate: The Rise and Decline of Mobile Homes.* Baltimore: Johns Hopkins University Press, 1997.

Wang, Tova Andrea. *The Politics of Voter Suppression: Defending and Expanding Americans' Right to Vote.* Ithaca, NY: Cornell University Press, 2012.

Wax, Amy. "Engines of Inequality: Class, Race, and Family Structure." *Family Law Quarterly* 41 (2007): 567–99.

Weisbrod, Carol. "On the Expressive Functions of Family Law." *UC Davis Law Review* 22 (1989): 991–1007.

Weiser, Benjamin. "New York to End Frisking Law Suit with Settlement." *New York Times*, January 31, 2014.

———. "Parting Words as Judge Steps Down, in Defense of Stop-and-Frisk Ruling." *New*

York Times, May 2, 2016.

West, Robin. "Submission, Choice, and Ethics: A Rejoinder to Judge Posner." *Harvard Law Review* 99 (1986): 1449–56.

White, James Boyd. *Heracles' Bow: Essays on Rhetoric and the Poetics of the Law.* Madison: University of Wisconsin Press, 1985.

Wieland, Lucy, and Jenny L. Nelson. "Aging out of Foster Care." *William Mitchell Law Review* 40 (2014): 1115–31.

Wiley, Lindsay F. "Shame, Blame, and the Emerging Law of Obesity Control." *UC Davis Law Review* 121 (2013): 121–88.

Williams, Timothy. "Jails Have Become Warehouses for the Poor, Ill, and Addicted, a Report Says." *New York Times*, February 11, 2015.

———. "A '90s Legacy That Is Filling Prisons Today." *New York Times*, July 5, 2016.

Wilson, William Julius. *The Declining Significance of Race: Blacks and Changing Institutions.* Chicago: University of Chicago Press, 1978.

———. *More Than Just Race: Being Black and Poor in the Inner City.* New York: W.W. Norton & Co., 2009.

———. *Power, Racism and Privilege: Race Relations in Theoretical and Sociohistorical Perspective.* New York: Macmillan, 1973.

———. *The Truly Disadvantaged: The Inner City, the Underclass, and Public Policy.* Chicago: University of Chicago Press, 1987.

———. *When Work Disappears: The World of the New Urban Poor.* New York: Knopf, 1996.

Wimberly, Catherine. "Deadbeat Dads, Welfare Moms, and Uncle Sam: How the Child Support Recovery Act Punishes Single-Mother Families." *Stanford Law Review* 53 (2000): 729–66.

Winslow, Don. "President Trump's War on Drugs Is Catastrophic." *Time*, June 20, 2017.

Witt, Whitney P., et al. "Neighborhood Disadvantage, Preconception Stressful Life Events, and Infant Birth Weight." *American Journal of Public Health* 105 (2015): 1044–52.

Wright, Erik Olin. "Class Analysis." In *Social Class and Stratification*, edited by Rhonda E. Levine, 143–67. Lanham, MD: Rowman & Littlefield, 1998.

Wrigley, Neil, Daniel Warm, Barrie Margetts, and Amanda Whelan. "Accessing the Impact of Improved Retail Access on Diet in a Food Desert." *Urban Studies* 39 (2002): 2061–82.

Yarbrough, Marlon N. "Trans-Racial Adoption: The Genesis of Minority Cultural Existence." *Southern University Law Review* 15 (1988).

Yarrow, Andrew L. "Falling Marriage Rates Reveal Economic Fault Lines." *New York Times*, February 8, 2015.

Young, Iris Marion. "Five Faces of Oppression." In *Rethinking Power*, edited by Thomas Wartenberg, 174–95. New York: SUNY Press, 1992.

Yuen, Nicky Gonzalez. "Oppression and Democracy." In *The Politics of Liberation*, 3rd ed., edited by Nicky Gonzalez Yuen, 12–15. Dubuque, IA: Kendall Hunt Publishing, 2000.

Zelizer, Viviana. *Pricing the Priceless Child: The Changing Social Value of Children.* New York: Basic Books, 1985.

Zenk, Shannon N., et al. "Relative and Absolute Availability of Healthier Food and Beverage Alternatives across Communities in the United States." *American Journal of Public Health* 104 (2014): 2170–78.

Zernike, Kate. "Why Are There So Many Single Americans?" *New York Times*, January 21, 2007.

Zywicki, Todd J. "Consumer Use and Government Regulation of Title Pledge Lending." *Loyola Consumer Law Review* 22 (2010): 425–62.

Index